PRAISE FOR *VALLEY OF THE BIRDTAIL*

"Offers gritty, eye-opening details about the history and present-day reality of this country. . . . A startling and optimistic way forward."
—*Toronto Star*

"A moving story that educates and provides potential paths to reconciliation. *Valley of the Birdtail* not only elicits empathy, but also moves us to action, shedding a shining light on our individual responsibility to respect each other's humanity. This is a masterfully written and accessible book which will resonate well beyond Canada as we work toward policies that create a better future for all."
—Shaughnessy Cohen Prize for Political Writing jury

"Meticulously researched and written with compassion, *Valley of the Birdtail* draws two parallel lines hopelessly distant, and then shows us a pathway through which they can come together. It's a work of trauma, of broken relationships, of how we perceive one another, but ultimately, it's a story of possibility and healing."
—DAVID A. ROBERTSON, author of *Black Water: Family, Legacy, and Blood Memory*

"This is a magnificent book. It's a new history of Canada, as lived in two communities—Rossburn and Waywayseecappo—who shared the same valley but never lived the same reality. I am haunted by what I learned and touched by the hope that these communities can teach us all how to live together in peace and justice. A truly extraordinary achievement: peeling back the layers of the history, searching through the records, but never once losing the characters, the detail, the grit of lives lived. I'm just so impressed."
—MICHAEL IGNATIEFF, author of *On Consolation: Finding Solace in Dark Times*

"A truly essential book. It's deeply researched and carefully constructed so that you come to love and respect each of the real-life characters, on both sides of the racial divide, and see the invisible hands at work in their successes and failures . . . and your own."
—JODY PORTER, award-winning journalist

"This is a remarkable book, combining wonderful stories with historical, legal, and political analysis on a subject that is critical to our future in Canada and around the world."
—BOB RAE, Canada's ambassador to the United Nations

"The most clear-eyed and compassionate book on the legacy of Indigenous inequality I've read. It's maddening in parts, wryly funny in other parts." —J.W. Dafoe Book Prize jury

"One of the most gripping books I've read this year."
—SHELAGH ROGERS, *The Next Chapter*

"An optimistic book that celebrates the human spirit."
—*Literary Review of Canada*

"Reads like a novel and feeds the mind like a first-rate textbook."
—Canadian Bar Association

"Should be read and owned by anyone who wants to learn how law can be a force for good or bad."
—GERALD LEBOVITS, New York Supreme Court Justice, and JESSICA WISNIEWSKI, *New York Law Journal*

"Narrative history at its finest." —*History Today*

"A stark and compelling picture." —*The Hill Times*

"Urgent, essential." —KATE HARRIS, author of *Lands of Lost Borders*

"An impressive piece of work—a thoughtful analysis of how racism develops and takes hold, a jarring insight into its impact, and a hopeful look at how reconciliation might work in practice."
—CHARLOTTE GRAY, author of *The Promise of Canada: People and Ideas That Have Shaped Our Country*

"If you know little about the relationship between Indigenous and settler people, this book is an excellent place to start." —*Prairie History*

ANDREW STOBO SNIDERMAN &
DOUGLAS SANDERSON (AMO BINASHII)

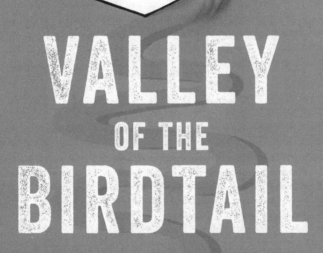

VALLEY
OF THE
BIRDTAIL

*An Indian Reserve, a White Town,
and the Road to Reconciliation*

HarperCollins*Publishers*Ltd

Published by HarperCollins Publishers Ltd

First published by HarperCollins Publishers Ltd in a hardcover edition: 2022
This trade paprback edition: 2023

HarperCollins books may be purchased for educational, business or
sales promotional use through our Special Markets Department.

HarperCollins Publishers Ltd
Bay Adelaide Centre, East Tower
22 Adelaide Street West, 41st Floor
Toronto, Ontario, Canada
M5H 4E3

www.harpercollins.ca

Map on pp. xiv to xv by Scott B. Henderson.

Library and Archives Canada Cataloguing in Publication

Title: Valley of the Birdtail : an Indian reserve, a white town, and the road to reconciliation /
Andrew Stobo Sniderman & Douglas Sanderson (Amo Binashii).
Names: Sniderman, Andrew Michael Stobo, 1983- author. | Sanderson, Douglas, 1971- author.
Description: Includes bibliographical references and index.
Identifiers: Canadiana 20230439691 | ISBN 9781443466325 (softcover)
Subjects: LCSH: Rossburn (Man.)—Social conditions. | LCSH: Rossburn (Man.)—
Economic conditions. | LCSH: Manitoba—Race relations—History. | LCSH: Manitoba—
Ethnic relations—History. | CSH: First Nations—Manitoba—Social conditions.
CSH: First Nations—Manitoba—Economic conditions.
Classification: LCC HN110.M35 S65 2023 | DDC 301.097127/3—dc23t

Printed and bound in the United States of America
23 24 25 26 27 LBC 5 4 3 2 1

For Mom and Dad, best of parents,
and Mariella, mon tesoro.
A.S.

For my grandmothers and grandfathers,
and for all of us still wrestling with the legacy of the
Indian residential school system.
D.S. (Amo Binashii)

CONTENTS

LIST OF PEOPLE

Waywayseecappo First Nation

Maureen Twovoice (*Binesi Ikwe*)	(1991–)	Student
Linda Jandrew	(1959–)	Maureen's mother
Michael Twovoice (*Niizhwaandem*)	(1920–1987)	Maureen's grandfather
Jim Cote (*Makade Makwa*)	(1941–)	Elder
Hugh McKay	(1919–1997)	Jim's stepfather

Town of Rossburn

Troy Luhowy	(1971–)	Gym teacher
Nelson Luhowy	(1943–)	Troy's father
Dick Yaskiw	(1888–1944)	Troy's great-grandfather
Maksym Yaskiw	(1851–1911)	Troy's great-great-grandfather
Dorota Yaskiw	(1855–1942)	Troy's great-great-grandmother

Government of Canada

Alexander Morris	(1826–1889)	Treaty negotiator
Hayter Reed	(1849–1936)	Indian agent
Clifford Sifton	(1861–1929)	Minister of the Interior

AUTHORS' NOTE

THIS IS A TRUE STORY, OR AS TRUE AS IMPERFECT MEMORIES and incomplete records allow.

In Canada, 330,000 people live on reserves, the tiny remainder of vast lands Indigenous Peoples once governed. Of those living on reserves, 120,000 are children; one in two grows up in poverty, which is triple the national average, and only four in ten graduate from high school, which is half the national average.[1] A child growing up on a reserve is more likely to end up in a jail cell than a university classroom.

Though these problems are vast, we opted to investigate them with a microscope. We looked for explanations in two neighbouring communities, in the lives of two families. We also looked inside government archives, where the dead continue to whisper their secrets. We examined thousands of records, catalogued by department and date, name and volume, box and file. It turns out there is nothing accidental or inevitable about poverty in Indigenous communities.

"We," Andrew and Douglas, didn't start this project as a co-author team. The book began as an article for *Maclean's* magazine written by Andrew in the summer of 2012, while he was a law student at the University of Toronto. A few years later, he wrote a follow up piece. Both times, he reported over the phone, from thousands of kilometres away. Haunted by what he had learned and determined to dig deeper, he booked a one-way flight to Manitoba in the fall of 2017 and first laid eyes on the valley of the Birdtail.

It became obvious to Andrew—a second-generation Canadian raised in Montreal with grandparents from Russia, Poland, and Wales—that he alone couldn't do justice to this story. So he reached out to Douglas, his former law professor.

Douglas grew up all over Western Canada—an Indian kid in cowboy towns. Later, at law school, he was asked why he wanted to pursue legal studies. He answered, "I want to know how the red man is being kept down."

Our paths first crossed in a classroom, with Andrew as a student in Douglas's property law seminar. In an early assignment, Andrew wrote that an Indigenous community had "roamed" an area of British Columbia. Douglas circled the word and added in the margin, "We could use all kinds of words to describe this: 'travelled,' 'crossed,' 'commuted,' 'perambulated.' Why 'ROAMED'?" Which was a polite way of saying: *Roaming is what animals do.*

With this unlikely beginning, an enduring friendship was born.

We wrote this book because schools on reserves have been grossly underfunded for decades. To reckon with this appalling fact is to discard the comforting notion that discrimination against Indigenous Canadians occurred in the distant past, perpetrated by strangers who are long dead. Rather, the combination of less funding and worse outcomes for Indigenous students persisted in our time, under Liberal and Conservative prime ministers. This book explains why, and shows how to ensure Indigenous children and their communities are given a fair chance.

We also address the fundamental question: How can Indigenous and non-Indigenous Canadians live side by side, as equals?

Together, we have tried to see the past more clearly, and to imagine a better future. The result is a story of villains and heroes, irony and idealism, racism and reconciliation. The story happens to take place in Canada, but if you listen carefully you can hear echoes of events in the United States, Australia, and throughout the Commonwealth.

Reconciliation is a process, and that process must begin with an honest assessment of our history. As Murray Sinclair, the former chair of Canada's Truth and Reconciliation Commission, has said:

"The truth will set you free. But first it's going to piss you off."

A NOTE ON TERMINOLOGY

WORDS USED TO refer to the earliest inhabitants in Canada—including "Indian," "Native," "First Nations," "Aboriginal," and "Indigenous"—have shifted over time. Words like "white," "non-Indigenous," and "settler" have their own upsides and shortcomings. The text of this book reflects language from primary sources and otherwise seeks to use terminology most fitting to a given context. This is easier said than done.

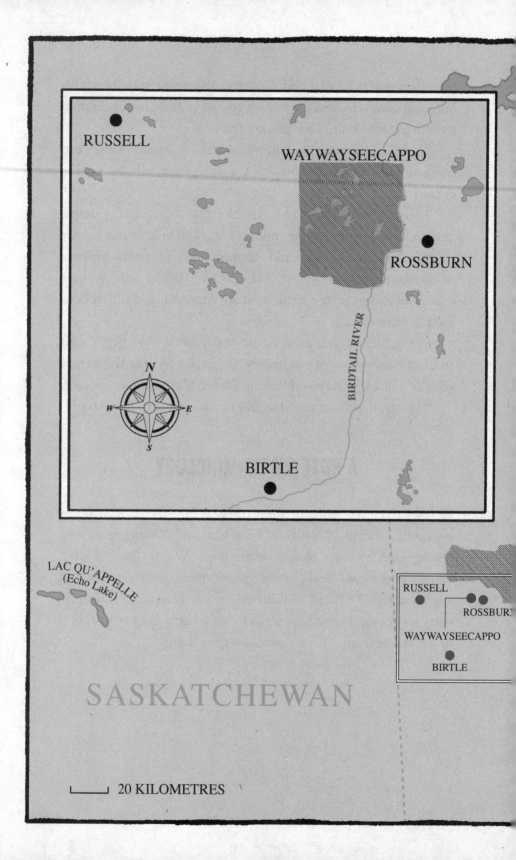

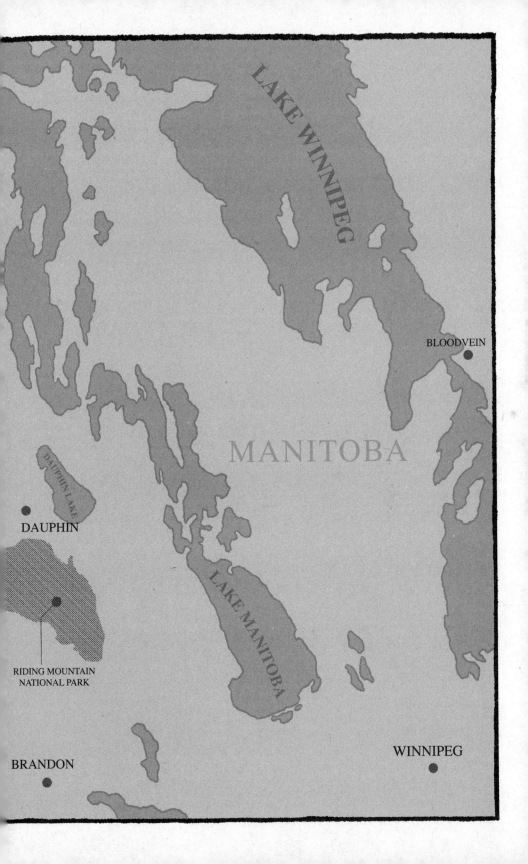

"THE VALLEY OF THE BIRDTAIL"

PEOPLE SAY MANITOBA IS SO FLAT THAT YOU CAN WATCH a dog run away for days. Not here, though—here, there is a valley, the parting gift of a retreating glacier. Along the floor of this valley winds the Birdtail River. It is not the mightiest of rivers; some maps acknowledge a mere creek. Still, the current was once strong enough to drown a boy. That's how the Birdtail River got its name, or so an old story goes.[1]

Sioux Indians on a buffalo hunt had set up teepees beside the river. The sun was high and bright when the Chief's son, a toddler, noticed an enchanting bird over the water. Its feathers were turquoise, except for its breast, which was as red as a raspberry. Transfixed, the boy walked to the edge of the river. As the boy watched, a hawk swooped from above to attack the colourful bird, which narrowly dodged the predator's talons with a sudden contortion. The movement dislodged from the bird's tail a single blue feather, which floated slowly downward, twirling in the breeze. It was falling close to the boy—so close that he reached out to grasp it. But he leaned too far and fell into the river.

Later, too late, the boy's body was recovered downstream, bobbing like driftwood. One of his tiny hands was balled into a fist. Inside was the bird's bright blue feather.

After the drowning, the river was called the Bird's Tail, which became, in time, the Birdtail. In 1877, federal surveyors marked out an Indian reserve near the river's western bank. The community assumed the name of its leader, Waywayseecappo, which means "The Man Proud of Standing Upright."

Two years later, a group of settlers decided to plant a crop of potatoes on the other side of the river. They called their new town Rossburn, in honour of the man who built its first school, Richard Ross. According to a local history written in 1951, "Nowhere in Manitoba is there a finer sight than the valley of the Birdtail, just west of the present town of Rossburn. It must have grieved the early settlers to find it set aside as an Indian Reserve."[2]

Waywayseecappo and Rossburn have been neighbours nearly as long as Canada has been a country. The town and the reserve are divided by a valley, a river, and almost 150 years of racism.

Today, the average family income in Rossburn is near the national average, and more than a third of adults have graduated from university. By contrast, the average family in Waywayseecappo lives below the national poverty line, and less than a third of adults have graduated from high school.[3]

This book is about how these two communities became separate and unequal, and what it means for the rest of us. The story of Waywayseecappo and Rossburn reflects much of what has gone wrong in relations between Indigenous Peoples and non-Indigenous Canadians. It also offers, in the end, an uncommon measure of hope.

WAYWAYSEECAPPO, FEBRUARY 2006

Maureen Twovoice's alarm first buzzed at 7:00 a.m., but she kept swatting the snooze button every five minutes. Eventually, her mom, Linda, got annoyed. "Maureen, come on," Linda called out. "It's time to get up!" Maureen grumbled, then farted in defiance. If the sun wasn't up yet, why should she be? A cool draft wandered through the house. Maureen was not keen to put her warm feet on the tile floor.

"It's *seven twenty*!" Linda yelled, her voice sharper now. "The bus is coming in fifteen minutes. I don't know why you say you want to stay in school if you're not willing to get up and go." This was enough to get Maureen out of bed and into the bathroom.

First, she washed her face, then she cupped hot water in each hand and ran it along her upper arms, just to heat them up a bit. Maureen showered at night, to save time in the morning, so before school she was content to sprinkle her wavy hair and brush it a few times to avoid the appearance of a full-blown nest.

She hurried to put together an outfit—colour-coordinated, as usual, with shiny bracelets and earrings—but she didn't have time to eat breakfast. On her way out the front door, she asked her mom for a single rolled cigarette to go. Linda picked her battles, and this was not one of them. Maureen put the cigarette in her pants pocket, hoping it would make the journey more or less intact.

Maureen lived near the corner of Cloud Road and Shingoose Road—not that there were any actual road signs on the reserve. She attended high school across the river, in Rossburn, ten minutes due east on Cloud Road, if you drove directly. But Linda didn't own a car, so Maureen had to settle for two separate school buses, which took more than an hour because they had to collect

kids from homes scattered all over the one hundred square kilometres of the reserve.

Maureen Twovoice (Courtesy of Maureen Twovoice)

The first bus picked Maureen up right outside her front
door, then headed north on Shingoose Road. Maureen propped
her backpack against the window and rested her head on it. She
would have loved a nap, but the bus shuddered and shook on
the gravel road. Even at this hour in the morning, in the inter-
lude without moon or sun, she could make out bluffs of pop-
lar and the occasional house. She knew these roads as well as
anyone. Maureen and her friends had made a habit of "borrowing" her grandmother's car keys so that they could drive around,
even though none of them had a licence yet. It was amazing how
much driving you could do around the reserve with just five or

ten bucks for gas. The important thing was to keep the windows rolled up, to avoid getting all that dust from the gravel roads in your hair.

Maureen's empty stomach was rumbling by the time the bus dropped her off at JJ's, the gas station at the corner of Shingoose Road and a road that didn't really have a name, unless you counted something like "that road where Jess and Germaine Clearsky live." JJ's was where Maureen and the other students from the initial pickup route waited while the driver picked up another group elsewhere on the reserve. Maureen used these spare twenty minutes to pop into the store and buy her breakfast/lunch: a six-inch bun filled with pepperoni, cheese, and tomato sauce, plus a can of Pepsi. She also had time to smoke the crumpled cigarette in her pocket. Even in the middle of winter, she was too cool to wear a hat or gloves, so she smoked with one hand in her coat pocket, alternating hands between drags.

Around eight thirty, Maureen boarded her second bus, which took Shingoose Road to Highway 45, the only paved road on the reserve. By now the sun had climbed over the horizon and sparkled in the snow-encrusted trees. When the bus reached the edge of the Birdtail valley, Maureen sat up in her seat to get a better view. This was her favourite moment on the ride, when the whole landscape unfurled before her. The bus picked up speed as it rolled down the slope. She could feel the descent in her stomach.

Off to the left stood the hockey arena where the Wayway-seecappo Wolverines, a team in the Manitoba Junior Hockey League, played for boisterous crowds of nearly a thousand people. Whenever Maureen attended a game, she imagined how it might feel to score a goal. Her father had been a good hockey player, good enough to earn the nickname "Fast." Family friends used to

5

call Maureen "Little Fast," but she didn't see much of her father and never really learned to skate. Her household had been too chaotic to get her to and from all those practices and games, plus the equipment had always been too expensive. Maureen had friends just as poor who somehow ended up with their own skates, but they were all boys.

As the bus approached the bottom of the valley, Maureen assembled her mental armour for the upcoming day in Rossburn. Waywayseecappo had its own school for children living on the reserve, but it only went up to Grade 8, so kids had to head across the river for high school. Nine of Maureen's Grade 9 classmates rode with her on the bus from the reserve, but most of the students at the school were pale, fair-haired teens from Rossburn with Ukrainian names full of *y*'s and *k*'s: Lysychin, Trynchuk, Olynyk. As far as Maureen could tell, there weren't really friendships between kids from Waywayseecappo and Rossburn. The boys from town barely even acknowledged her presence. "They probably thought we were all troubled," Maureen later said.

The average student from Waywayseecappo starting at Rossburn Collegiate was two to four years behind academically. Most ended up dropping out. Maureen got a reminder of the attrition rate during her morning bus commute: the number of students in each grade decreased the closer they got to Grade 12. None of Maureen's three older siblings had made it beyond Grade 11. Neither had her parents, who didn't study beyond Grade 10.

Maureen wanted something more for herself—what exactly that was, she couldn't say, but she was certain that she didn't want to spend the rest of her life eating crappy welfare dinners like fried baloney and Kraft Dinner, waiting for a biweekly government cheque that didn't buy much. *If I can get through high school*, she thought, *I can get a job. And if I can get a job, I can find another way.*

The bus engine groaned as they headed up the other side of the valley. To her right was the Birdtail River, frozen solid enough to walk on. For a brief moment, she could see a long stretch where the serpentine river split the valley, marking the line where Waywayseecappo ended and Rossburn began. Maureen crossed that line every day to get to high school.

ROSSBURN, SEPTEMBER 2006

Troy Luhowy woke up at 7:00 a.m., the same time Maureen's buzzer was going off on the other side of the Birdtail. But Troy was not a snooze button kind of guy. He didn't even bother with an alarm. He just woke up on time, battery charged, ready to roll. After a quick shower, he put on the work clothes he had laid out the night before: a monochrome tracksuit, black or blue, with a collared golf shirt and running shoes. A perfectly respectable outfit for a gym teacher.

Breakfast was a bowl of cereal—Vector, the healthy option, or Frosted Mini-Wheats, the usual. Then he made a cup of instant coffee, fastened the lid on his travel mug, and was out the door of his mobile home and into his Ford Explorer by seven thirty.

Troy could count on a quick drive to work. He didn't have to worry about traffic, or even traffic lights. The whole town fit within a single square kilometre. The tallest building was the grain elevator, which loomed next to rusting tracks that hadn't borne a train in a decade. At this time in the morning, there were never more than a few vehicles on the road. Students wouldn't be dropped off at school for another hour or so, plus the streets these days were quieter than they used to be. The town's population had peaked at 694 a quarter century before, when Troy was ten years old.

Troy drove past the modest houses lining his residential street, then turned right on Main Street. Up ahead and to the left stood the town hall where his parents had held their wedding reception And there, just beyond, was the post office. He had mailed some letters there a few days before.

"Troy, good to see you," the postmaster had said. "I hear you've moved back."

"Yeah, I'm working in Wayway now."

"Oh," the postmaster said, pausing an extra beat. "Good luck straightening that out!"

Troy usually let that kind of comment go. He had heard far worse about Waywayseecappo from friends and family. "Ah, it's not bad," he said this time. "It's, you know, they're just kids."

The building after the post office was the hardware store. When Troy was growing up, a group of men from the reserve used to hang out there, carrying bottles in paper bags and flashing uneven smiles. People in town called them "the Veterans." Troy could tell by looking at them that they were sleeping outdoors. Sometimes they slept in rusting cars that sat abandoned at the edge of town, or in the small park next to the train stop. Other times they made it no farther than bushes outside the Rossburn Hotel bar, around the corner from the hardware store.

"Fucking Indians," Troy heard neighbours complain. "They shouldn't be allowed here."

When Troy was older, close enough to the legal drinking age, he would spend his Friday nights at the hotel bar. It was the most racially mixed place in town—"Moccasin Square Gardens" is what he and his friends sometimes called it. Inside, wooden beams running along the ceiling were covered with

paper money in various denominations, signed by patrons looking to buy a little piece of immortality. Troy had left a two-dollar
bill, signed with his nickname, Heavy. (This was a joke, as his
limited mass had been the primary defect in an otherwise promising hockey career.) Nearby, a $100 bill had "FUCK U" writ-
ten on it. In this bar, as in others, the odd punch was clumsily
thrown for forgettable reasons. Sometimes, it was enough that
"you're Indian and I'm not," as Troy later put it, though on such
occasions he considered himself more of a peacemaker than a
main combatant.

Troy sipped his coffee as he kept driving along Main Street,
which was lined on each side with a single file of elm and oak
trees. As he approached the corner of Main and Cheddar Avenue,
he checked to see if his dad's lights were on, which would mean
he was getting ready for work. Nelson still lived in the two-storey
house where Troy grew up as an only child. The family's religion
had ostensibly been Catholic, but mostly Troy was expected to
worship the Montreal Canadiens.

At thirty-five, Troy was not quite the formidable hockey
player he once was. His knees bore the scars of nine surgeries. For
a time, he had thought his hockey days were over, but recently a
few old friends coaxed him out of retirement. Now he was playing twice a week, and he'd never had more fun, with none of the
pressures of old. His pre-game routine just needed a couple of
adjustments: he popped two or three Advils, lathered stiff joints
with a balm that made his skin tingle, and slid on knee braces he
rarely washed. Troy still loved the way locker rooms everywhere
stank the same.

A few short blocks after his dad's place, he passed by Rossburn
Collegiate, his old high school. In its library sat a copy of the
1990 yearbook, which contained a picture of him in his senior

year, along with an assessment by his peers: "Troy Luhowy—We don't know what he's on, but we all want some." The boy in the yearbook, with his fresh face and plentiful hair, looked more like a stranger with each passing year. But Troy hadn't lost that way about him, that aura of undaunted, infectious energy. It made him nearly impossible to dislike.

Troy Luhowy (Courtesy of Troy Luhowy)

The drive through town was over in less than a minute. Troy didn't encounter a stop sign until he reached Highway 45, which was lined on both sides by farms. The last crop standing was canola, now fast approaching the shade of radioactive yellow that would signal harvest time.

Troy didn't have long on the highway before he turned onto Cemetery Road to take a shortcut to work. On his left, a small clearing contained rows of tombstones, many with names obscured by moss or rubbed out with the passage of time. The cemetery held no special significance for Troy, as he didn't have family there. This was a resting place for the town's old Anglo-Saxon stock. The Ukrainians, Troy's people, were buried elsewhere.

Just beyond the last row of tombstones, the road plunged sharply into the valley's steepest parabola. Some people called this descent Cemetery Hill; others called it Suicide Hill. Troy rode the brakes all the way down. This was where the lid on his mug came in particularly handy. To his right, the morning sun lit up a bend in the Birdtail River.

Down then up Troy went, until he reached the far edge of the valley. Had he continued straight ahead, along Cloud Road, he would have ended up at Maureen Twovoice's house, but at this point Troy still hadn't met Maureen, who was spending her days at school in Rossburn. He instead turned left, toward the Waywayseecappo Community School, which had a green metal roof and brick walls painted an earthy brown.

Troy enjoyed spending his days with kids, but he wasn't really planning on sticking around as a teacher in Waywayseecappo. The pay was lousy, and he had too many classes with thirty-five or so students. Typically a few students in each class had fetal alcohol syndrome, and an uncomfortably large number of students arrived at school hungry and wearing the same clothes as the days before. All this made teaching on the reserve particularly challenging, so when teachers got the chance to relocate, they almost always did. The students noticed, of course. They came to understand that their school was something to be endured and escaped.

All told, Troy's drive to work took six minutes. Each morning and afternoon, he and Maureen criss-crossed the Birdtail valley from opposite directions, with destinations less than five kilometres apart. It felt a lot farther than that.

PART I

"MASTERS OF THEIR OWN DESTINY"

I

"DEAR DIARY"

HER MOM GAVE HER A DAY TO PACK. MAUREEN, AGED ten, wanted to stay in Winnipeg, but Linda was tired of raising kids alone in a jagged corner of the city. Maureen knew better than to ask too many questions. She grabbed a camo-patterned duffle bag and filled it with a few of her favourite books and a disproportionately red wardrobe. The last item she packed was her teddy bear, a Christmas gift from recent foster parents. It was white, soft, and huggable, with a crimson hat and matching suit. One of her sisters used to have the same bear from the same foster parents, until her brother ripped its head off.

Maureen's favourite thing about Winnipeg was her public school, Greenway Elementary, where she wrote rhyming poems in the quiet library and had a quirky teacher who wore a jean dress backwards during Spirit Week. Maureen liked school so much that she tagged along when her younger sister, Samantha, had been forced to attend summer classes.

One day after school, Maureen was running in a park, through a row of trees, figure-eight style. She raced with arms outstretched, enjoying the whoosh in her ears. "I'm Pocahontas!" she shouted to her older sister, Jacinda. Maureen had just seen the Disney film, so nothing was cooler than being like Pocahontas. Jacinda laughed and said, "You know that's what we are, right?" Actually, *no*. Until that moment, Maureen had never thought of herself as Indigenous.

Now her mom was moving them to the reserve, whatever that meant.

"Mom, what is a reserve?" Maureen asked.

"It's where our family lives."

Maureen had already been there once, when she was seven, to spend time with a stranger named Maurice whom her mom had introduced as Maureen's dad. He had picked her up in Winnipeg and then they drove to Waywayseecappo, just the two of them. He let Maureen sit in the front seat. As he spotted cows in the fields, he shouted, "Hamburger! Hamburger!" Maureen was relieved to have something to laugh about.

When they arrived at her dad's home, she was struck by the quiet. Compared with the cacophony of downtown Winnipeg, everything felt impossibly calm and spread out. She spent a lot of time playing alone among the trees, all those willows and poplars, and caught dark green lizards that felt cold to the touch. Under a canopy of branches, she came across a pocket knife, half-buried in the ground. It was sharp and rusty. She took it back to show her dad, who gently folded the blade into the handle and set it aside.

After that trip, Maureen started writing her father elaborately decorated holiday cards. "Merry Xmas dad, I love you!" Maureen pictured her dad sticking the cards on his fridge, smiling at the thought of his brilliant daughter. But Maureen never actually mailed anything to him. She was too scared that he wouldn't write back.

Three years after that first visit, Maureen was returning to the reserve with her mom, sisters, and teddy bear, this time to stay.

The drive from Winnipeg to Waywayseecappo takes about three and a half hours by car, but Linda didn't own a car, so it took closer to six on a Greyhound bus. Maureen sat alone in a separate row and stared out the window, lost in whys and whats and wheres. The flatness, which extended all the way to the horizon, left even more room for the sky. The bus travelled north and mostly west, through farmland frosted by snow.

Linda tapped Maureen on the shoulder. "We're getting close." The bus stopped with a hiss. "Ross-BURN," the driver announced. Maureen watched a few passengers get off in a town that looked like little more than a main street. "Next stop, Way-way-see-CAPPO."

Just beyond the outskirts of Rossburn, the bus dipped into a valley, giving Maureen a momentary flutter in her belly. Soon, the bus dropped them off in front of a strip of low-slung buildings at the side of the highway. Linda headed to a payphone to call her father, Alvin, for a ride. Maureen was sitting on her camo bag when her grandfather pulled up in a yellow Oldsmobile. It was so low to the ground it reminded Maureen of a boat.

Before long, they arrived at a three-bedroom house made of wood and painted brown and white. Alvin had vacated it to give Linda and the kids a place to stay. Inside, the house smelled older than it looked. A film of dust covered nearly everything except the rocking chair and its green cushion. The walls were bare.

On the upside, Maureen and Samantha each got their own room, which was definitely a step up from their smaller apartment in Winnipeg. And Maureen liked that she couldn't see any neighbours. She could go outside to sit on the front steps and just listen to the stillness. At night, far from city lights, Maureen could not believe how bright the moon looked. Sometimes it felt like the moon was parked directly above the house, shining a spotlight on them.

THE HARDEST PART of the move for Maureen was changing schools. Her mom knew it wasn't ideal to switch halfway through the year, but she hoped Maureen would fit in easily among other Native children. For her first day, Maureen wore her favourite outfit: black sweatpants and a red V-neck sweater, plus lip gloss that tasted like watermelon. Her classmates thought the new girl looked like a tomboy.

For the first time in her life, Maureen found herself surrounded by hundreds of students who shared her skin colour and dark hair. "There are lots of kids that look like me," she recalls thinking. "I was just, like, looking at people. They were probably wondering why."

Inside the classroom, Maureen was in for an even bigger adjustment. In math class, a girl sitting next to her whispered, "This is so hard. I can't do it." Maureen did not know what to say: she found the material almost laughably easy. It didn't take long for her Grade 5 teacher, Tammy McCullough, to realize that Maureen was far advanced compared with her peers. When McCullough took Maureen to a quiet corner of the classroom to perform a standardized reading and spelling assessment, it became obvious that Maureen was well above her grade level. That year, she would average 98 percent on her spelling tests.

Even the way Maureen carried herself stood out: standing tall, shoulders back, confident. McCullough recalls the way Maureen smiled when she put up her hand to show she had completed an assignment first: "Some kids can be rude, like, 'I'm done first, yay for me.' Maureen wasn't that type of kid. She wanted extra assignments." Maureen was also quick to raise her hand whenever McCullough asked a question. "Anytime I called on her, she was always right," McCullough says. Sometimes McCullough pretended not to see Maureen's raised hand, just to give other students a chance.

Maureen read ahead, which left her even more bored in class. "I could see how behind they were," Maureen says. "I kept thinking: this is weird, why are we relearning what I already know?" She passed the time by helping other students with their homework or doodling increasingly elaborate renditions of her name.

"I just kept waiting to learn," Maureen says. "I felt like an alien."

AT HOME, MAUREEN faced other challenges.

When her mom was drinking, Maureen tried to hide in her room, though this didn't work particularly well because there was no lock on her door. Linda would wobble in and sit on Maureen's bed, crying and muttering about times she had been humiliated and abused as a girl at residential school. Maureen could see the hurt in her mom, could see it in the shadows that darkened her face. Still, Maureen thought: *Mom, come back sober. I shouldn't have to listen to this.*

"I remember feeling so lonely," Maureen says, "and sometimes wished I had a different, loving family." She could not remember her mom ever saying the words "I love you."

Sometimes Maureen came home from school, took one glance at her mother's unsteady lean, then went right back outside for a long walk. Her cousin Tamara lived within walking distance, and Maureen visited so often she wore a path through the field of waist-high prairie grass that separated their homes.

Maureen went to Tamara's place when things were particularly rough at home. It got to the point where Maureen didn't even have to ask Tamara's parents if she could sleep over. "I just went over," Maureen says. "'Camping.' That's the word we used. They'd say, 'Are you going to camp here tonight?'"

Maureen poured her frustrations into a diary. She would sit on the couch with her legs folded into her chest and the purple notebook resting on her knees. She had been keeping a detailed record of her thoughts ever since she had read Anne Frank's diary while she was living in Winnipeg. Maureen imagined that one day people would pore over her every word, so she took the time to write in her best handwriting. Every day she wrote, in bubbly cursive, about her frustrations at school and at home. A typical entry posed a question and then tried to answer it. "Dear Diary," she always began.

"Why is life like this?"

"How come schoolwork is so easy?"

"Why does my mom have to drink all the time?"

"Why is there nothing on the walls?"

MAUREEN'S REPORT CARDS document a slow and steady slide. In Grade 6, her second year in Waywayseecappo, a teacher wrote that Maureen had "started showing little enthusiasm." Back when she lived in Winnipeg, she had loved school. Increasingly, it was a source of boredom. In Grade 7, Maureen concluded that middle school most definitely sucked. Just getting out of bed in the morning felt daunting. On days when she was really not feeling it, which was more and more often, she tried to sweet-talk her mom into letting her stay home. Occasionally Linda caved and called the school to report that Maureen was feeling sick. Usually, though, Linda did her best to nag Maureen into submission. "Why, Maureen? *Why* don't you want to go to school?" Even while Linda was herself struggling, she never stopped encouraging Maureen to go to school.

When Maureen did show up, her favourite activity became hanging out in the girls' bathroom with one of her cousins. They squeezed into a stall together, sharing the toilet as a seat. They talked about teenage stuff: notably, boys, and, before long, the cousin's pregnancy. Sometimes they worried that a teacher would bust them for skipping class, but they always got away with it. Maureen liked to stand up on the toilet to doodle on the ceiling. A typical entry memorialized a crush. "Maureen & Craig: forever and always," she wrote, framing the words with a heart.

One of Maureen's various schemes to skip class involved complaints that she needed glasses. She had perfect vision but pretended the whiteboards appeared blurry to her. The closest ophthalmologist was in the town of Brandon, 150 kilometres away and a veritable metropolis compared to other towns closer to the reserve. Brandon was Maureen's favourite place to shop for clothes. She was also vaguely aware that her mom had once attended a school there, and that she had never made it beyond Grade 8.

For a time, it was not clear whether Maureen would make it past Grade 7. Homework was easy, but she didn't bother to do it. Trying to fit in better, she became a half-hearted badass. She was one of those teenagers who knew what she *ought* to do but did the opposite to get attention. She talked back to teachers, missed too much class, fought at recess. An evaluation in Grade 7 showed that she had fallen below the standard reading level—a sign either that she didn't take the test seriously or that she was indeed falling behind.

In November 2003, Maureen was suspended for three days for fighting. She was also caught smoking, and the principal sent a letter to Linda emphasizing the school's zero-tolerance policy. In January, Linda received another letter from the principal, saying that Maureen was harassing a student and threatening to fight her. "Watch your back," Maureen had reportedly told another girl, who was so scared that she stopped going to school. "If this doesn't stop immediately," the principal wrote, "I will be informing the RCMP"—the Royal Canadian Mounted Police.

That spring, after another fight, Maureen received an indefinite suspension. "Dear Diary," she wrote. "Am I going to graduate?"

Maureen doesn't remember much about what she did next. She chilled a lot. At some point near the end of the school year, she belatedly realized she was facing the prospect of repeating Grade 7 in the same class as her younger sister, Samantha. Maureen begged the school to let her write the final exams in English, math, science, and social studies. After the school agreed, Maureen barely studied but still managed to pass. For her, this was a stark reminder of just how far ahead she had been when she arrived on the reserve a couple of years before.

In Grade 8, though, Maureen's behaviour, attendance, and grades didn't get any better. Her first report card showed her failing seven of her nine classes, with an attendance rate of about 50 percent. In their comments, teachers made copious use of exclamation marks. "Poor attendance and participation!" "Many assignments were not handed in!" "More effort required!" "Does not use class time wisely!" "Poor attendance / Poor achievement!"

Seeing Maureen struggle pained Linda, and she tried to offer encouragement. "I know I drink," she told Maureen. "I know it's hard. But you have to go to school. Look at me, I only made it to

Grade 8. You've still got a chance." Maureen tuned her out, thinking, *If it's that important, Mom, why didn't you finish?*

Maureen listened more carefully to her grandfather, Alvin, who was less inclined to tell her what to do. "He wasn't one to go on a big lecture about life," Maureen says. They spent the most time together during the winter, when he would drive her to the local hockey arena to watch the Waywayseecappo Wolverines play. Alvin would describe life on the reserve when he was young. Mostly, he talked about what the land used to look like. There were more trees, for one thing, and plenty of elk, moose, ducks, and partridges. During the car rides, Alvin made a point of asking Maureen how she was doing at school. He himself had only made it to Grade 5, he told her. When Maureen confided that, actually, things weren't going great, Alvin tried to give her a boost. "You can make it," he would say. "You can do something, you can be somebody." She wanted to believe him. When she was alone, in her darkest moments, Alvin's words glowed like fireflies. *Do something*, she told herself. *Be somebody*.

Maureen kept writing in her diary, day after day, month after month. Over time, she accumulated a pile of booklets. Whenever she flipped through the pages and reviewed old entries, the level of detail in her catalogue of disappointments amazed her. Writing made her feel better, but reading her own words made her feel worse. Sometimes she started a new notebook even when plenty of blank pages remained in an older one. "I changed notebooks because what was inside was so ugly," she recalls. "I thought maybe if I started over it would be better."

Maureen also found other, more destructive ways to deal with her feelings. When they were thirteen, Maureen and her best friend, Amanda, started drinking regularly. Getting their hands on a bottle wasn't particularly hard, even though the reserve was officially dry. That just meant people bought their booze in Rossburn. That same year, Maureen registered her first email account: chug4life666@hotmail.com.

When Maureen and Amanda found themselves particularly bored and despondent on weekends, they took turns choking each other. They would sit facing each other on the couch, then Amanda would put both her hands around Maureen's throat and squeeze. When Maureen felt sufficiently dizzy, she gave Amanda a tap. It was a good feeling, that whirling in her head. *Yeah*, they thought, *this is the shit!* Sometimes one of them blacked out, but it never lasted long enough to really scare them. Even as they hurt each other, they took comfort in being together.

Maureen also started cutting herself when she was alone. She sliced near her wrists and hid the scabs and scars with long sleeves. She found a kind of grim satisfaction in her own pain. One night in her room, she used a piece of glass she'd recovered from a smashed bottle. She accidentally cut deeper than usual and was scared by all the blood—more gush than dribble. She wanted to scream but stayed mute, paralyzed, while she bled. Fortunately, her uncle Matthew picked that moment to open the door to say hello. "Maureen, *what* are you doing!" he exclaimed, loudly but not angrily. He rushed to get a tea towel and pressed it firmly on her arm. Maureen just sobbed.

The next morning, Maureen found her mother seated at the dining table, waiting for her. She asked Maureen to sit down. "You know," Linda said, "when people take their lives they don't go anywhere. Their spirit just stays on the earth, wandering, sticking around until the time they were actually supposed to go." As she said this, she remained perfectly calm. Linda had a habit, when she was in a really deep conversation, of making a fist and wrapping the other hand around it as though she was going to crack her knuckles. This is what she was doing now. "If you chose to do that to yourself," Linda said, "your spirit wouldn't be at peace." Maureen began to cry.

Linda talked about how sad she would be if she lost Maureen, and then she talked about Maureen's siblings and nieces and nephews. How would they feel? What would Linda tell them? Maureen stayed quiet, her cheeks wet with tears. Part of her appreciated that her mother was showing how much she cared. Another part of her wanted to say, "Mom, you're part of the reason why." Maureen hated coming home and wondering whether her mom was going to be drunk. But Maureen didn't mention that, and after Linda was done talking, the two of them hugged for a long time in silence. Linda didn't tell Maureen she loved her—it just wasn't something she did in those days—but Maureen could feel love in that hug.

After a particularly taxing stretch in Grade 8, Maureen decided to burn her diaries, hoping that would give her the fresh start she needed. That afternoon, her mom's partner, Earl, had lit a fire in the backyard to burn leaves and garbage, as he often did. A towering spruce tree stood a few paces away from the firepit, close enough that the smoke curled through the outstretched branches. Earl was poking the fire with a stick when he saw Maureen come out the back door carrying a large wooden chest she had made at school. The industrial arts teacher had asked his students to create a hope chest where they could store their most prized possessions. Building that chest was probably the highlight of Grade 7 for Maureen. She had painted it blue and black and decorated it with a few squiggly red flourishes. Inside, she had stacked her diaries.

Maureen put the chest down next to the fire. She fished out the purple diary, her first one ever, then ripped out a few pages.

With what she imagined was a dramatic flourish, she tossed the pages into the fire. She was close enough to the flames to feel their warmth on her face. It felt quite good, actually. Earl watched on with a look that said, *Really?* But he said nothing. Maureen proceeded to burn the diaries one at a time, oldest to newest. She thought, *Now I can let go of what I wrote.* And so what if future generations never read her beautiful cursive. She cherished a rare wave of relief as she looked at the ashes, a growing heap of grey streaked with dancing orange. She burned to forget.

Maureen kept no more diaries after that.

In Grade 8, after repeatedly talking back to teachers and getting caught smoking and fighting, Maureen was expelled and told there was no way back. She enrolled in a "transition program" for students on the reserve who were not coping with the regular school. Maureen felt she had really messed up this time. She became convinced she wasn't where she was supposed to be. This made her feel dumb, though deep down she suspected she was smart. She heard her grandfather urging her on. *Do something. Be somebody.*

A teacher in the program recommended that Maureen try to publish an article in *Say Magazine*, a national publication looking for submissions from Indigenous youth. Maureen decided to give it a try. To her surprise, the magazine accepted her submission and published it in the Winter 2006 issue. "I'm Maureen Lynn Twovoice," she began, "a fourteen-year-old Anishinaabe from the Waywayseecappo First Nation in Manitoba. I'm finishing up Grade 8 in a Co-Op Program." She wrote about her favourite music (powwow) and her "huge mistake" (giving up on school). She described her volunteer work at a home for the elderly in

Rossburn, which was a mandatory part of her program. She was helping with baking, hairstyling, and nail painting. She had even learned how to make perogies, a beloved Ukrainian dish. "I talk and listen to what they have to say and I tell you they have lots to say," Maureen wrote. "Some people just don't take the time to listen."

She also wrote warmly about her mom, who had encouraged Maureen "to finish school so I could be successful" and taught her "not to judge someone by his or her looks." Maureen felt happy to write about her mom like that. She knew that Linda, for all her faults, had been trying. "My mom was a single parent who raised me without my dad," Maureen recalls. "This was a way to acknowledge her."

A copy of the magazine arrived shortly after Maureen started Grade 9 in Rossburn. Linda was so proud that she cut out Maureen's article and framed it on the wall. In the final sentence of the essay, Maureen wrote, "I want to be an inspiration to other youth."

2

LINDA'S SHOES

AS A LITTLE GIRL GROWING UP IN WAYWAYSEECAPPO, Linda Jandrew bathed in the Birdtail River, which was so clear she could count the minnows darting along the bottom. Her kokom—"grandmother" in Ojibway—kept a close watch from the shore, even though the water came up only to Linda's belly button. The current was gentle, a caress.

Every August, Linda joined her kokom for berry-picking around the reserve. "*Naadinaan mskomnak jimiijyan*," her kokom said. "Get the berries to eat." As Linda went from one bush to the next, she had to watch out for thorns, which could cut right through the thin rubber soles of her shoes. She carried a plastic bucket to put the raspberries in. "*N-ji kenndaam wedodamaan kinaawin. Kaayi memech gda mamaa jibaayaat zaam minitwe pane*," her kokom said. "We know what to do ourselves. It is not necessary that your mother come along. She drinks too much, all the time."

Linda lived with her grandparents, parents, and older brother, Matthew, in a three-bedroom house on the reserve. On the back door, her mooshum (grandfather) hung his traditional medicine bag and skin drum, which he took along to Sun Dances.

When Linda's parents were drinking and yelling and fighting, which was too often, her grandparents took her and her brother to a special hiding place, a tent made of tan-coloured canvas within walking distance of home. Sometimes they spent days at a time out there, but they never wanted for food. Her mooshum would disappear for a few hours and return with a snared rabbit. Her kokom would cut off its head and paws, then skin and gut it. Some of the meat was sliced into ribbons and hung on a branch to dry just beyond the reach of their bounding dog. The rest of the meat went into a soup, which slowly boiled in a large pot on an open fire. For dessert, Linda's favourite was bannock sprinkled with sugar. At dusk, they burned sage to ward off the mosquitoes. This was a time for stories, told in Ojibway.

Linda fondly remembers one night in particular. Inside the tent, her kokom laid down a thin blanket that she had stitched together out of purple and black squares. Linda could still feel the ground through the blanket, but she didn't mind. She was resting back-to-back with her kokom, who wore a one-piece cotton dress in a flowery pattern. They whispered to each other as all around them frogs croaked and crickets chirped and owls called. Then, in the distance, wolves began howling.

"Shhh," her kokom said. "Do you hear them?" Linda and her brother went perfectly still and they all lay there, listening. The howls lingered as they cascaded through the valley. Linda loved the way her back pressed up against her kokom's when they inhaled deeply at the same time.

This was one of the last times in Linda's life she felt truly safe.

★ ★ ★

IN THE FALL of 1965, Linda was told that she had to go to boarding school. She didn't understand why, and when an unfamiliar bus full of other children from Waywayseecappo came to pick her up, no one mentioned that the destination was 150 kilometres away, near the town of Brandon. Linda was six years old.

The Brandon Indian Residential School, an imposing brick structure with limestone trim, loomed on a hillside, visible from the main road into town. It looked so grand, so modern, so impressive that it awed many who drove by. To the students inside, however, it felt like prison.

The Brandon Indian Residential School, circa 1910 ("Brandon Industrial Institute," United Church of Canada Archives, 93.049P/1396)

When Linda arrived, she was instructed to remove her clothes and given a bath. Then her long, dark hair was cut into a short pageboy style, which is the way mandatory trims would keep it for years to come. After the haircut, a full bottle of anti-lice mix was poured on her scalp and roughly kneaded in. Even after a cold shower, a foul chemical taste lingered in her mouth for hours, and in her memory forever.

Linda slept with dozens of other girls in a large dormitory with single beds arranged in a grid several rows deep. Her bed-sheets smelled like mothballs. If a girl had the misfortune to wet her bed at night, she would be punished in front of the others with a strap on the hand or across the backside. Yet somehow this regime of terror did not have the desired deterrent effect on the girls' bladders.

The atmosphere at the school was severe and oppressive. As Linda later put it, "Not often, we were allowed to laugh." Students had to obey all kinds of rules and orders, which was particu-larly challenging for Linda at first, because she did not understand English well. When a supervisor heard her speaking Ojibway, he slapped her across the mouth. "I couldn't speak my language," she recalls. Her older brother, Matthew, was already at the school when Linda arrived, but they rarely saw each other because most activities were organized by age. The school did not even permit siblings to hug.

For breakfast, they were served porridge, always porridge, which Linda grew to loathe. She ate as much as she could get anyway, because she was hungry all the time. There was never enough food.[1] The exceptions were the few occasions when family members were permitted to visit, such as on Thanksgiving, Christmas, and Easter, when the school served heaping portions of ham and potato salad. "They would try to impress the people visiting us, so they didn't think we were getting starved," Linda says. "That's the only time we really got to eat." On these occa-sions, her lone visitor was her aunt.

And the shoes. Linda will never forget the shoes: black oxfords, which all the students had to wear. They were a mandatory part of the school uniform, affixed to the feet of every Indian child on the assembly line to Anglo-Saxon respectability. Their heaviness surprised Linda; they felt clunky at the end of her spindly legs. She was made to shine them until she could see her face in the leather. And, most important of all, she was not allowed to leave her dormitory without them. Civilized people wore shoes. Don't ever forget them, the students were warned.

BY THE TIME Linda arrived, the Brandon Indian Residential School had been operating for seventy years. Its doors opened in 1895 as one of many residential schools funded by the Canadian government and run by churches. Their purpose was to sever the link between Indigenous children and their culture, in order to assimilate Indians into the Euro-Christian mainstream. The government sought to keep its costs low by partnering with churches, which were more interested in souls than salaries. Between the opening of the first such school in 1880 until the closing of the last one in 1996, more than 150,000 Indigenous children attended such institutions, including both of Maureen's parents and all four of her grandparents.[2]

In the beginning, many Indigenous communities welcomed government promises to provide education, believing new schools could offer a bridge to a better future. Treaty agreements with Indigenous Peoples often specified that these schools would be situated in Indigenous communities. Nevertheless, churches and the government favoured more distant locations, because they believed children could be more easily reformed if kept away from the supposedly malign influence of their parents. As Prime

Minister John A. Macdonald put it, "When the school is on the reserve, the child lives with its parents, who are savages, and though he may learn to read and write, his habits and training mode of thought are Indian. He is simply a savage who can read and write."[3]

The case of the Brandon school was typical. In the late 1880s, Methodists petitioned the federal government to start a school and insisted on avoiding "the serious disadvantage of having such an institution in or near an Indian Reserve."[4] For its part, the city council of Brandon warmly welcomed the opportunity to host a federal school, notably because it would bring more government investment into the area.[5]

Chief Jacob Berens (Nauwigizigweas in Ojibway) was the leader of a reserve in northern Manitoba and a pious Methodist himself. When he heard about the plans for a new school in Brandon, he expressed his opposition in a letter to the secretary of the Methodist Mission Society in Toronto, Reverend Sutherland. Though Chief Berens and his community welcomed a new school, Brandon was too far away: "Our hearts are sad for one cannot think of sending our children away such a long distance from their people & homes. No, we love our children like the white man & are pleased to have them near us."[6] Reverend Sutherland wrote a condescending response in which he expressed doubt that Chief Berens was the real author of the letter written in his name, and opined that Berens had in fact written "at the suggestion of others" who were hostile to the church.[7]

Chief Berens replied that the reverend's letter was "very ungenerous and unchristianlike" and criticized him for presuming to know the best interests of the community "without consulting our views."[8] Berens also wrote a letter to the federal government to argue against putting the school in Brandon: "We cannot really think of ever sending any of our children so far away from our reserves even for the purpose of getting an education."[9]

Nauwigizigweas (Chief Jacob Berens) (Archives of Manitoba, 1909, Item Number 1, Coloured Negative 117, Still Images Collection, Personalities Collection)

In the end, Berens's forceful protestations were ignored. Brandon it would be.

The school's first principal, Reverend J. Semmens, doggedly travelled around Manitoba seeking prospective students. In his personal journal, he described the territory around Lake Winnipeg as his "recruiting field." He reached many communities by canoe, portaging between "stormy lakes," and at times he found "the mosquitoes intolerable."[10] But his greatest obstacle by far was skeptical parents. The reverend recorded the questions they asked him after he made his sales pitch:

> "Will the Government keep this promise or break it as they have others made in like beautiful language?"
>
> "Can the children return at their own wish or at the wish of the parents before the term at School expires?"
>
> "Is it the purpose to enslave our children and make money out of them?"
>
> "Is it the object of the Gov't to destroy our language and our tribal life?"[11]

It is unclear what, if anything, Semmens said in response, but the truth would have confirmed their worst fears.

Reverend Semmens wrote to the Department of Indian Affairs to report the widespread reluctance he was encountering. In response, an official recommended that Semmens remind parents of "the powers vested in the Department," which would compel attendance if parents did not "evince their willingness to have their children educated."[12] Under the revised Indian Act of 1894, parents who refused could be jailed.

For years, parents in Waywayseecappo, as those in other communities, resisted sending their children to faraway schools. A government official overseeing Waywayseecappo (one of the so-called "Indian agents" who was in charge of enforcing federal policy on reserves) reported in 1907, "I am quite safe in saying that very few parents voluntarily bring their children to school."[13]

One reason was surely the mortality rate. In 1902, for example, at least six students died at the Brandon residential school. The following year, nine more died, which prompted a statistically minded government official to note: "a larger percentage than the average number of deaths has occurred."[14]

Carpentry class at the Brandon Indian Residential School, circa 1910 (United Church of Canada Archives, 93.049P/1368N)

Heavy farming equipment crushed at least one student during field labour, but mostly the killers were preventable diseases such as scarlet fever, pneumonia, tuberculosis, and typhoid, abetted by a crowded building that incubated illness. "From time to time sickness came," wrote Reverend Semmens in his journal. "It was sad beyond measure when we had to bury a pupil so far away from home and friends. Distress keen and trying was felt when in hours of extreme illness the dear children longed for their dusky mothers and their humble wigwam homes."[15] Of course, it was the reverend who had separated the children from their families in the first place.

A recruiter of students wrote to a Methodist leader in 1907 to say that parents in Manitoba had become "dumb to entreaties" to send their children to the Brandon school. The student deaths "completely knock the attempts re: Brandon . . . in the head. They just sit right down on a fellow. And one must shut up because there is at least a degree of justice on their side."[16]

Across Canada, thousands of students died at residential schools. It is hard to say with much precision how many, because of shoddy record keeping and unmarked graves, but the number is at least 4,400 and possibly many multiples of that.[17] They died from disease, from malnutrition, from neglect. Duncan Campbell Scott, a bureaucrat who oversaw the residential school system for two decades, wrote in 1913: "It is quite within the mark to say that fifty per cent of the children who passed through these schools did not live to benefit from the education which they had received therein."[18] The second principal at the Brandon school, Reverend Doyle, kept a portrait of Campbell Scott hanging in his office.

══

As the years went on, more and more students from Waywayseecappo attended residential schools in the towns of Brandon and Birtle, largely as a result of unrelenting pressure by zealous missionaries and Indian agents. In a characteristically patronizing report, a federal inspector noted in 1914, "Education now occupies a prominent place in their minds, and it is now the desire of the band that their children shall receive an education not inferior to the average education of the white child. Slowly the light of civilization is penetrating and the marks of progress are apparent."[19]

The United Church took over the Brandon school from the Methodists in 1925 and oversaw a major renovation to the main building, including adding a limestone trim to the facade. In 1930, the revamped school published a promotional pamphlet saying that its students were being trained "to become happy, successful, and useful citizens when they go out to take their place in life."[20] According to the then principal Reverend Doyle, "a wholesome and balanced diet is being followed."[21]

Students and their concerned parents reported otherwise. In 1935, a mother with a child at the Brandon school wrote to the Department of Indian Affairs to report that students were so hungry that they were resorting to shoplifting in town stores. She accused the principal of "training the children to be thieves" by leaving them with no choice but "to steal to fill their empty bodys." A student who attended the school in the 1940s later detailed the experience he and hundreds of others endured: they ate food that was "prepared in the crudest of ways" and "served in very unsanitary conditions," including "milk that had manure in the bottom of the cans and homemade porridge that had grass-hopper legs and bird droppings in it." The students also faced "cruel disciplinary measures ... such as being tied to a flag pole, sent to bed with no food, literally beaten and slapped by staff."[22] Under these conditions, it is not surprising that so many students tried to escape.

A RELIABLE GAUGE of student abuse at the Brandon school was the steady stream of runaways. In 1942, twelve children between the ages of ten and fifteen fled the school. The problem worsened when Reverend Oliver Strapp became principal in 1944. Previously, Strapp had been principal at a residential school in Ontario, where the year before he faced complaints of "improper conduct" with female students.[23] There was no formal investigation, and the United Church shuttled him to Brandon. An Indian agent described Strapp as "an aggressive type" and a "strict disciplinarian."[24] Jim Cote, a former student from Waywayseecappo, recalls Strapp's fondness for corporal punishment with a leather belt: "He certainly earned his name."

Reverend Oliver Strapp (Manitoba Historical Society, "Memorable Manitobans: Oliver Bailey Strapp," Courtesy of Gayle Strank)

There were so many runaways during Strapp's time that the problem came to the attention of Tommy Douglas—preacher of gospel, pioneer of medicare, and premier of Saskatchewan. On September 23, 1946, RCMP officers forcefully removed Clifford Shepherd, aged fourteen, and his sister Verna from a day school on the Moose Mountain Reserve, in Saskatchewan, against the wishes of their parents. The two children were transported two hundred kilometres away to the Brandon residential school. A few days later, Premier Douglas sent a telegram to the federal minister of Indian affairs:

CLIFFORD AND VERNA CHILDREN OF JOHN SHEPHERD OF MOOSE MOUNTAIN RESERVE AT CARLYLE WERE FORCIBLY REMOVED FROM DAY SCHOOL LAST MONDAY BY RCMP AND SENT TO BRANDON INDIAN SCHOOL –STOP– FATHER AND MEMBERS OF BAND HAVE PROTESTED ARBITRARY ACTION [. . .] –STOP– SCHOOL PRINCIPAL AND [INSPECTOR OF INDIAN AGENCIES IN SASKATCHEWAN] OSTRANDER REFUSE TO TAKE ACTION TO RESTORE CHILDREN TO RESERVE ALTHOUGH DAY SCHOOL AFFORDS ADEQUATE ACCOMMODATION AND INSTRUCTION –STOP– THIS MATTER REQUIRES YOUR IMMEDI-ATE ATTENTION FOR WHICH I THANK YOU –STOP–[25]

On October 9, Clifford ran away from the school when students were let outside to play. Two days later, the RCMP tracked him down in the town of Redvers, Saskatchewan, 150 kilometres southwest of the school and most of the way home. He was taken into custody and dropped off at the Brandon school at three thirty in the morning of October 12.

Three weeks later, Clifford escaped again. This time, he made it all the way home, travelling most of the distance by stowing himself in a boxcar of a freight train. The RCMP eventually located him on his reserve. When apprehended, Clifford was wearing a tweed cap, an air force jacket, and a grey-and-blue shirt with matching overalls. Once again, the officers drove him back to the Brandon school.

In early December, Clifford escaped a third time, along with two other boys from the same reserve, aged nine and eleven. Principal Strapp himself set off in pursuit, driving his car along the highway headed west, asking farmers about errant children. Later that day, Strapp and RCMP officers found Clifford and the other two boys walking along the Canadian Pacific rail line, twelve kilometres west of the school, where they were "successfully apprehended," according to an RCMP report. The boys were then driven back. "Just as we entered the school," Strapp later wrote, "Clifford made an attempt to run away again and put up quite a fight." During the struggle, Clifford managed to land a kick to Strapp's groin—a fact that Strapp himself did not acknowledge, though an RCMP report did. "I was compelled," Strapp said, "to use considerable force to remove him to the dormitory." The principal pinned Clifford to a bed and sent another student to retrieve a strap.

After inflicting corporal punishment, Strapp asked Clifford to give his word that he would not attempt another escape. Clifford refused. Strapp then decided to lock Clifford into a room alone and without clothes. In the days that followed, Clifford remained in confinement, naked, with meals delivered at regular intervals. According to an RCMP report, Clifford "threatens openly that he will leave the minute his clothes are returned to him."

Shortly thereafter, Tommy Douglas once again wrote to the minister of Indian affairs to demand that something be done to remedy the situation. Douglas had heard that "the boy, Clifford, has again run away from the Brandon Residential School and returned home by hitch hiking and on foot. I understand that he travelled through a severe blizzard and returned home ill-clothed and in a weakened condition." And Douglas had heard of others running away, too. "These incidents," he wrote, "have caused grave concerns among the Indians of the district," who worried that "the children in the Brandon Residential School are not properly cared for, that they do not receive sufficient supervision or training, and that the food is inadequate." Douglas urged the minister to reconsider the possibility of "returning these children to their parents" and sending them to a nearby day school.

A copy of the premier's letter found its way to Reverend G. Dorey of the United Church, which was then responsible for administering the school. The reverend joked to a colleague that if Premier Douglas accepted allegations of Indians "at their face value . . . all I can say is that he will have plenty to do looking after the Indians . . . without being able to give much time to his duties as Premier."[26]

On January 6, 1947, Douglas wrote directly to Principal Strapp to emphasize that "neither [Clifford] nor his parents desire that he continue as a student of your school." Douglas added, "I do think that it is improper to coerce a lad of fourteen years into remaining at your school by locking him in his room and depriving him of his clothing. I am certain you will agree with me on this score."

Clifford was allowed to return home three weeks later. When questioned by the RCMP, Strapp blamed Clifford's escapes on encouragement from the boy's parents and relatives. As for the federal minister of Indian affairs, he assured Douglas that the school was well run and providing a "satisfactory" diet. Of course, this wasn't true—not then or long after.[27]

STRAPP STAYED. MORE students fled. Bleak reports about the Brandon school continued piling up. In 1951, a visiting nurse observed, "The overall picture of the institution is pretty grim."[28] That same year, a regional supervisor for Indian Affairs wrote, "There is certainly something wrong as children are running away most of the time. . . . The sooner we make a change the better."[29]

One of the runaways was Jim Cote, a boy from Waywaysee-cappo. Jim was twelve when he arrived at the Brandon school in 1953, having been expelled from the residential school in Birtle for refusing to let a teacher inflict corporal punishment on him. Jim had dared to snatch the strap out of his teacher's hand and chase the teacher around the room with it.

As a student in Brandon, Jim spent half his days doing physical labour, cleaning the barn and milking a cow he nicknamed Elsey. Jim talked to Elsey while he pumped her udders, hoping she didn't kick. "Hey Elsey," he said. "How are you doing today?" He milked her at dawn and dusk. Elsey provided more milk than the other cows, but the school officials didn't know that because Jim was sneaking in a full cup in the barn twice a day, a supplement to the school's otherwise execrable diet.

At night in the dormitory, Jim listened to boys sniffling and crying, talking about their homes. "We suffered humiliation, physical abuse, sexual abuse," he recalls. It wasn't long before he resolved to escape. The fact that the school was 150 kilometres from his home in Waywayseecappo did not deter him. "I didn't tell anyone I was going to run away," he says. "I was afraid of a snitch."

One morning, he ran out of the building and kept running. "I just ran, I was happy, I was headed home to see my mom and dad and that gave me the strength to go. I was running far from that damn school and barn, away from Elsey!"

Jim stayed away from the main roads to avoid capture. When it became too cloudy to orient himself by the sun, he carefully examined trees because he knew moss grows best on the north side of the trunks. At night, he found a quiet spot in a wooded area and sheltered himself from the wind with branches he gathered. As Jim listened to coyotes howl in the dark, he imagined his family's dog, Sparkie, lying in a nearby bush to protect him.

Jim fed himself by sneaking into the gardens of "white folks" and stuffing as many potatoes, beets, carrots, and turnips into his pockets as he could run with. "I ate potatoes like apples," he says. He recalls that one pilfered carrot was a good seven inches long—"I never ate a carrot that tasted so good." He also gorged on dark saskatoon berries and rosy-red chokecherries, which were so tart his lips puckered.

After three days of flight, entirely on foot, Jim finally made it back to Waywayseecappo. He had covered more than the distance of a marathon each day. "I was a tough little bugger," he says. When Jim arrived home—exhausted, triumphant—his mother gave him a big hug. Then she told him to brush his teeth, which were blackened by all the berries.

It wasn't long until his father, Hugh, said, "You know you're going to have to go back, right?" Since truancy remained a federal offence for which Jim's parents could be sent to jail, the family had no meaningful choice.[30] When Waywayseecappo's Indian agent found out that Jim was with his parents, he promptly drove him back to Brandon. Jim's three-day escape was undone by three hours in the back of a flatbed truck.

Strapp was finally removed as principal in 1955. Jim recalls that when students heard the news, they let out a loud cheer. "It was like we got rid of a devil." Incredibly—or, perhaps, not too surprisingly—the United Church then appointed Strapp principal at another school, this one in Alberta. He was reprimanded five years later by a government official for the "poor diet" his students were receiving.[31] Strapp retired the following year, at the age of sixty-nine, and lived peaceably into his late eighties.

Problems at the Brandon school persisted after Strapp's departure. A senior government official told a colleague in 1956 that he was "disturbed about the serious danger of the adverse publicity which is likely to arise from the unsatisfactory operation of the Brandon school"—as if the prospect of bad publicity was the most disturbing thing.[32]

DURING THE YEARS Linda walked the school hallways in her black oxfords, the principal, Ford Bond, regimented the school like an army barracks. They recited prayers four times a day: after breakfast, before class, after supper, and before bed.

In the evening, the students were lined up for showers, counted, and given half a teaspoon of baking soda to wash their teeth with. Supervisors counted the children multiple times a day to make sure nobody had strayed or run away. Linda's brother, Matthew, once made a daring escape by tying a makeshift rope with bedsheets and lowering himself from the third-floor window of the boys' dormitory. He was caught by the road, along with two other fugitive students, and welcomed back with an exemplary strapping.

The school's assistant administrator was the hawk-eyed Mrs. McKay, who was known to stalk the halls with a long ruler in her right hand. She had worked her way up from head of the sewing room and was now in charge of all the female students. "We had to go by what she said," Linda later said. "She was kinda—well, the boss." When the students lined up outside the dining room for a head count before every mealtime, Mrs. McKay insisted on absolute silence. She used to say that she wanted "to be able to hear a needle drop."

FIFTY YEARS LATER, Linda says she would prefer to forget about her four years at the Brandon school, but she can't. "No matter what I went through, I always remembered," she says. "Ha ha ha!"

Linda's laugh takes some getting used to. She often says unfunny things, then bursts into joyless laughter, typically in spurts of three with enough force to empty her lungs. It is a smoker's laugh, raspy, as close to a cough as a laugh can be. "We all cope in different ways," she says, speaking of residential school Survivors. "Some become alcoholics, some don't. I chose to drink my life away, ha ha ha!"

Linda has repeatedly sought help for her addiction. She checked herself into treatment centres five times: in 1974, 1986, 1995, 2001, and 2005. In her fifties, she developed cirrhosis, a disease often caused by a liver drowning in booze. Her doctor told her she would die if she didn't stop drinking. Linda's mother, who also attended a residential school, developed the same condition sooner in life. She died at forty-two. Linda is sober now, except on the worst days.

Her favourite activity is spending time with her grandchildren. She makes a point of speaking to them in Ojibway and saying she loves them—two things she had rarely done with her own children.

Linda never says "residential school." She says, simply, "residential"—as in, "after residential, I felt guilty for years anytime I grew out my hair." She has tried to push the memories away, but they might as well be nailed into her. She remembers her loneliness. She remembers her fear. She remembers that her mother never visited. "Mom was always drunk, ha ha ha!"

Linda speaks little and softly. In conversation, she angles her face slightly to the left as she listens. That's because she's deaf in her left ear.

One day, Mrs. McKay rang the bell for dinnertime. Linda was six years old, and had been at the school for only two months. Fifteen minutes were allotted for supper, and students had mere seconds to form a straight, orderly line outside the dining room, which was in the basement of the school building. "As soon as the bell would go, there was no time," Linda says.

As Linda found a place in the queue, she realized that she had forgotten her shoes. She had rushed from the dormitory upstairs, belly growling with hunger, without realizing her mistake. Now Mrs. McKay was standing at the entrance of the dining room, counting each student she let in, and there was no time for Linda to do anything except look guilty. Sure enough, when Linda's turn came, Mrs. McKay noticed she was in her socks and asked where her shoes were. At first Linda didn't respond, frozen with fear and unsure of her English, but then she tried to explain she had forgotten them. Mrs. McKay stepped toward Linda, cocking her right arm as she approached. With an open palm, she struck Linda hard on the left side of her head. Linda staggered, then began to cry. Mrs. McKay told her to retrieve her shoes.

"I remember crying and holding my left ear and running upstairs to get my shoes," Linda later said in sworn testimony. After finding them, she sat down on the edge of her bed and put her hands over her ears—the ringing in her head was overpowering. By the time she returned to the dining room wearing her black oxfords, the only food left to put on her plate was a piece of bread.

After that, Linda always remembered her shoes. And she never heard with her left ear again.

Ha, ha, ha.

3

"AN INDIAN THINKS"

ICHAEL TWOVOICE, MAUREEN'S PATERNAL GRAND-
father, was born in 1920. He came to be seen as one
of Waywayseecappo's greatest minds and orators.
"He could out-talk any white man," his friend Jim Cote fondly
remembers. According to family lore, the name Twovoice comes
from the sounds that follow a nearby lightning bolt: first a boom,
then a rumble.

Michael loved words. He read constantly—newspapers,
magazines, books, whatever he could get his hands on. He even
liked to carry around a dictionary, just in case. One time, after
he spotted a cougar prowling the reserve, friends asked him to
describe it. To Michael, the animal wasn't "fast" or "quick" but,
rather, "fleet-footed."

Michael's way with words made him Waywayseecappo's go-to
MC for holiday parties and charity events. He chaired community
meetings. He occasionally preached in the reserve's Presbyterian
church, though he wasn't the pastor, or even a Presbyterian. He
was a Catholic, but that didn't seem to bother anyone because

he sure knew his Bible. Beside his bed, he kept a copy with an Ojibway translation.

Michael Twovoice (Courtesy of Maureen Twovoice)

Michael walked with a limp, slightly stooped over to his left side. As a young man, he had lost a lung to tuberculosis, so strenuous activity left him huffing and puffing. He did not own a car, and when walking from the reserve to Rossburn he needed to take breaks. Sometimes, while he caught his breath, he lit a cigarette. You could hear the phlegm in his voice.

Michael, his wife, and their children lived on the reserve in a modest two-bedroom house with little insulation. When it was cold in the winter, Michael kept the fire going all night. On particularly hot summer days, he went shirtless. That's when his children could see the six-inch scar below his left armpit that looked like a zipper.

A dedicated writer, Michael often worked at a small brown desk in the corner of the living room. His daughter, Hazel, could always tell when he was thinking deeply about something, searching for just the right words: he would prop his elbows on the desk, look out the window, and chain-smoke. He couldn't afford a typewriter, so he wrote by hand, his letters looping and elegant, his glasses slipping halfway down his nose. He kept his papers neatly ordered in the desk's six drawers to protect them from the entropy of his children. "Don't touch my paperwork," he gently reminded them. "There's important stuff in there."

In 1951, Michael published an essay in the *Rossburn Review* titled "An Indian Thinks."[1] It begins like this: "It often amuses me, when I am among white strangers, to have them look at me intently, quite unaware that I am observing them. As they gaze at my expressionless and impassive features, I know they are wondering what goes on in an Indian's mind. What does go on in an Indian's mind? I shall attempt to answer this question in part."

For Michael, as for others, the answer was complicated.

MICHAEL DEVOTED MUCH of his life to politics. As one of the few Indians of his generation to get his high school diploma, he tended to be thrust into roles that involved writing. After serving in the Canadian military during the Second World War, Michael worked as the secretary to Waywayseecappo's Chief, Prince Astakeesic. He then became the secretary for the Manitoba Indian Association, an organization that dedicated itself to reforming the Indian Act, the federal law that set out rules that applied only to Indians and detailed the many ways in which bureaucrats were empowered to micromanage them.

At a fundamental level, Michael believed that Indians needed more control over their own lives. "Things will never change," he told his son Maurice, "as long as those guys over there are calling the shots." His finger wagged vaguely towards Ottawa and the Department of Indian Affairs. "We will progress more as Native people when we can govern ourselves," he said.

Michael insisted that his children "never, ever look down on anybody or judge anybody by the colour of their skin, whether they're black, Chinese, or white." Michael didn't mention any of his own experiences with discrimination. "He went to residential school," Hazel says. "Maybe that's where he learned about racism."

In 1951, the Indian Act was amended. Michael welcomed some of the changes: restrictions on Indian ceremonies and dancing were removed, as were limitations on hiring lawyers. But Michael thought that more drastic change was still urgently required. He applauded Indians who continued "appealing for justice to the Canadian government." They were "right in fighting for their security and other humanitarian rights which, at this date, are not given. . . . It is only just and fair that the Parliament of Canada should heed their plea." Real progress would not occur, he wrote, unless "barriers which are hedging in the Indian of today, in matters of handling their own affairs, are broken down."

At the time, federal Indian agents still enjoyed immense, and virtually unchecked, power over life on reserves. For example, an Indian on reserve could not sell their produce or cattle off reserve without the specific permission of an Indian agent. This was typical of the kind of paternalistic government that Michael despised. "We can't just obey anymore," he said. "Let's do things on our own. We don't need any help from the Indian agent."

In 1952, a new Indian agent, Fred Clarke, arrived in Waywayseecappo, along with his wife, Lillian. Fred wore his pants high, well above his hips, which did not so much obscure his considerable belly as make his upper body look compressed. While Fred worked as the Indian agent, his wife worked in the community as a nurse. The Clarkes went on to spend five years in Waywayseecappo, until Fred was rotated to another reserve in 1957. Upon their departure, Lillian published a letter reflecting upon their experience. "The years we spent on Wayway were very happy ones," she wrote. "We had a comfortable four bedroom home but no telephone, electricity and no water!" Mrs. Clarke was probably not aware that people on the reserve used to sardonically refer to her home as "God's house."

"Most of the Indian people," Mrs. Clarke wrote, "are very reserved and withdrawn until a white person proves himself to them and gains their respect and trust. They always seem to expect persons in authority to treat them as an inferior class." Perhaps Mrs. Clarke had some sense why. In any case, she believed she and her husband were different: "Our friends on Wayway soon found out that they were to be treated as equals."[2]

She did not mention the fact that her "equals" were still not allowed to vote in federal elections, a right they wouldn't receive until 1960, the same year Premier Tommy Douglas observed that Canada was still treating the Indian as "a second-class citizen." "We are going to have to make up our minds," Douglas said, "whether we are going to keep the Indian bottled up in a sort of Canadian Apartheid."[3]

Fred Clarke served as Waywayseecappo's Indian agent during a time when many of the community's children were being hauled off to residential schools. One of them was Jim Cote. When Jim escaped from the Brandon Indian Residential School and ran 150 kilometres to give his parents a hug at home in Waywayseecappo, Fred Clarke was the Indian agent who promptly drove him all the way back.

★ ★ ★

ON JANUARY 17, 1957, residents of Rossburn gathered at the town hall to fete the Clarkes before their departure. The evening featured songs and hymns, an accordion solo, a piano-accordion duet, and a tap dance. The next day, another goodbye ceremony was held in Waywayseecappo. There, a local man rose "on behalf of all the members of the Waywayseecappo Reserve" to thank the Clarkes. He said news of their departure had left the people of Waywayseecappo "with heavy hearts." The Clarkes had arrived soon after new revisions to the Indian Act. "We needed someone to guide us and lead us through it all. Then through God's holy providence you were sent to us."

"Although you were vested with much authority over us," the speaker continued, "you met us on our level. You were not prejudiced because our colors were different, you thereby gave us a chance to cast aside our cloaks of inferiority complex." In time, the community had "learned to love and appreciate you."[4] In concluding, he bade the Clarkes farewell and offered a pair of lamps as a gift.

A reporter from the *Rossburn Review* was so impressed by the speech that he typed up the whole thing for publication in the following week's paper. The speech concluded with these words:

> *Thank you for what you have done for us and please forgive us*
> *if we haven't done too much for you.*
> > *On behalf of my people, I am*
> > *Michael Twovoice*

Indeed, it was Michael Twovoice, dedicated opponent of the Indian Act, who so effusively praised an Indian agent. Was this simply a tactical curtsy to power, or a sign of something else? What *was* going on in Michael's mind?

Michael left behind his published words, fossils of a vibrant mind. Unfortunately, his personal papers, which he had scrupulously ordered and archived, were lost in a fire after his death. The remaining fragments do not resolve his paradoxes but deepen them.

In 1959, two years after his speech in honour of the Clarkes, Michael published a short and telling history of Waywayseecappo in the *Rossburn Review*.[5] He started back at the beginning, when Waywayseecappo and his braves roamed in peace over a "vast tract of land" that was "rich in game, fowl and fur." Then "the Great Queen Victoria's representatives [came] to stipulate lasting treaties with the Indians across the breadth of the Prairies to the Rocky Mountains." After Chief Waywayseecappo signed a treaty and his band moved to the reserve, the "only enemy" that remained was "the onslaught of the deep-freeze of winter." Michael commended the government for being "benevolent" to Chief Waywayseecappo "and his braves."

The government should be "given full credit" for improving "the Welfare of the people" and "steering them in the things of life that are good," Michael wrote. "The Indians of Waywayseecappo feel forever grateful for this, as they have been well cared for from the earliest times." These are hardly the words of a revolutionary.

Michael went on to praise the "unceasing labor in the spiritual welfare of the people" by the Presbyterian and Catholic missionaries. "Much can be said of both churches in administering to the Indians," he wrote. They established the first schools on the reserve, though these were "given up when Residential Schools were built in centrally located places to serve a greater number of Reserves." Michael's history included no criticism of these residential schools.

In 1960, Michael did appear before Waywayseecappo's band council to address a concern he had about residential schools. The concern was this: Michael wanted to ensure that Roman Catholic children had access to Roman Catholic instruction.[6] The next year, Michael was asked by the band council to personally escort a child to the Brandon Indian Residential School, because the parents did not seem to be providing adequate care at home. Michael drove along the same roads that Agent Fred Clarke had taken when driving Jim Cote back after his escape.[7]

When it came time for Michael's own children to be sent to residential schools, his daughter Hazel recalls, "There was sadness. But he never said, 'You aren't going to go.' You had to accept it. They just took us."

MICHAEL TWOVOICE WROTE in his 1951 essay that, for Indians, "it is one of their greatest ambitions to be assimilated generally into all phases of Canadian life—social, political and economical."

Assimilate. That was a word the government of Canada had been using for a long time. Prime Minister John A. Macdonald said, "The great aim of our legislation has been to do away with the tribal system and assimilate the Indian people in all respects with the other inhabitants of the Dominion, as speedily as they are fit for the change."[8] For the Canadian government, assimilation was both means and end.

Did Michael Twovoice embody Macdonald's grand plans? As a child, Michael attended the Qu'Appelle Indian Industrial

School in Saskatchewan, also known as the Lebret Residential School. A history of the school, published in 1955, was dedicated to "the great missionary pioneers, men and women, who spent their lives . . . for the civilization and the Christianization of the Indian Nation."[9] No doubt Michael's time at this school left a lasting mark. As Jim Cote puts it, "Mike was a smart man, educated. He was well taught at residential school."

Unlike many of his contemporaries, Michael cultivated ties in Rossburn. In 1952, he posted an ad in the Classified section of the *Rossburn Review*: "POSITION WANTED—Desire job as assistant in any town establishment. Have qualified Junior Matriculation. Nationality – Indian. Steady employment preferable. Contact Michael Twovoice."[10]

The fact that Michael felt the need to disclose his Indian "nationality" says a lot about the norms of the time, and his willingness to abide by them. In any case, he got what he wanted: his ad landed him a job . . . working at the *Rossburn Review*, as an assistant editor. Years later, after a fire damaged his family's home, Michael received gifts of clothing and supplies from people in town. Afterwards, he published a letter in the newspaper on behalf of his family: "We would like to extend our thanks to our friends in Rossburn."[11] On another occasion, Michael was the one receiving public thanks in the paper for his contribution to a charity bake sale in Rossburn.

Michael's daughter, Hazel, remembers trips to Rossburn's butcher shop with her dad, who took pleasure in bantering with the staff. Hazel saw that her dad wasn't afraid when he spoke to white people. She loved that about him.

"See," Michael told his daughter, "that's why you go to school. So you can talk with these people." Michael always insisted that she stay in school, no matter how frustrated she got. "You have to learn," he told her. "You have to learn the white man's ways to survive. We're living in their world." The point of all this, as far as Hazel could tell, was that her dad wanted her to have access to everything Canada had to offer. "That's why education was so important to him," Hazel says. "So we could communicate with all kinds of people, so we could work with them." Michael knew there was a system restricting the social mobility of Indians, and he wanted his children to have a pass.

IN 1951, MICHAEL was thirty-one years old, father to three children, and infected with tuberculosis, which had destroyed his left lung and threatened his life. He went to a sanatorium in Brandon, where a surgeon removed a rib and the infected lung. Michael penned his essay "An Indian Thinks" during his convalescence— his side aching, his fresh stitches itching, and the site of the surgery still just a patched wound, not yet a scar. Michael had just sacrificed one lung to protect the other. Now he was asking himself what he was willing to concede to survive in Canada.

Michael refused to renounce his culture. "I, for one, am proud to have been born an Indian," he wrote. "I take pride in our traditions and heritage as Canada's own children of nature." Michael spoke Cree and Ojibway fluently. With his children, he stuck mostly to Ojibway. And he attended local Sun Dances, though not as often as some others. In a photo taken at a Sun Dance, Michael is seen standing alongside his wife, Annie, as a spectator, not participating as a dancer in regalia. He is present and supportive, yet somehow apart.

At the same time, he served as an informal intermediary between the government and Waywayseecappo. One of his friends on the reserve, Norbert Tanner, saw him as a bridge. On many occasions, when a government official visited Waywayseecappo, community members would ask Michael to speak on their behalf. He was tasked with explaining to Indian agents like Fred Clarke the concerns of his community. In turn, Michael often appeared before Waywayseecappo's band council to explain in Ojibway what the government was trying to do. "He talked to both sides, to make sure everyone had a clearer understanding of what was going on," Tanner says. "Mike was an interpreter." To help his community as best he could, and to survive the challenges he had faced in his own life, Michael Twovoice had learned to speak with two voices.

Despite everything Michael had seen and endured, he was still convinced that the government meant well, that Canada could change, that the future could brighten—if not in time for him, at least for the generations to follow. "In this country, with its democratic principles and its great opportunities for achievement," Michael wrote, he hoped for a future in which Indians "shall not be discriminated against or retarded in any way." Michael wanted to believe in Canada's promise, even though Canada had always relegated him to second-class status. The residential school where he had learned to write was premised on the idea that his culture was backwards and worthless. As of 1951, when Michael wrote his essay, Canada still did not trust him enough to cast a vote or buy a beer. The Brandon Sanatorium where he was receiving treatment for tuberculosis was a segregated facility. Indian patients were not allowed to mix with white patients, even though they were all suffering from the same disease.

Michael knew what it was to be separate and unequal, and that's not what he wanted for his children. He believed they would have to adapt, as he had, as he would continue to do. He thought that the best hope for his children was "a good education."

From his bed in the sanatorium, he concluded his essay: "It gladdens my Indian heart to visualize the future in which I see my people working side by side with their palefaced brothers, making of this wonderful country a still greater Canada. I think of the inevitable day when I shall have reached with my children the parting of the ways. . . . As they stand proudly on the threshold of their futures, I shall say to them, 'Children, there lies your Canada, yours by heritage. Make use of its vast opportunities.'"

As early as 1948, the federal government could see that residential schools were failing.[12] At that time, there were seventy-two residential schools in operation, educating 9,368 children, but the attitude in the Department of Indian Affairs, according to one history, "was that the sooner the residential schools were done away with the better."[13]

Economic considerations drove the government's about-face. The population of Indian students was rapidly increasing, and bureaucrats wanted to avoid building and maintaining yet more costly residential facilities. The first alternative was opening more day schools on reserves, where students could be educated while living at home. An analysis by the Department of Indian Affairs determined that the cost per student at a residential school was nearly four times more than the cost at a day school.[14] A senior bureaucrat argued that "the education requirements of the great majority of the Indians could be met by day schools to the decided benefit of the Indians and to the financial benefit of the taxpayer."[15] Schools on reserves also happened to be what treaties between the government and Indigenous leaders in the nineteenth century had explicitly called for, though this did not seem to be a factor in the policy shift.

In a total reversal, the government came to doubt the wisdom of educating children away from their parents after all. In the new era of "educational services," according to one government memo following the change, "everything possible will be done to enable families to stay together so children will not have to be separated from their parents needlessly."[16] In Waywayseecappo, the result of the shift was the opening of two day schools in the 1950s. A majority of students from Waywayseecappo, including Linda Jandrew and Jim Cote, continued to be sent away to residential schools in Brandon and Birtle. But more and more were being educated on the reserve, close to their homes and families. (It would still take almost five decades to close all these schools, largely because of staunch resistance from some of the churches running them.[17] That is why Linda could still be put on a bus to the Brandon residential school in 1965.)

Meanwhile, the federal government was also developing another option that it preferred most of all: the integration of Indian students into provincial public schools. Again, the prospect of lowering expenditures weighed heavily. The cost of integrated education "would in the end be substantially less" than the cost of running a separate school system, federal bureaucrats concluded.[18] The Department of Indian Affairs became "convinced that where possible, Indian children should be educated in association with children of other racial groups."[19]

In the United States, a parallel movement was taking place to integrate Black children into public schools. "Separate educational facilities are inherently unequal," the United States Supreme Court ruled in a ground-breaking judgment in 1954, Brown v. Board of Education. "To separate [Black children] from others of similar age and qualifications solely because of their race generates a feeling of inferiority as to their status in the community that may affect their hearts and minds in a way unlikely ever to be undone."[20] This argument—that racial separation was necessarily harmful—gained traction in Ottawa as well. The Canadian government came to believe that racial integration in public schools was the best recipe for equality. By passing more time with white peers, officials noted, Indians could "quicken and give meaning to the acculturative process through which they are passing."[21] Which is to say: the method was changing, from segregated to integrated schools, but the goal remained assimilation.

By the late 1950s, the Department of Indian Affairs was pressuring Waywayseecappo to send its children to study in Rossburn and selling Rossburn on the merits of opening its schools to students from the reserve. The incentive for public school boards to accept Indigenous children was simple: more funding. The federal government paid school boards for every Indian pupil attending a public school and also promised to invest in upgrades to elementary and secondary school buildings. In exchange, school boards had to agree that "there will be no segregation in the schools by reason of race or colour."[22]

On March 30, 1961, Rossburn's school board agreed to accept students from the reserve. The only remaining hurdle was approval by Waywayseecappo's elected band council, which scheduled a meeting on April 11 to debate the measure. The question was whether it would be better for their children to receive a segregated federal education, on the reserve and at residential schools, or an integrated education in the provincial public school system.

Four days before the band council meeting, a teacher at Waywayseecappo's day school, C.M. King, wrote to the federal government to express doubts about integrated education in Rossburn. King was "deeply agitated" because he doubted children from the reserve would "cope with the troubles that a minority group meets in an integrated situation." He did not think that Rossburn's teachers were aware of the distinct needs of Indian children or would "take the time to give . . . the extra consideration" these students might need. Instead, he worried that Rossburn was just allowing Indian students to enrol to "reap the harvest of many more dollars to pay for their new school expenditures." He added: "I feel that integration of all children is the coming thing, but I also feel that it is not yet time for total integration. . . . It looks to me that Rossburn School has more to gain than the Indian child."[23] None of these prescient warnings were heeded.

When Waywayseecappo's Chief and four band councillors met on April 11, they voted unanimously to close the day schools on the reserve and send their students into Rossburn. One of these councillors was Michael Twovoice, then serving in his first term as an elected member of the council. He signed the resolution in his refined cursive.[24]

Michael, a product of residential school, helped usher in the era of integrated education. "Children, there lies your Canada, yours by heritage," Michael had written hopefully a decade before. "Make use of its vast opportunities." For too many children in Waywayseecappo, and on reserves across Canada, it didn't work out that way.

4

"WHITEWASH"

B Y THE TIME THE BRANDON INDIAN RESIDENTIAL
School fully closed in 1970, about half of all Native students across Canada were attending provincial public
schools. Linda had left Brandon the previous year, after finishing Grade 4. She was "discharged," as the Department of Indian
Affairs records put it, as if she were leaving a prison or a hospital.
Linda returned home to live with her aunt and enrolled in Grade 5
at Rossburn Elementary, where the experiment in integration
had been under way for a decade. Linda found herself among 160
students from Waywayseecappo studying in town.

Linda was glad to escape the horrors of Brandon, but now
she had to deal with white classmates in Rossburn calling her
a "wagon burner." The expression never made any sense to her,
but apparently Indians were known to torch cowboy wagons in
Hollywood movies. "Dirty Indian" was another favourite, along
with "savage," the classic. As a girl, Linda could expect to be called
a "squaw." "The teachers didn't really stop the white students
from saying these things," Linda remembers. "On the playground,

white students stood in little groups of four or five and called me names. They thought they were smart. They weren't. I tried to ignore them. It hurt."

Linda had struggled as a student ever since Mrs. McKay had struck her in the ear. The assault shattered her trust in authority figures like teachers. She took to sitting at the back of class, where her impaired hearing made it even more difficult for her to follow lessons. She also avoided raising her hand. "I was scared to ask anything after I got hit."

In Rossburn, Linda often felt like white students were laughing at her, but she never really understood why. And she didn't find the teachers, all of whom were white, much better. "I always felt unwanted," she says. "The teachers couldn't care less if we were there or not. They were always yelling at us. They were more on the white side." Linda retreated behind the thickest shell she could muster and kept to the company of other students from Waywayseecappo whenever possible. "I stayed away from whites as much as I could," she says. "I felt unsafe all the time. I wanted to get away from there. We could have gotten hurt on the playground and teachers wouldn't have done anything about it. They didn't give a shit, ha ha ha."

Linda made her own lunch every morning: two fried eggs, which she placed in a plastic sandwich bag before embarking on her thirty-minute walk to school. The school also provided a small carton of chocolate milk at noon to all the students from the reserve, paid for by Waywayseecappo's band council. Still, Linda had to fight to protect her lunch from hungry students who tried to take her cold fried eggs. "I felt bad for kids who had no lunch," she says. "But I thought, it's not my fault. I wasn't going to walk home on an empty stomach."

Former teachers from this period attest to difficult conditions facing many of their students from Waywayseecappo. One teacher says she kept spare towels and soap in the classroom, so that her students from the reserve could slip away as discreetly as possible for a hot shower, something that was often not available in their homes. A former principal, Con Erickson, recalls that during the bitter cold of the winter, many students showed up at school without hats and mittens, so a group of his teachers collected winter gear so that every student could safely go outside during recess.

One of the school's greatest challenges was regular attendance. "In order for a kid to get to school," Erickson says, "the kid has to get up, get dressed, eat if there is anything to eat, and be on the bus at eight in the morning. And if mom and dad are not helping, that's a pretty hard thing." Erickson recalls spotting children from the reserve hanging around town late at night because they had to wait for the adults to finish up at the bar.

Linda was living with her aunt, whose place was a thirty-minute walk from school, and Linda relied on her own legs to get to school and back. But when she was a little girl, before she was sent off to Brandon, she had once been one of those children, waiting outside the Rossburn Hotel in the dark, just wanting to go home.

IN 1969, PRIME Minister Pierre Trudeau's government unveiled a plan to deal with the separateness and inequality of Native peoples once and for all.[1] This proposal became enduringly known as "the White Paper." As the policy was unveiled, Minister of Indian Affairs Jean Chrétien said, "This government believes in equality." The central premise of the White Paper was that the best way to improve the living conditions of Indians was to treat them exactly like everyone else: "The separate legal status of Indians and the policies which have flowed from it have kept the Indian people apart from and behind other Canadians. . . . The treatment resulting from their different status has been often worse, sometimes equal and occasionally better than that accorded to their fellow citizens. What matters is that it has been different."

The White Paper approach was consistent with Trudeau's view of Quebec, which he insisted should be a province like the others, without distinct status or powers. For Indians, as for Quebec, Trudeau saw different treatment as fundamentally at odds with the ideal of equality. As long as Indians were treated differently and kept separate, the White Paper argued, they would not become equal. The reserve system should accordingly be abolished, and services like education should be administered wholly by the provinces, not the federal government. The ongoing integration of Indian students into public schools would be just one aspect of a larger process of integration. "The traditional method of providing separate services to Indians must be ended," the White Paper continued. "The legal and administrative discrimination in the treatment of Indian people has not given them an equal chance of success. . . . Discrimination breeds discrimination by example, and the separateness of Indian people has affected the attitudes of other Canadians towards them." Here, the document might as well have invoked the attitude of many people in Rossburn, who harboured suspicions that the federal government, in dealing with Indians separately, was according them preferential treatment.

At this time, a man named Arnold Minish was superintendent of the Pelly Trail School Division, which included Rossburn's schools. Minish had become chair of the school division in 1968 and quickly earned the respect of Rossburn's high school principal, who described him as "young, dynamic, knowledgeable, aggressive and well-organized."[2] Minish was six foot four, with a booming voice. A former colleague remembers Minish as someone who "pushed his view forward as hard as he could. He was a little bullish."

On April 22, 1970, Minish mailed a letter to Minister Chrétien. "Dear Sir," Minish wrote,

> The Pelly Trail School Division . . . wishes to bring to your attention the utterly deplorable conditions on the Waywayseecappo Indian Band living on the Lizard Point Indian Reserve located at Rossburn, Manitoba.
>
> Indian students integrated into the Rossburn Elementary and High School systems . . . come from homes where work opportunities are nil, where moral standards are nonexistent, and where drunkenness and debauchery are the order of the day.
>
> The Pelly Trail School Division Board would like you to appear at a meeting to be held at Rossburn at your convenience to discuss ways and means of launching a frontal attack on the conditions of this reserve before they spill out into the surrounding community to a greater extent than they do now and destroy the surrounding civilization and particularly the school system.[3]

Chrétien's assistant replied that the minister was "sorry" to hear about the "problems" but believed "that this situation may be remedied with the cooperation of all involved."[4] Representatives from Waywayseecappo, the school board, and the federal government assembled in Rossburn in late June. The most senior federal official present was J.R. Wright, the district superintendent of education for Indian Affairs, who took extensive notes.[5]

Minish started the meeting with a lengthy presentation about the problems with Indian students in Rossburn's schools: their attendance was terrible and getting "progressively worse"; teachers expended disproportionate time and resources on them; their "general health and cleanliness" was questionable; many were too old for their grade; they were passive and showed "little interest" in their courses. Minish was also troubled that "Indian children were robbing lunch pails of non-Indian children." There were only a few thieves, he said, but they were disrupting the entire school. The underlying problem seemed to be children from Waywayseecappo arriving at school without lunch and having eaten no breakfast. As far as Minish was concerned, integration of Waywayseecappo's students into Rossburn's schools was not working. He "stressed that the climate in the school was getting worse and worse each year as the problems seem to mount rather than diminish."

The meeting then turned to a video recording of Dan George, a former Chief of the Tsleil-Waututh Nation in British Columbia, who discussed the challenges of integrated education from a Native point of view. (That same year, George starred alongside Dustin Hoffman in a Hollywood film called *Little Big Man*, for which he received an Oscar nomination.) In his recorded speech, George said:

> *You talk big words of integration in the schools. Does it really exist? . . . Unless there is integration of hearts and minds you have only a physical presence and the walls are as high as the mountain range. Come with me to the playgrounds of an integrated high school. . . . Over here is a group of white students and see over there near the fence a group of Native students . . . and a great chasm seems to be opening up between the two groups.*[6]

According to the meeting notes taken by J.R. Wright, several people then argued that the deeper issue "was a Waywayseecappo-Rossburn problem, that any lasting and useful solution would have to be the result of day-by-day communication between the people of Rossburn and the people of Waywayseecappo. Until such communication was in effect there would be hostilities between the two communities."

Wright concluded his report of the meeting with his own assessment:

The people on the Waywayseecappo Reserve must come to under-stand that they are masters of their own destiny and that the effectiveness of the education program for their children depends to a large extent on their willingness to create an environment on the reserve which will promote good learning habits on the part of the students. . . .

Just as the band members at Waywayseecappo must take action . . . so must the community around Waywayseecappo reassess their historical attitudes towards the Indian people in the area and must come to respect them as people having rights and privileges as do all the other people in the area, as people who are to be respected and treated with respect and trust by their neighbours in the larger community. There has been many, many years of mistrust and it can therefore be assumed that this change in attitude will require several years.

In the months that followed, Minish and Wright continued exchanging cordial letters, one superintendent to another, about the unfolding disaster. "The attendance of the Indian children in the Rossburn school is not good," Minish wrote on October 23, 1970.[7] For years, he had been trying to hire a truancy officer to help get more students from Waywayseecappo to school. Waywayseecappo's band council had even passed a resolution in 1968 approving the idea. But Minish had been unable to hire anyone because, he wrote, "the white people refuse to take the job of going onto the reserve to bring the Indian students to school." Minish settled for asking local RCMP officers to keep an eye out for students skipping class.

"I think it is indeed unfortunate," Wright replied five days later, "that no one in the Rossburn area will go on to the reserve for the purpose of enforcing school attendance, but this is perhaps understandable when one realises the hostility that has existed between the people at Rossburn and Waywayseecappo over the last many years."[8] It is not clear whether either man considered hiring someone from Waywayseecappo to perform the role.

At the end of 1971, Minish again wrote to Minister Jean Chrétien, this time to plead for additional federal funding.[9] He explained that providing remedial services for Indian students required resources that the school board could not afford. He acknowledged that the school board could, in theory, raise additional funds with "a special levy to help educate these children," but that would amount to an extra tax on families in the school district, and that was not going to happen. "We are in a dilemma," Minish explained, "as the Pelly Trail Board has established policy whereby they refuse to further subsidize the education of Indian children." Rural taxpayers felt they were carrying an unfair burden, and they'd had enough.[10] In years to come, this was to be a recurring theme in relations between Waywayseecappo and Rossburn.

In February 1972, Wright wrote a long and heartfelt letter to encourage Minish to make changes to help Indian students succeed:

71

I think all of us who are involved in implementing joint school projects were quite naive at the time as to the implication of the action that we were proposing. The result was that in many cases our joint school project was simply an exercise in which Indian children attended a provincial school, but where no real tangible changes in the Provincial school program were put into effect in order to meet the educational needs of the Indian children. The result has been that in almost every Division we have still large numbers of drop outs. . . . . Almost all the students go through the system without really gaining a pride in themselves or their heritage, two things which are essential if people are to live a happy life.[11]

Around that time, only 4 percent of Indian students across Canada were graduating from high school.[12] Wright offered a series of concrete suggestions: offering Ojibway language classes; changing the name of the school to the Rossburn-Waywayseecappo School; and teaching all students, not just Indian students, more about Native history and culture. "By this," Wright wrote, "I do not mean Indian culture that comes from the stereotype image that many people have gained about Indian people, but a real attempt on the part of the teaching staff and students to learn about Indian people in their area." Above all, he asked Minish to "insist that all education officials are committed to the fact that Indian children have the same basic intelligence as other children" and "can learn." If Minish did these things, he could create "really joint schools in fact as well as in name."

Minish did not stick around long enough to try. Later that year, he transferred to another school division.

By then, Linda had also left Rossburn after only one year in the elementary school. At the end of Grade 5, she was removed from her home by Manitoba's child welfare agency. Over the course of the next six years, she would live with nine white foster families, in places all over Manitoba. This was possible only because of a 1951 law that authorized provincial child welfare agencies to apprehend Indian children. Over the following three decades, more than twenty thousand Indian, Métis, and Inuit children were taken from their homes and sent out for adoption to primarily white families across Canada and the United States. Those not adopted outright were placed into foster homes. This widespread removal of Indian children from their homes is sometimes called the Sixties Scoop, but the practice was common through the 1980s.[13]

The United Way was the organization charged with arranging Linda's foster placements. At one point—Linda doesn't remember exactly which year—the United Way sent a photographer to take her portrait. In this photo, Linda is holding a rose. It is an image she vividly remembers because it ended up on the cover of a widely distributed pamphlet about adoption. In subsequent years, whenever Linda came across any of these pamphlets, she would pick them up, crush them inside her fist, and throw them into the closest garbage can.

As ARTHUR MINISH and J.R. Wright swapped letters about Waywayseecappo's students in Rossburn, Indigenous opponents of integrated education were mobilizing. Trudeau and Chrétien's White Paper had been resoundingly opposed by Native peoples. Cree leader Harold Cardinal described the government's policy as a "thinly disguised programme of extermination through assimilation" and ridiculed the government for trying to solve the "Indian problem" through "gallons of white paint liberally applied."[14]

The Manitoba Indian Brotherhood, an organization representing Manitoban Chiefs, gathered in 1971 to articulate a new vision for relations between Indians and non-Indians. Among those gathered was Hugh McKay, a friend of Michael Twovoice, who was then serving a two-year term as Waywayseecappo's elected Chief. The assembled leaders produced a manifesto called *Wahbung: Our Tomorrows*. It began with a declaration of "confidence in the integrity and goodwill of the majority of the people of Canada."[15] It also demanded an end to integrated education.

Wahbung called on the federal government to "recognize the total failure of the present education system for Indian people." Integrated education, the Chiefs believed, was just the latest iteration of education without "relevance to the Indian reality." The architects of integration had sought to bring Indians into the Canadian mainstream, and not without a measure of good intentions. But in the end, the new policy amounted to another "invitation to participate in the annihilation of our culture and our way of life. The government had simply rephrased this long standing invitation." Indian students continued to feel like strangers in the classroom, in schools that offered no instruction of Native cultures and languages. "Many non-Indians believe that we have failed education," *Wahbung* stated, "but the truth of the matter is that education has failed us." Across the country, Indian communities were protesting against integrated education in public schools.

The following year, another watershed document, titled "Indian Control of Indian Education," was released by the National Indian Brotherhood, or NIB. "Until now, decisions on the education of Indian children have been made by anyone and everyone, except Indian parents," the document declared. "This must stop." The NIB proposed locally controlled education aimed at two primary goals: first, to "reinforce . . . Indian identity," and, second, to prepare students to make "a good living in modern society." Twenty years earlier, Michael Twovoice might have advocated for similar objectives, but he had believed integrated education was compatible with them. Increasingly, Indian leaders and parents like Hugh McKay were convinced otherwise. Instead of empowering Indian students, integration had too often left them experiencing feelings of "inferiority, alienation, rejection, hostility."[16]

In response, Minister Chrétien, erstwhile champion of the White Paper, acknowledged that public education for Indigenous students continued to be "a whitewash" that equipped students "with white values, goals, language, skills needed to succeed in the dominant society," but with "very little recognition of the importance of cultural heritage in the learning process."[17] Instead, these schools were offering a "cookie-cutter education" in order "to turn out functional and identical Canadians." Chrétien admitted that this approach was not working. An integrated school "of the whitewash variety" could "serve no purpose in a child's world. Rather it alienates him from his own people." Under heavy political pressure, Chrétien conceded the proposition that Indian communities should have a greater say over schooling their own children. It would take some years yet to implement, but the shift was clear, and fundamental.

IN 1980, MAUREEN Twovoice's uncle, Lyle Longclaws, was elected president of the Manitoba Indian Brotherhood on the third ballot of a closely contested election.[18] He was only twenty-five years old and his winning campaign focused on education. "Indian schools should be controlled by Indians because our children receive a poorer quality of education than the average Canadian," he said. "We're tired of seeing taxpayers' dollars funneled into a solution that won't work," he added, shrewdly undermining the stereotype that Indians heedlessly devoured public resources.[19]

The numbers in Waywayseecappo told a dismal story. In the two decades that followed Michael Twovoice's 1961 vote for integrated education in Rossburn, 80 percent of students from Waywayseecappo dropped out of school by Grade 8. From 1965 to 1982, only a single student graduated from Grade 12.[20] The proportion of students completing Grade 10 and beyond actually diminished between 1954 and 1983.[21] In most cases, students who continued beyond Grade 8 in Rossburn were funnelled into a special program called the Occupational Entrance Course, commonly known as OEC. This was a euphemism for "dummy classrooms" where students learned little and had no route to a high school diploma, according to Waywayseecappo Elder Bryan Cloud. *Our kids aren't dumb*, parents and community leaders thought as their children struggled in Rossburn's schools. *This can't be right.*

Meanwhile, Waywayseecappo's band council was paying the public school division full year's tuition, even for students who often dropped out before Christmas. Tuition was paid out based on the "nominal roll," which was calculated in October, the second month of the school year. "They were glad to take our bucks but weren't interested in helping our children," Bryan Cloud recalls. "So we said, 'Screw that.'"[22]

In the spring of 1982, Waywayseecappo's band council announced that all of the community's 155 students in Rossburn's schools would be withdrawn the following academic year. For the public school board, this meant a loss of about $300,000 in revenue, which led to staff layoffs. Despite the financial loss, the reaction of many in Rossburn was, to a great extent, *good riddance*. The chair of the public school board insisted, "We have done everything within our power to accommodate them."[23] It is difficult to take this assertion seriously, given how little was done to create an environment where Native students and their culture were respected. Notably, none of J.R. Wright's suggestions to create "joint schools in fact as well as in name," outlined a decade before, had been implemented.

For Waywayseecappo, the most pressing challenge became finding an alternative place to educate their children. The best option, as it happened, was the hockey arena. The federal government had financed an indoor hockey rink on the reserve in 1978, but it turned out that the water available from nearby wells contained so much zinc and salt that forming ice was almost impossible. In the four years following the arena's construction, no one had skated in it. In order to finance the construction to convert the useless arena into a school, Waywayseecappo received a federal grant. The band council also took out a $400,000 loan from the Rossburn Credit Union, with an interest rate of 18.5 percent (the prime lending rate plus 1.5 percent).[24] Waywayseecappo was evidently willing to pay a high price to establish their own school. By the end of summer, fourteen extra-large classrooms had taken shape inside the hockey arena, and this still left plenty of room for a colossal gym.

In September 1982, Waywayseecappo became the twentieth reserve in Manitoba to establish and manage its own school. The community greeted the opening with euphoria. There would finally be formal Ojibway language instruction, and even adults who had been out of school for years decided to return to classrooms that smelled like freshly cut wood. In the school's first three years, attendance rose to 85 percent, about double the previous attendance rate in Rossburn. "If the Indian People of the

Waywayseecappo Band are to survive," Chief Robert Shingoose wrote in the first school yearbook, "we must develop and control our own education. Education has always been seen by our Indian Leaders as one of the major tools that would help us strike off the shackles of poverty." In the same yearbook, Grade 2 student Kevin Mecas wrote, "I like Wayway school because ... the teachers here are better friends than the other teachers in Rossburn school. I like learning Ojibway best."[25] The school's first Ojibway teacher was Jim Cote, Hugh McKay's stepson.

In Waywayseecappo, the new school became a symbol of renewal. One community member, Ron Rattlesnake, wrote that "the transformation of the arena into a school in my opinion has been the greatest accomplishment in the history of Waywayseecappo."[26]

The federal government was less impressed. Since the school construction was done with plywood and with great speed, the building had become a certifiable fire hazard. An internal memo of the Department of Indian Affairs noted, "The school facility was built ... generally to unacceptable standards, and fire, health and physical safety deficiencies are major concerns." (It is not clear what, if anything, was done to mitigate these risks.)

A new body called the Waywayseecappo Education Authority was created to oversee the school. Hugh McKay became its first chairman, eleven years after calling for the end of integrated education. In one of his first letters to the federal government in his new role, he wrote, "We want it clearly understood that the Waywayseecappo Education Authority is in control of the situation." And this is how he signed off: "Yours in Recognition of Total Control of Indian Education, Hugh McKay."[27]

Two decades after Michael Twovoice voted for integration, his friend Hugh McKay's vision of separation prevailed. For

Hugh, a separate school was not an end in itself—it was a way to give Waywayseecappo's children an opportunity to grow up with dignity, in a country that had long sought to impose a choice between being Canadian and being Indian. Michael had been more willing to celebrate Canada's abstract ideals, more generous in his assessment of Canada's ability to change. But it was Indigenous students who had been asked to make all the concessions, in exchange for a so-called "good education."

Hugh McKay and Michael Twovoice were contemporaries, born a year apart. They both attended residential schools. They both served in Canada's armed forces and heard the same grandiloquent speeches about Canada's contribution to the global fight for freedom. Each still professed loyalty to Canada—in 1967, they marched, side by side, as representatives of Waywayseecappo in a parade held in the nearby town of Russell marking Canada's centenary. But Hugh and Michael had different notions of what Canada really was, and they reached different conclusions about how Indians could flourish within it. Hugh held the more pessimistic view, and in his lifetime he seemed to have the more accurate understanding of Canada's enduring racism. Unlike Michael, Hugh never had a good word to say about assimilation. By 1982, most parents in Waywayseecappo shared his belief that a separate school for their children was a better way to secure equality. Even Michael had become disillusioned by how Native children were faring in Rossburn, and came to support the idea of a school on the reserve.

Within the span of a few decades, Waywayseecappo's students had gone from involuntary racial segregation (in Indian residential schools), to racial integration (in provincial public schools), to voluntary separation (in a school on the reserve). The hope was to be separate *and* equal.

It did not take long for a dispute to arise between Waywayseecappo and the federal government about funding for the new school. Waywayseecappo had achieved more local control but still relied on federal money, a paradox that continues to plague most reserves. "There is a need for more financial assistance," Waywayseecappo's Chief wrote to the Indian Affairs Department in 1983, "and we feel that there should be identical rules . . . for all—rules that take a realistic look at what Indian people are trying to accomplish."[28] Jim Manly, a member of Parliament for the area, contributed his vocal support of the reserve's educational efforts. "The entire system is stacked against Indian control of Indian education," he wrote in a letter to the minister of Indian affairs, John Munro. "Please take action to enable these people to control their own educational institution without being completely starved for funds."[29]

Munro's response was by turns frank and evasive. "You are no doubt aware that my Department, as is the case with all Government departments, is under extreme resource constraints," he wrote. (At the time, the federal government was running a deficit.) He also noted that it was "fair" and "appropriate" to compare the costs of the Waywayseecappo school with the costs of neighbouring provincial schools, but insisted that Waywayseecappo's school was not receiving less.[30] This claim—that students on reserves like Waywayseecappo were receiving fair and equal treatment—would become more and more difficult to sustain as time wore on.

AFTER FOUR YEARS of educating all its students in elementary and secondary grades, Waywayseecappo concluded in 1986 that it did not have enough students to justify its own high school program. The closest provincial high school was in Rossburn, just down the road, but community leaders and parents preferred to send students to a particularly well regarded public high school in Dauphin, a hundred kilometres away, even if it meant that students would have to live in residences away from home. That is how desperate the parents of Waywayseecappo were for quality, non-discriminatory education for their children, and how convinced they were that no such education was to be found in Rossburn.

Waywayseecappo asked the Department of Indian Affairs for reimbursement of the lodging costs in Dauphin, but they were turned down on the basis that there were perfectly good public schools nearby, notably in Rossburn.[31] Waywayseecappo's director of education replied to explain that Waywayseecappo had "deliberately" removed its students from Rossburn a few years before and that it would be "ridiculous" to send them back to a place where their students had underachieved for two decades.[32] Their experience in Rossburn had been too disappointing and the acrimony between the communities ran too deep.

Yet federal officials would not budge, which infuriated Robert Shingoose, Waywayseecappo's Chief. In a letter to the government, he asked, "Where in the hell is this so called Local Control?"[33] In the end, Waywayseecappo opted to bus its high school students to and from the town of Russell, twenty-five kilometres away.

In the fall of 1990, six students from the reserve decided to enrol in Rossburn's high school—partly because of mixed experiences in Russell, and partly because of the shorter commute. It had been eight years since Waywayseecappo removed all its students from Rossburn.

Almost as soon as the six students arrived, things went badly. They were called the same old names and reportedly told to "go to your own damn school."[34] Julia Mecas, aunt of one of the six

students, promptly drove to Rossburn to share her concerns with
the principal. During this meeting, a few students from Rossburn
snuck out to the parking lot and propped nails behind one of
Julia's tires. When she later backed out of her parking spot, her
tire went flat with a hiss. She and the six students were furious,
and the students promptly decided to collectively withdraw from
the school. They had been attending classes for less than a week.

Outraged family members published a letter in the *Rossburn
Review* in which they decried discrimination against Native students just like in "years gone by." They concluded:

> *It's sad to say that racism and prejudice is still so evident in
> Rossburn; to our way of thinking racism is a learned thing. It
> is passed from one generation to the next. It is instilled in chil-
> dren when they are very young. The intent here is not to stereo-
> type all the white society as being racist against Natives. Those
> people who have been a party to racist teachings know who
> they are. Are these the same "Good Christians" who appear in
> church on Sunday mornings and teach each other to "Love thy
> Neighbour?"*[35]

One of the concerned parents, Norbert Tanner, told a
Brandon Sun reporter that nothing seemed to have changed
since Waywayseecappo pulled out all its students almost a decade before. "We had hoped there was a better understanding
and a better acceptance. . . . You feel it when you go to town.
Nobody talks to you. It is as if they are ashamed of standing
beside a native. . . . They have got to accept us. We are here. We
are here forever."[36]

Rossburn's student council hastily composed an apology letter and sent it to Waywayseecappo's band council. "We hope you

do not condemn our whole staff and student body for the actions of a small minority," they wrote. "It is unfortunate that we did not have the opportunity to become friends." One of the letter's young authors told a reporter from the *Winnipeg Free Press*, "We were sort of disappointed they didn't give us a second chance." Presumably, this teenager knew little about all the prior chances that had come and gone.

Rossburn's principal blamed separation for the persistent racial discord. "The real problem," he said, "is that during the developmental period in their lives, the kids have no contact with each other. So they never have the opportunity to mix and learn and see other people in the educational system. As a result, our kids, the image they get of native people comes from the few they see who spend the afternoon in the hotel." The principal ignored the not-so-distant failure of integrated education less than a decade before. For so many, for so long, mere proximity between Waywayseecappo and Rossburn had not led to greater understanding. Rather, in the absence of respect, contact tended to provoke yet more discord.

One of the six students from Waywayseecappo, Carolyne Longclaws, spoke to the same *Winnipeg Free Press* reporter. "I just hope they can change," she said about people in Rossburn. "They probably won't change inside, but they might change outside. The way they really feel about us inside, I don't think that will change."[37]

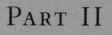

PART II

"THE CUNNING
OF THE WHITE MAN"

"LET US LIVE HERE LIKE BROTHERS"

W HAT I HAVE TO TALK ABOUT CONCERNS YOU, YOUR children, and their children, who are yet unborn," the treaty negotiator Alexander Morris said to hundreds of Cree and Ojibway Indians gathered inside a cavernous tent three hundred kilometres northwest of Winnipeg. "What I want is for you to take the Queen's hand, through mine, and shake hands with her forever."[1]

The year was 1874, and Canada was seven years old. Politicians in faraway Ottawa dreamed of a railway stretching from the east coast to the Pacific Ocean bearing goods and settlers. With this spine of iron, Canada could stand up to the United States. But a major obstacle was blocking this grand plan: Indigenous Peoples claimed to own the land over which these trains would run. So the government sent Morris, a lawyer and politician with a gift for metaphor, to make a series of deals.

Morris arrived with two armed battalions dressed in Her Majesty's signature red coats—113 men in all, along with a two-hundred-pound cannon. Indians made up the majority in the prairies, and Morris estimated that they could field as many as five thousand warriors for battle, if it came to that.[2] But he did not want a fight. The federal government had neither the will nor the means to conquer the West with soldiers and bullets.[3] Ottawa preferred to avoid the kind of bloody, drawn-out "Indian wars" that were then roiling the American Midwest. Prime Minister Alexander Mackenzie instructed Morris that "our true policy was to make friends of [the Indians] even at a considerable cost."[4]

At these treaty talks in the fall of 1874, Morris was charged with securing control of 120,000 square kilometres without firing a shot. Negotiations began on September 8, just as the landscape was darkening from green to brown following the first overnight frosts. The soldiers accompanying Morris had erected a marquee tent on the shore of Lac Qu'Appelle—the "Calling Lake," named for its echoes. At dawn, a layer of mist covered the water, but the white veil lifted as the sun climbed. Morris dispatched a bugler to announce the start of the first meeting. The blasts from the brass horn rolled across the water.

Like other statesmen of his day, Alexander Morris was an unabashed imperialist. He hoped "Christianity and civilization" would replace "heathenism and paganism among the Indian tribes."[5] Yet he did recognize what he called the "natural title of the Indians to the lands," as had Canada's first prime minister, John A. Macdonald, who characterized Indians as "the original owners of the soil."[6] Morris's job was to settle their claims.

The year before, in 1873, Morris had received a letter from a group of Chiefs in the prairies who had spotted white surveyors marking off land. The Chiefs wished to "inform your Honor that we have never been a party to any Treaty . . . made to extinguish our title to Land which we claim as ours . . . and therefore can not understand why this land should be surveyed." One of the Chiefs was identified as Wahwashecaboo, an early spelling of Waywayseecappo.[7]

Alexander Morris (Library and Archives Canada, Topley Studio fonds/a025468)

Cree and Ojibway negotiators knew their long-standing ties to the land and ongoing presence gave them some leverage, but they also understood that their bargaining position had been deteriorating. Recent smallpox epidemics in the prairies had subjected each

Native life to a coin toss: one in two died.[8] And the buffalo that had provided them with food, clothing, and shelter were depleted, owing in part to a concerted American campaign to slaughter the herds. ("Every buffalo dead is an Indian gone," a U.S. Army colonel once boasted.)[9] Indians on the prairies were in acute need of new livelihoods.

They also sensed that trickles of white settlers augured a flood. As one Cree leader put it, Indians could not "stop the power of the white man from spreading over the land like the grasshoppers that cloud the sky and then fall to consume every blade of grass and every leaf on the trees in their path."[10]

Another threat lay to the south: American traders who crossed the border were showing no qualms about killing Indians who got in their way. Morris referred to these incidents as the "constant eruptions of American desperadoes."[11] During one incursion of heavily armed traders across the Canadian border in the summer of 1873, more than twenty Indians were killed in what came to be known as the Cypress Hills Massacre.[12] And the cavalry of the United States Army was feared even more—Indians referred to them as the "long knives."[13] For the Cree and Ojibway Indians who gathered at Lac Qu'Appelle, a deal with the Queen's redcoats seemed like a safer bet than the alternatives.

Morris, a seasoned negotiator, knew which strings to pluck. "We are here to talk with you about the land," he said to those gathered in the marquee tent. "The Queen knows that you are poor. . . . She knows that the winters are cold, and your children are often hungry. She has always cared for her red children as much as for her white. Out of her generous heart and liberal hand she wants to do something for you, so that when the buffalo get scarcer, and they are scarce enough now, you may be able to do something for yourselves."[14]

In response, two Cree Chiefs, Kakushiway and Kawacatoose, sought to unnerve Morris. They arranged for bags full of soil to be carried into the tent and laid at Morris's feet. Kawacatoose asked Morris how much money he had brought, because for each sack of dirt Morris would need a full sack of money. Then Kawacatoose said, "This country is not for sale."[15]

One of the main Ojibway spokespeople was Otakaonan (translated to English as "The Gambler"). He belonged to the band led by Chief Waywayseecappo, who had not himself travelled to Lac Qu'Appelle for reasons lost to history.

Otakaonan, "The Gambler" (Provincial Archives of Saskatchewan, R-11962, photo by Edgar C. Rossie)

Speaking through a translator, Otakaonan opened by recalling how his people had welcomed European settlers to the plains. "When the white skin comes here from far away I love him all the same," he said to Morris.[16] Yet Otakaonan objected to the way the government had recognized land rights claimed by the Hudson's Bay Company, a British trading group that had been operating in the area. Four years before, in 1870, the federal government had paid £300,000 to the company to purchase these supposed land rights.[17] Otakaonan did not think the Hudson's Bay Company should have been paid for territory it did not rightfully own.

"When one Indian takes anything from another we call it stealing," Otakaonan said.

"What did the Company steal from you?" Morris asked.

"The earth, trees, grass, stones, all that which I see with my eyes."

Morris was unmoved. "Who made the earth, the grass, the stone and the wood?" he asked. "The Great Spirit. He made them for all his children to use, and it is not stealing to use the gift of the Great Spirit." Morris pointed out that the Ojibway had themselves arrived on the prairies only a few generations before, after migrating west from the Great Lakes region in the eighteenth century. (Morris left unspoken the fact that aggressive Euro-Canadian settlement was a cause of the Ojibway migration.) "We won't say [the Ojibway] stole the land and the stones and the trees," Morris continued. "No ... the land is wide ... it is big enough for us both, let us live here like brothers."[18]

This sentiment met with approval from an Indian named Pahtahkaywenin, who agreed on the need for cooperation: "God gives us land in different places and when we meet together as friends, we ask from each other and do not quarrel as we do so."[19] To reach a deal, Morris offered one-time cash gifts, annual payments, and hunting rights on land that remained unsettled. He promised 640 acres for every family of five on "reserves," land that would be protected from encroachment by settlers. The government would also provide agricultural assistance so that, in time, farms on reserves would provide the livelihood that buffalo no longer could. And the government pledged to build schools on the reserves and send teachers, so that Indians might "learn the cunning of the white man."[20]

"We won't deceive you with smooth words," Morris insisted. "We have no object but your good at heart."

"Is it true you are bringing the Queen's kindness?" a Chief asked.

"Yes, to those who are here and those who are absent," Morris replied.

"Is it true that my child will not be troubled for what you are bringing him?"

"The Queen's power will be around him."[21]

AFTER SIX DAYS of negotiations, a document titled "Treaty No. 4" was finalized on September 17, 1874. Morris had likely arrived at Lac Qu'Appelle with a pre-drafted template that left only a few blank spaces for dates, names, territorial limits, and payment amounts.[22] The final text of Treaty 4 was virtually indistinguishable from another treaty Morris had negotiated the year before ("Treaty No. 3"), which applied to another massive expanse of territory in Ontario and Manitoba. Morris would ultimately negotiate four similar treaties dealing with land between the Great Lakes and the Rocky Mountains.

It is highly doubtful that government and Indian negotiators shared the same understanding of what Treaty 4 meant.

The text was written in English, which the Indian negotiators could not read. When Morris instructed a translator to read the document out loud before the parties formally signed, a white observer found it "immensely amusing" to watch the translator's "look of dismay and consternation" as he attempted to hold the "bulky-looking document" and convert the English into Cree and Ojibway.[23]

According to oral history, the Chiefs believed that the treaty represented a partnership that bonded Indians and settlers into one family, with a commitment to share the land and bring mutual aid.[24] The government would take a more narrow view, relying heavily on the legalese affirming, among other things, that with their signatures the Chiefs agreed to "cede, release, surrender and yield up . . . all their rights, titles and privileges whatsoever, to the lands."[25] (This provision became known as the "surrender clause.") Morris would later describe the terms of the treaty as "fair and just."[26] One hundred years later, a group of Indigenous leaders in Manitoba would describe Treaty 4, and other treaties like it, as "one of the outstanding swindles of all time."[27]

After a signing ceremony,[28] Morris travelled two hundred kilometres east to Fort Ellice, where he was to meet with more Indian leaders who had not been present at the Lac Qu'Appelle negotiations. Among them was Chief Waywayseecappo, who was then around fifty years old.[29]

At least as far back as 1859, Waywayseecappo had been trading furs at the Hudson's Bay Company outpost in Fort Ellice, in exchange for cloth, flints, knives, tobacco, and ammunition.[30] A company trader described Waywayseecappo as "a giant in size and ancient in days and devilment."[31] Morris wanted Waywayseecappo to sign Treaty 4 on behalf of the fifty families in his band, which Otakaonan had not had the authority to do at Lac Qu'Appelle.

"What we offer will be for your good," said Morris. "I think you are not wiser than your brothers."[32]

A witness to the meeting sketched Waywayseecappo's profile with a lump of charcoal, leaving his only surviving likeness.

Chief Waywayseecappo
(Library and Archives Canada, Sydney Prior Hall fonds/e010999415)

Chief Waywayseecappo, who could not read or write English, signed the treaty with an "X." His name, transcribed as "Way-wa-se-ca-pow," was translated as "the Man proud of standing upright."[33]

It is difficult to say what Chief Waywayseecappo thought about the treaty, but shortly after signing it he demonstrated his good faith. Reports reached him that a Métis man named McIver had killed a white settler near Fort Ellice. After hearing this, Waywayseecappo picked four of his ablest men to join him in a hunt for the killer. They successfully captured McIver and brought him to the nearest detachment of Mounted Police. (McIver was convicted of murder the following year.) Canada's governor general, Lord Dufferin, was so impressed when he heard what Waywayseecappo had done that he sent a message to the Chief expressing "great appreciation of his conduct, and that of his 'braves,' in having given so practical a proof of their desire to assist the government in carrying out the laws of the country."[34] This would not be the last time Chief Waywayseecappo showed his loyalty to Canada.

It was not long, however, before the federal government turned its laws against Indians. In 1876, two years after the signing of Treaty 4, Parliament passed the first incarnation of the Indian Act, a law that defined who would be counted as Indian and detailed how they would be controlled. First Nations were to be treated not as equal partners but as wayward children. As the minister of Indian affairs said, "Our Indian legislation generally rests on the principle, that the aborigines are to be kept in a condition of tutelage and treated as wards or children of the State"—until, that is, the government could successfully lift Indians into a state of "higher civilization."[35] The long-term goal of the Indian Act was to assimilate Native peoples into the Euro-Canadian mainstream, building on a prior law that was more revealingly called the Gradual Civilization Act.

Parliament assumed it had the power to pass a law like the Indian Act because Canada's 1867 Constitution had granted the federal government exclusive control over "Indians and lands reserved for the Indians." The Fathers of Confederation did so, of course, without consulting any actual Indians. The "overall effect" of the Indian Act, as the Royal Commission on Aboriginal Peoples would later note, "was ultimately to subject reserves to the almost unfettered rule of federal bureaucrats."[36]

THE WAYWAYSEECAPPO RESERVE and the town of Rossburn were created within two years of each other, and not by coincidence.

After signing Treaty 4, Chief Waywayseecappo requested reserve land in an area where his band had planted its summer gardens since the early 1800s, inside a far larger Traditional Territory where they had lived, hunted, and traded for the previous century.[37] The reserve was formally established in 1877, and some two hundred people moved there. Among them were families named Longclaws, Keewaytincappo, and Jandrew—names that later featured in some of the thickest branches of Maureen Twovoice's family tree. For a time, the government referred to the community as Lizard Point, a name inspired by the dark green salamanders that were ubiquitous in the area after extended periods of rain. An early map of the reserve—formally known as Indian Reserve #62—shows that it is bordered on the east by the Birdtail River.[38]

Treaty 4 simultaneously authorized the creation of reserves and declared "that it is the desire of Her Majesty to open up [land] for settlement, immigration, trade and such other purposes." And so it was that a mere two years after the Waywayseecappo reserve was established, a wave of settlers made their way to the valley of the Birdtail, just as Her Majesty Queen Victoria had supposedly desired. Among them was Richard Rose Ross, whose family had come to Manitoba by way of Scotland, Manhattan, and Ontario.

In 1879, Ross set off from Winnipeg along with a small group of men wheeling a half-dozen carts. They dreamed of a fertile new home with enough hills to protect crops from flash floods. They headed north as far as the town of Portage, then continued west through sleet and storm and a "sea of mud."[39] "Foremost in their minds," according to a chronicle of the trip, "was the thought of owning land which extended for hundreds of miles, large tracts inhabited only by Indians."[40] Thanks to Alexander Morris, these Indians were no longer considered much of an obstacle.

After walking 221 kilometres from Portage, Ross and his companions found what they were looking for. Near the banks of a gurgling river, they planted their first potatoes. They claimed the land as squatters.[41] Later, each man applied under federal law for a homestead of 160 acres. In exchange, they paid a modest fee of ten dollars (the equivalent of about $325 today) and promised to build a house and cultivate twenty acres of land within three years. It was not long until "old Mr. Ross," as he was affectionately known, helped build a school, store, and post office.

Early relations between the new town and the reserve appear to have been largely friendly. Indians from Waywayseecappo visited Rossburn to trade moccasins, baskets, and rugs. They also sold tanned moosehides, dried elk meat, and fish from the largest lake on the reserve. Some settlers in Rossburn were given Ojibway names: one elderly man was called Wapawayap—"white eyebrow." A few of Ross's sons even learned to speak Ojibway. A Rossburn resident later remembered "what fine men some of the braves were when the settlers first came in, big strapping healthy fellows—ideal pictures of Indians."[42] According to an 1882 report by a federal official, "These Indians are all very well disposed towards the settlers, and whenever trouble has arisen it has, on all occasions which I have investigated, been directly attributable to the settlers, who dislike to see the Indians in possession of desirable locations."[43]

Chief Waywayseecappo himself developed friendships in town. Toward the end of his life, though the old Chief had gone blind, he continued to travel by foot with the assistance of his wife, who held out a stick to guide him. One day, Waywayseecappo walked with his wife all the way to Rossburn, grasping the guiding stick with one hand and holding a gun with the other. He was looking for one settler in particular. When he found him, Waywayseecappo greeted his white friend warmly and handed him the gun, as a gift.[44]

It is possible to imagine how the relationship between Waywayseecappo and Rossburn might have deepened over time, built on respect, trade, and friendship. But that is not how things turned out—not at this time, not in Canada.

The overwhelming majority of people living in Waywayseecappo continued to regularly travel far beyond the borders of the reserve. In December 1881, when a federal agent recorded census data, 190 of 220 band members were off reserve, hunting in the Riding Mountain area to the northeast.[45] This was part of the long-standing seasonal rhythm of the community: they hunted goose and duck in the spring, deer in the summer, and elk, moose, and prairie chicken in the fall.[46] Yet big game was growing scarcer, and the arrival of ever more settlers was restricting traditional hunting. Band members had established a wide network of trails to hunt in land around the reserve, but with the arrival of more settlers around Rossburn, the reserve's border was slowly becoming more meaningful. "As the valley became more thickly populated," one settler recalled, "the Indians frequented the valley less and less. . . . Their old trails finally disappeared as fields were plowed and fences erected [by settlers]."[47]

One particular incident seems to capture a shift in the relationship between the two communities. In 1884, two settlers built a stone grist mill with a water wheel along the Birdtail River. The purpose of the mill was to produce flour, but one of its effects was to block fish from making their way up the river to the reserve. That year, Waywayseecappo's residents "complained of starvation" to a federal official, in part because of the effect of the mill on their access to fish.[48] At the time, the federal Indian agent responsible for the area was Lawrence Herchmer, who showed little sympathy. Rather, Herchmer believed hunger would motivate more industrious farming, which he saw as a necessary step in the civilizing of Indians. "A little starvation will do them good," he wrote.[49]

Just as families in Waywayseecappo struggled with an abrupt and painful transition from traditional livelihoods, so did many other communities that had been abruptly transplanted to reserves. To make matters worse, aberrant weather caused widespread crop failures in 1883 and 1884. Across the prairies, the overwhelming majority of Indians were depending on government food rations of bacon and flour to survive.[50] It was called "the Time of the Great Hunger."[51]

In the summer of 1884, within a decade of Alexander Morris's grand pronouncement during treaty negotiations, a group of two thousand Cree Indians assembled near Duck Lake (in present-day Saskatchewan). They discussed fears of being "cheated" by a government that had made "sweet promises" in order to "get their country from them." They claimed that the government had not been living up to its treaty commitments, including the promises of agricultural support and supplies, and said that Indians had been "reduced to absolute and complete dependence upon what relief is extended to them." They told a federal official that "it is almost too hard for them to bear the treatment received at the hands of the government," yet they were "glad the young men have not resorted to violent measures."[52]

The peace did not last another year.

6

"IRON HEART"

ONE OF THE 113 SOLDIERS WHO ACCOMPANIED Alexander Morris to the Treaty 4 negotiations in 1874 was a young man named Hayter Reed, who had a wispy moustache and mutton chops venturing well below his jawline. Hayter marched forty-five kilometres a day, for a total of almost five hundred kilometres, to get from his military base at Fort Garry (near present-day Winnipeg) to Lac Qu'Appelle. There, he "came in close touch with the Redman," as he later put it.[1] Hayter was struck by the "picturesqueness" of the Indians, with their painted faces, multicoloured beads, and ceremonial feathers.[2] This was the beginning of Hayter's lifelong fascination with Indians, whom he described as a "human creature that sickens beneath our civilization, and dies midst our prosperity."[3]

Born in 1849 and raised in Toronto, Hayter turned eighteen the same year that Confederation made Canada a country. By then, Hayter was already barking orders as a drill instructor for the Kingston Rifle Battalion. He later said that marching with his regiment to the tune of a brass band was the highlight of his young life.[4] At the age of twenty-two, he jumped at a chance to join a battalion deploying to the North-West, which at that time referred to all of Canada west of Ontario and east of British Columbia. In time, this is where Hayter would attain fame, and infamy.

Hayter Reed (McCord Museum of Canadian History, portrait 53878, 1880, Notman & Sandham)

But first, young Hayter had to actually get to the North-West, which was no small undertaking in the days before a national railroad. Hayter's battalion of four hundred men headed westward in the final months of 1871, just as winter's white blanket was snuffing out the last embers of fall. Their final destination, Fort Garry, was two thousand kilometres away, almost exactly midway between the Atlantic and Pacific oceans. A steamship carried them as far as the western shore of Lake Superior, where the harder work began. The troops were divided into groups of two dozen and assigned to small boats they would have to row through hundreds of kilometres of rivers, streams, and lakes. As they traversed this "immense volume of water," Hayter later wrote, they encountered "every kind of waterfall, from chutes to cataracts."

Hayter had headed west looking for adventure, and it didn't take long for him to find something to boast about. "To shoot the many Falls or the numerous Rapids, to lift and haul the boats from the whirling rush of water and launch them by the edge of a whirlpool—all had more or less a spice of danger."[5]

The battalion avoided the most perilous stretches of water by making overland portages as long as six kilometres, over which the men had to haul their boats along roughly cut trails featuring occasional inclines of sixty degrees. Each man carried a backpack with fifty kilograms of equipment and rations. Hayter came to resent the "heavy military tents," "cumbersome iron camp kettles," and "iron shovels without number" that had been assigned by clueless officers at faraway headquarters.

Travel by boat was no less strenuous. Sometimes a waterway would start to freeze as the men rowed and they would use their oars to stab at the ice and cut a way forward. As the weeks wore on, Hayter wrote, "the blades were entirely worn off the oars so that we were towards the end of the journey driven in some instances to the use of shovels for paddling—the only use we ever found for these shovels by the way."

Finally, after twenty-six days of rowing and portaging, the men reached what is now the town of Kenora, near Ontario's border with Manitoba, where they left their boats behind. The last stretch to Fort Garry was a 175-kilometre march "through deep and fine dry snow, making it very much like heavy loose sand to walk in," Hayter recalled. With thermometers reading minus fifteen degrees Celsius, the men reached the fort "in the pink of health, though rugged, ragged and torn." Of all those who had undertaken the journey, "there was not one who had a pair of trowsers [*sic*] reaching below the knee—the bottoms having been torn and cut off."

With Fort Garry as its base of operations, Hayter's battalion fended off cross-border raids by armed groups from the United States that had "the idea they could snatch Canada . . . away from the British Empire," Hayter wrote.[6] (Strange as it sounds today, the threat arose from Irish revolutionaries called Fenians, whose roundabout plan to support Irish secession from the United Kingdom involved attacks in North America).[7]

During his military service, Hayter also found time to pursue legal studies, an early sign of his uncommon drive and ambition. Within a year of his arrival in Manitoba, he was called to the bar. He became only the sixteenth person in the province to be recognized as a lawyer there. He swore two oaths: an oath of allegiance and an oath of attorney. First, to "Her Majesty Queen Victoria," he pledged to "defend Her to the utmost of my power against all traitorous conspiracies." Second, he swore to act "honestly" as a lawyer, "according to my best knowledge and ability. So help me God."[8] In the years to come, he proved more adept at punishing perceived traitors than acting honestly.

Hayter's military unit was disbanded in 1880, and he left the military as a major. He then worked briefly as a land guide for settlers, directing them to their new homes in the North-West.[9] Hayter was the first point of contact for every prospective settler who passed through Winnipeg. It is entirely possible that he sang the praises of a promising settlement along the Birdtail River, which had a view of the most beautiful valley in Manitoba. Yet his job as a land guide was only part-time, and he kept looking for work that was more suited to his talents.

Then, in 1881, Hayter embarked on a path that would transform his life for the better—and the lives of countless others for the worse—when he was appointed Indian agent with the federal Department of Indian Affairs.[10] His job was to enforce federal law and policy regarding the Native population in the Battleford region of Saskatchewan, a role that infused Hayter with considerable power over the daily lives of more than a thousand Indians.[11] Hayter's predecessor in the Battleford region had left the job because he feared the Indians he sought to govern, but Hayter was undaunted. He embraced "the labourious and often dangerous work of transforming Bands of Savages into peaceable agricultural labourers," as he put it.[12] To civilize, he was willing to die, and even, it later became clear, to kill.

Hayter described the life of a federal Indian agent as "a state of practical exile," in which the agent is "debarred from all the pleasures of the world, from society, from civilization."[13] Hayter oversaw a sprawling area of more than twenty-two thousand square kilometres, which he traversed on horseback and by dogsled, in the "heat of summer and extreme cold of winter," sometimes travelling eighty or even a hundred kilometres a day.[14] During his arduous travels, he would be overcome by "strange weird feelings" when he looked at "the unending vision of sky and prairie," he wrote. "I very doubt if it be possible to place before your mental vision anything like a true picture of the loneliness of endless space."

As Hayter travelled the plains, he spent many nights in Indian encampments, where he was welcomed as a guest. He watched as men danced naked "without surprise or comment," though women appeared to be "more decently clothed." "Many and many a time," he wrote, he was kept up all night "by the revels of the young Indians, in which the tom tom or Indian drum was incessantly beaten."[15] Hayter's notes of such encounters evince only a limited understanding of what was happening around him and the cultural significance it might have held.

Hayter claimed to have witnessed Indian bands preparing to launch attacks on one another. "I saw them perform their dances and sing their war songs and go through the different rites and ceremonies preparatory to such expeditions," he wrote, "resulting in either the taking of scalps, or stealing of horses or both." He rode along on a few such "marauding undertakings," to watch as much as possible before slipping away in advance of any fighting. He said he was never directly involved in any of these skirmishes, though "in one or two instances I was closer to them than I fancied, as upon one occasion a young brave rode up to me where I was encamped on the plains, and held up a scalp from which the blood was still running, and offered it to me as a present." Hayter accepted the gift and went on to keep the scalp for decades as a memento. (He eventually donated it to McGill University, along with his vast collection of "Indian relics," though the item has since gone missing.)[16]

Such intimate experiences with Indians—and, no doubt, Hayter's colourful recounting of them—earned him a reputation within the government as an expert. His boss, Edgar Dewdney, commended him for "having a knowledge of the Indian character possessed by few in the country."[17] Indeed, during his time on the plains, Hayter claimed to have identified the "great difference between the Indian and the Civilized people." It was not their degree of intelligence or their brand of religion, he insisted.

Rather, it was morality: Indians had none. As far as Hayter could tell, the concepts of right and wrong had no meaning for an Indian, who "remained a savage simply from a lack of a code of morals." Instead, "all was Right that he wished to do, all was wrong that opposed him."[18]

Hayter concluded that allowing "an ignorant savage to determine his own course for himself" was as foolish as allowing children to raise themselves.[19] Rather, "what the Indian requires to have brought to bear upon him are the influences of Christian civilization." Amazingly, Hayter acknowledged that if the "advantages of civilization" were only offered rather than imposed, "the Indian may not covet them for himself, or for his children." That is why consulting Indians was pointless.

The Royal Commission on Aboriginal Peoples would later describe some Indian agents as "petty despots who seemed to enjoy wielding enormous power over the remnants of once powerful Aboriginal nations."[20] Hayter Reed, it seems, was of this type. The sudden disappearance of the buffalo and the abrupt transition to life on reserves had left thousands of Cree, Ojibway, Lakota, Assiniboine, and Blackfoot Indians on the prairies reliant on government food rations. Within the area he purported to administer and control, Hayter established a simple rule: "If a man would not work, he would not eat."[21] Rations would be denied to the idle. This policy, which was soon emulated by other Indian agents, won praise from the Department of Indian Affairs.

Of course, Indian agents were the ones who dictated what counted as real work. Typically, this meant farming, which the government saw as the Indians' surest path to civilization. Hayter insisted that his firm approach was best in the long run, both for Canada and for Indians themselves, and he resented critics who portrayed Indian agents as dishonest tyrants. Hayter said he was willing to endure a stream of complaints from Indians, though from time to time he felt the need to retreat from his office "in order to obviate the constant nagging, noise and stench."[22] He once warned a superior who was planning a visit to the area that he would probably "be greeted on setting foot in this Agency, with sorrowful tales of my hardheartedness."[23]

Hayter proved so inflexibly harsh that he earned the nickname "Iron Heart" from Indians under his supervision.[24] As for Hayter, he described some of his charges as "the scum of the Plains."[25] Nevertheless, Hayter's superiors viewed him as a model Indian agent. He was praised for being "very faithful" and "an indefatigable worker."[26] In 1882, the highest-ranking Indian Affairs official in the prairies reported to the prime minister that Hayter had "been of good service, his legal training being of much assistance."[27] Hayter would soon receive a succession of rapid promotions, giving him ever more power over yet more people.

Those who witnessed Hayter's work on the ground were more skeptical. A colleague described him as "entirely lacking in sympathetic understanding of the Indians" and attributed "much of the unrest existing amongst the different bands" to Hayter's "management or mismanagement."[28] A settler in Battleford accused Hayter of "immoral behaviour" with two Indian women and of fathering an illegitimate child, calling Hayter "a libertine" with "no respect for the virtue of women."[29] Hayter denied everything and escaped the episode without official censure.

Hayter distinguished himself by helping create the first government-sponsored residential schools, which he embraced as a "solution of the Indian problem."[30] He later bragged that "the Indian Industrial Schools, from Winnipeg to the Pacific, were all established by me."[31] He fiercely advocated for the suppression of Indigenous languages at the schools. He wrote: "Use of the native tongue in the schools, for any purpose whatsoever, is one which I feel convinced should on no accounts be allowed."[32] Tellingly, he refers to the students at residential schools as "inmates."[33] After opening one school in (present-day) Saskatchewan, Hayter insisted on personally giving an Indian boy his first bath, which Hayter claimed to have caused "great amusement." Who exactly was so greatly amused he does not specify, though perhaps no one more than Hayter.

Hayter also helped establish the Qu'Appelle Indian Industrial School in Saskatchewan, which Michael Twovoice later attended. The school's principal, Father Hugonard, once wrote to Hayter to thank him for helping to get police to pick up "our fugitives"— that is, students who had fled the school.[34] Hayter also personally reviewed and modified the architectural drawings for the building that would become the Brandon Indian Residential School, where Linda Jandrew was later sent.

In 1883, Hayter faced his greatest challenge yet. Thousands of Cree and Assiniboine had gathered in Treaty 4 territory, in the Cypress Hills near the U.S. border. (Hayter estimated their number at eight thousand, though his boss put the number closer to three thousand—an indication of Hayter's unreliability as a narrator.)[35] The encampment was led by two Cree Chiefs, Payipwat (Piapot) and Mistahimaskwa (Big Bear), both fierce skeptics of the treaties negotiated by Alexander Morris. Piapot and Big Bear were particularly unhappy with how the scattered reserves stranded their people on small pockets of undesirable land they called *iskonikan*, "leftovers."[36] The Chiefs wanted to consolidate reserve land into a larger, contiguous territory with more autonomy.[37]

Of course, spreading out bands to weaken their collective power was a key aspect of government policy. "The Canadian system of band reserves has a tendency to diminish the offensive strength of the Indian tribes,"[38] Morris had noted. Likewise, Hayter praised the government for having the "wisdom" to avoid establishing "large Reservations," so giving Indians "less opportunity for hatching mischief."[39] He had previously reported that "Big Bear and his followers were loath to settle on a Reserve," and he anticipated that they would gather to "test their powers with the authorities."[40] For the Canadian government, this would not do. Hayter was dispatched to defuse the situation and get the Indians back on their assigned reserves.

Hayter's first move was to cut off the provision of government rations—he would starve Big Bear, Piapot, and their followers into submission. After three months of watching their children wither to skin and bone, the Cree dropped their demands and agreed to return to their reserves without violence. Hayter, never one to overlook his own ingenuity and daring, attributed his success to months of "hard work," with "not a little risk of life."[41] To get the Indians moving, Hayter's men "pulled tents down."[42] Hayter described the scene as thousands decamped and headed northward:

> The wild cavalcade stretching out for a mile or so in length and some hundreds of yards in width that wended away with its paint and war-plumes fluttering, trophies and savage embroidery. . . . Old squaws mounted on shaggy meagre looking ponies with perhaps one or two painted children seated behind them clinging to their tattered blankets. Young squaws with faces of various colors, red, green, white and yellow with necklaces of brass or other beads, gaudy colored earrings of shells or metal. . . . Tall, lank, young men on their best ponies with a defiant air leading the way. . . . Some carrying long lances, some with guns and rifles, most with bows and arrows at their backs, all headed by Chiefs

Piapot and Big Bear . . . with their war bonnets and bearing their shields which fluttered with eagle feathers. This will never be seen again.[43]

Perhaps what comes out most clearly in this description, despite Hayter's florid efforts to characterize it otherwise, is the dignity displayed in the darkest of times by Piapot, Big Bear, and those who accompanied them.

The following spring, in April 1884, Hayter wrote a memo warning of possible new attempts by Indians to "congregate in large numbers." To "prevent these gatherings," Hayter advised, "if the slightest pretext offers, to arrest some of the ringleaders before the Indians have assembled—the law might have to be strained a little to meet a particular case, but in the interests of the country at large as well as the Indians themselves such a course would I think be advisable."[44] This was an early sign of government tactics still to come.

AS INDIAN RESENTMENT of the federal government festered on the prairies, about fifteen hundred Métis living along the Saskatchewan River were coming to see that they too were under threat. The Métis were the descendants of Euro-Canadians and Indians who had intermarried. Since the end of the eighteenth century, they had forged a distinct identity, with their own customs and laws. Many referred to them as "half-breeds." One Protestant missionary, similarly keen on descriptions based on fractions, characterized the Métis as "one-and-a-half men"— that is, "half Indian, half white and half devil."[45] The prime minister, John A. Macdonald, referred to them simply as "those wild people."[46] The federal government was controlled at the time by Anglo-Saxon Protestants, and the Saskatchewan River Métis were largely French-speaking and Catholic. This meant they had "three strikes" against them, as Jean Teillet notes in her history of the Métis Nation. They were "too Indian, too Catholic and too French."[47]

By the spring of 1884, the Métis living along the Saskatchewan River felt squeezed, and the pressure kept mounting. Euro-Canadian settlers were coming from Ontario and claiming land that the Métis had occupied for at least a generation. Métis custom was to divide land abutting the river into "rangs"—long, skinny rectangles that ran along the water for eight hundred feet and stretched away from the river for two miles. This arrangement gave more families direct access to the water, which they relied on for irrigation as well as transportation. But the federal government would only recognize settlement on square plots and was quick to credit claims made by Euro-Canadian new-comers.

Back in 1874, Alexander Morris had excluded Métis from formal Treaty 4 negotiations but insisted at the time that the Queen would "deal generously and justly with them" in due course.[48] Instead, their claims continued to be ignored. Starting in 1878, the Métis community started sending petitions to Ottawa in an effort to have their land rights recognized. In 1882, for example, they wrote to Prime Minister Macdonald: "We appeal to your sense of justice . . . and beg you to reassure us speedily, by directing that we shall not be disturbed on our lands" occupied in "good faith."[49] This petition, like dozens of others, received no response.

The Métis eventually turned to the one person they thought might be able to get the federal government's attention, a man many Métis considered their "national apostle": Louis Riel.[50]

Louis Riel (Provincial Archives of Manitoba, N-5733)

In 1869–70, Louis Riel had led a Métis resistance against a federal plan to annex what is now Manitoba without any regard for the rights and customs of eight thousand Métis who constituted the majority of the people living there. Prime Minister Macdonald believed the "impulsive half-breeds . . . must be kept down by a strong hand until they are swamped by the influx of settlers."[51] Yet Riel, then aged twenty-six, emerged as the leader of his people and the Métis took up arms to seize control of the territory. They sought a negotiated settlement with the federal government, which ultimately made some grudging concessions.[52] Yet despite assurances of amnesty for those who had participated in the Métis resistance, a warrant was issued for Riel's arrest. Even as an outlaw, Riel managed to be elected to Parliament twice, in 1873 and 1874, though he was never allowed to take his seat in Ottawa. He eventually accepted an amnesty deal in 1875, in exchange for five years of exile. He settled down across the U.S. border in Montana, where he worked as a teacher and lived with his wife and two children. This is where, in the spring of 1884, a Métis delegation seeking his help found him. Riel agreed to come and serve his people as best he could.

In the months after his return from Montana, Riel pursued a peaceful strategy, putting his faith in persuasion and yet more petitions. He sought a more representative local government and recognition of valid land claims, including those of recent settlers. Riel also sought to make common cause with Indians. "When I came to the North West in July [1884]," Riel would later say, "I found the Indians suffering."[53] Government agents noted with alarm that Riel spent two days in August 1884 in talks with the Cree Chief Big Bear, who had disbanded the mass gathering at the Cypress Hills only a year before.[54] Riel became increasingly convinced that Indians, like the Métis, were being denied their true rights to land, and references to Indian interests made their way into his petitions. By February 1885, Hayter Reed warned the prime minister that Indians "were beginning to look up to [Riel] as the one who will be the means of curing all their ills and of obtaining all their demands."[55]

Still, Ottawa continued to ignore Riel and the Métis petitions. On March 3, 1885, Riel wrote in his diary, "O my Métis people! You complain that your lands have been stolen. Why, how can it be that you have not yet recovered them? You hold all the cards, you are strong enough."[56] The following week, Riel and a council of Métis leaders assembled near the town of Prince Albert to draft a Revolutionary Bill of Rights. Most of the demands related directly to the Métis, but the seventh item urged that "better provision be made for the Indians."[57] Riel ensured that a copy of this latest petition reached the local member of Parliament, Lawrence Clarke, with an urgent request to get it to the prime minister. This was the eighty-fourth petition the Métis had sent to Ottawa since 1878. It would be Riel's last.

While the Métis waited for a response, Major Lief Crozier of the North-West Mounted Police telegrammed his superiors with an assessment of a growing threat: "Halfbreed rebellion likely to break out any moment. If Halfbreeds rise Indians will join them."[58]

On March 18, the Métis received an unofficial message from Ottawa via Clarke, who said the latest petition would be "answered by powder and bullet."[59] Clarke also claimed that a detachment of police was on its way to arrest Riel. As it happens, this was not true, but the lie escalated an already tense situation.[60] The next day, Riel and a few hundred of his followers, mostly Métis and some Cree, declared a provisional government and overran the town of Batoche.

As Riel and his men seized control of the Saint-Antoine de Padoue Catholic Church, the resident priest said, "I protest your touching the church." Even in this fateful hour, Riel did not miss a chance to indulge his love of puns. "Look at him," Riel said, pointing with amusement at the priest. "He is a protestant!" Then Riel, a Catholic, added, "We are protesting against the Canadian Government, he is protesting against us. We are two protestants in our own ways."[61]

Riel was by now convinced that the federal government had "usurped the title of the Aboriginal Halfbreeds to the soil" and that "we are justified before God and men to arm ourselves, to try to defend our existence rather [than] to see it crushed."[62] Riel expected to rally support among Indians disgruntled with their treatment in the aftermath of the treaties. "I hear the voice of the Indian," he wrote. "He comes to join me. . . . He is in the mood for war."[63] Riel's greatest hope—that an alliance between the Métis and the Plains Indians would emerge—was the government's greatest fear.

On March 26, Major Crozier led ninety-nine men outfitted in red coats, a mix of mounted police and volunteer militia, to confront Riel. The two forces faced off near the town of Duck Lake, some five hundred kilometres northwest of Waywayseecappo and Rossburn.

Major Crozier and a translator met two Métis at the midpoint between the front lines. But the talks went badly and a scuffle broke out, culminating in one of the Métis negotiators being shot in the head. Crozier ran back toward his men, yelling, "Fire away, boys!" As the first bullets started to whistle and whine, Riel surveyed the scene from a hollow to the north. He sat atop his horse to get a better view, even though this left him exposed within gunshot range. He was armed with only a crucifix.

Riel's men had Crozier outflanked. They had also secured higher ground and taken positions among willow trees and dense brush. Sharpshooters flung blankets on the snow, lay down on their stomachs and started firing their Winchester rifles at the redcoats down below. Another group of Métis found cover in a nearby log cabin and shot from the windows.

Crozier's men, by contrast, were badly exposed. The luckier ones crouched behind their sleighs that were loaded with supplies, and some even resorted to placing their cooking stoves on top to secure a few extra inches of protection. Many had no cover at all and made easy targets as they lumbered through a metre of snow crusted with ice. Crozier did have command of a 224-pound brass cannon, which was their only chance against the Métis snipers in the log cabin. The first four cannon shots sailed beyond their mark, but got closer each time. Then a jittery soldier mistakenly loaded a fifth shell before inserting powder, which rendered the cannon useless.

Sensing that the battle was lost, Crozier ordered a retreat. There was no time to collect the dead, though the major ensured the disabled cannon got dragged along. The wounded left behind a bloody trail in the snow, crimson blots on a white canvas. Riel opted against pressing his advantage and ordered his men not to pursue. "For the love of God," he said, "don't kill any more. There's too much blood spilled already."[64] Notwithstanding Riel's display of mercy, a haunted police officer recalled, "The Indians were all painted like demons."

In thirty minutes of fighting, Riel had lost four men, Crozier twelve.[65] Hayter "Iron Heart" Reed, a man whose career had prepared him for exactly this kind of crisis, reported, "It is probable that an Indian war is on our hands."[66]

WHEN NEWS OF the battle at Duck Lake reached Ottawa, the government urgently summoned a company of infantry from Toronto and two companies of field artillery from Kingston and Quebec City. Most of the call-ups were not full-time soldiers. In Toronto, a colonel barked, "I don't care who a man is, or what he is doing, but I want every man in the regiment to be under arms and ready!"[67] Departure was delayed by a full day because the Toronto City Council needed more time to collect enough underwear, boots, and mufflers to keep the departing troops warm.[68] They would be travelling in open railcars through territory still under the dominion of winter. When the militiamen finally pulled out of the train station, they were cheered on by a raucous crowd of thousands caught up in a patriotic delirium. They sang, "We'll hang Louis Riel on a sour-apple tree."[69]

The train ride west was less thrilling. For days, the troops caught no sight of the sun or moon; the sky offered only snow and sleet. They ate rations of salted pork and biscuits smeared with rancid butter. "There were fifty of us to a car, piled one on top of each other, drenched by the rain which fell on our backs in torrents," a soldier wrote. "For the first time, we really knew what misery was."[70] Along the way, one man died from exposure.

In Rossburn, reports of Riel's resistance spurred settlers to volunteer for the front lines. Among them were James Stitt, Alex Brown, and James McBride.[71] The trio headed 120 kilometres southwest to the nearest recruiting station, in Moosomin. When they arrived, primed for action, military officials were still working out logistics. So Stitt, Brown, and McBride had to endure a few days of boredom. During this languid period, a measure of doubt crept in. McBride thought of his wife and children. He decided that maybe his country wasn't worth his life after all, then mounted his horse and headed back to Rossburn. Brown, too, lost his passion for the fight. According to Stitt, Brown was "looking forward to the choice of several blondes who had come into the district." Off Brown went, chasing greater glories.

That left Stitt, who decided to stick it out. Only a few hours after his friends departed, he received orders to head farther west. Each man received ten bullets and a rifle. The weapons were so rusty that it seemed to Stitt that they "had not been used since the battle of Waterloo, I am sure, and were much more dangerous than an Indian skirmish."

Louis Riel, too, was working to rally more support to his cause, following his victory at Duck Lake. Runners carried his letters to Métis communities and Indian reserves across

Saskatchewan and Manitoba. Riel predicted that "the struggle will grow, Indians will come in from all quarters."[72] This would turn out to be wishful thinking.

In the next few weeks, the forces Riel did manage to assemble seized control of two government forts. At Frog Lake, a group of Cree Indians in Chief Big Bear's band killed two priests, five white settlers, and two federal officials, one of them an Indian agent who, in the mould of Hayter Reed, had denied rations to the starving. A few of the dead bodies were mutilated and two white women were taken hostage.[73] Newspaper headlines announced the "Frog Lake Massacre."[73] Big Bear had actually tried to prevent the killings, but he ultimately could not control his more militant warriors. "It was as if they were trying to lash out against years of abusive deprivation, abuse and wounded pride," write historians Blair Stonechild and Bill Waiser.[74]

With a wider war looming, the mood in Rossburn darkened. The town's residents heard that a Native uprising was under way in Saskatchewan, led by that rascal Riel, and now the Indians in Waywayseecappo seemed to be behaving suspiciously. "Fear of the Indians was a constant worry," a settler recalled. "They would come with their paint and feathers requesting food or simply staring about in their silent way. . . . The uncertainty of what they would do next . . . was ever present."[75] Others recalled how "some of the young bloods in the reserve here became truculent in manner" and "asked questions about the ownership of stock. We thought that they were sizing up the possibility of owning them soon."

From the edge of the valley just west of town, a large encampment of Indians on reserve land was visible. "There were so many tents it looked like the area was covered with giant puffballs," one settler said.[76] "We were, you might say, surrounded by the Indians," said another.[77]

A town councillor, Robert Carson, hosted a group of men at his home to discuss how to prepare for an Indian attack. They considered digging an underground hideaway but ultimately decided against it because their children probably wouldn't keep quiet enough. The meeting adjourned without a plan.[78]

The next day, Carson passed anxious hours whittling a fallen branch into a tool called a double tree, used to connect horses to a wagon. By dusk, his handiwork still just looked like a big stick. He went home for supper and rested his work-in-progress outside the entrance. It was a windy night. After supper, Carson and his wife tucked their children into bed and went to sleep. But a loud thud on the front door startled the family awake. A gust of frigid air whistled through the house, which could only mean that the front door was ajar. Carson was "sure the Indians were upon us" and rushed from his bedroom to confront the invaders.

What he saw was this: The front door wide open, and his whittled branch lay on the floor. Carson laughed nervously. It was just the wind, just a stick. The Indians had not attacked. Yet.

ALL TOLD, THE Canadian government mobilized eight thousand troops to face Louis Riel, who had mustered only a few hundred fighters to his cause. Hayter Reed was assigned to advise General Middleton, the man in charge of Canada's military efforts. Within two months, Riel's resistance was overcome. Roughly one hundred people lost their lives in the fighting; hundreds more were wounded. Stitt, the brave bachelor from Rossburn, never even fired his rusty rifle, while the Métis defended their stronghold of Batoche until they ran out of bullets.

Government troops overtook Batoche on May 12, and Riel turned himself in three days later. A central factor in his defeat was the refusal of the vast majority of Indians in the North-West to assist him. Once signed, the treaties signalled a commitment to peace, and the Indians took that seriously. According to a history written by Maureen Twovoice's grandfather Michael, Chief Waywayseecappo "staunchly sided his sympathies with the Government" during the "unrest" of 1885. The Chief "counselled his braves for peace and ensured that they kept it."[79] Yet again, Chief Waywayseecappo provided a clear demonstration of his loyalty to Canada, his treaty partner.

The local Indian agent, Lawrence Herchmer, gave himself most of the credit for keeping the peace. "The outbreak of the rebellion naturally greatly excited my Indians," he wrote in a memo to headquarters. "I am happy to report, however, that I had no difficulty during that trying time in managing [them]."[80]

In Rossburn, settlers soon began to regain their optimism. "Riel had been crushed and the fear of the Indian rebellion removed," one resident recalled. "Now the West was on its way."[81] Another settler admitted that their anxieties had been overblown: "As a matter of fact, the Indians were never dangerous to any but mental well-being. . . . There was a certain fear of the Indians, although no single story of harm from them was ever told."[82]

But even as Rossburn's fears dissipated, the government was intent on making sure the Natives could never cause so much trouble again. The West needed to be made safe for settlement, once and for all. It fell to Hayter Reed to devise a plan. "I have a few radical changes to suggest," he wrote to his superior.[83]

On July 20, 1885, Hayter delivered a document entitled "Memorandum on the Future Management of Indians." Among other draconian measures, his plan proposed a "pass" system to keep "rebel Indians" on their reserves unless they received signed permission to leave. "The dangers of complications with white men will thus be lessened," he reasoned.[84]

Hayter also prepared a list of Indian bands in Canada, accompanied by notes on the extent of each band's loyalty during the recent violence. He deemed the Ojibway of Keeseekoownin "Loyal" and the Sioux of Standing Buffalo "Very Loyal." The Chippewas of Kinoosayo were among the "Disloyal." And for the Cree of Okemasis, near Duck Lake, Hayter simply wrote, "Ditto."

Waywayseecappo received a more ambiguous assessment:

Way-way-se-cappo, Salteaux (Ojibway)
Bird Tail & Lizard Pt.   *A few became impudent*

Altogether, twenty-eight bands were deemed outright disloyal. Hayter recommended a pass system for these treacherous Indians. Prime Minister Macdonald agreed but proposed to extend the measure to *all* reserves. "As to disloyal bands," Macdonald instructed, the pass system "should be carried out as the consequence of their disloyalty." Then the prime minister added, fatefully: "The system should be introduced in the loyal bands as well and the advantage of the changes pressed upon them."[85]

The pass system was born.

MEANWHILE, LOUIS RIEL was charged with high treason, punishable by death. According to government prosecutors, Riel "most wickedly, maliciously and traitorously, did levy and make war against our said Lady, the Queen." By contrast, Riel believed that all his actions could be justified—that he was a patriot, not a rebel. "I have the honour to answer the court that I am not guilty," he said at the beginning of his trial.[86] "I have acted reasonably and in self-defence."[87]

His lawyers submitted a defence of insanity, despite Riel's forceful objections. Even though it was probably his best chance to avoid execution, Riel was not interested in procuring his survival at the expense of his dignity. "Here I have to defend myself against the accusation of high treason, or I have to consent to the animal life of an asylum. I don't care much about animal life, if I am not allowed to carry with it the moral existence of an intellectual being," he wrote.[88] He went on to undermine his lawyers' insanity argument by defending himself with two cogent speeches in English, his second language. Rather than rely on a claim that he was himself mad, Riel insisted that he had been "contending with an insane and irresponsible government."[89]

An all-white, all-anglophone, all-Protestant jury found Riel guilty. The jury recommended clemency, but the judge sentenced him to "be hanged by the neck till you are dead." Two subsequent appeals came to nothing, and his hanging was eventually scheduled for November 15, 1885. Shortly before his execution, Riel wrote: "I have devoted my life to my country. If it is necessary for the happiness of my country that I should now soon cease to live, I leave it to the Providence of my God."[90] He was hanged shortly after eight in the morning.

Eighty-one Indians were also formally charged with taking up arms against the government, of which fifty-five were convicted. Eight Cree Indians received death sentences, the largest collective death penalty in Canadian history. Hayter Reed expressed hope that public executions would cause those who supported Riel to "meditate for many a day" on their "sound thrashing."[91] Prime Minister Macdonald said, "The execution of Riel and of the Indians will, I hope, have a good effect on the Metis and convince the Indians that the white man governs."[92]

On the day of the scheduled mass hanging, before a crowd of Indians and settlers, the eight condemned men remained defiant. Standing atop the scaffold, their ankles tied together and their heads shaved by their captors, they spoke their final words. Among them was Big Bear's son, Imasees (Little Bear). According to an eyewitness, Little Bear "told the Indian onlookers to remember how the whites had treated him—to make no peace with them." Another of the condemned urged Indians "to show their contempt for the punishment the government was about to inflict on them."[93] Then the executioners drew black caps over the prisoners' faces and bound their hands. With the pull of a lever, the scene came to a macabre end.

THE FOLLOWING YEAR, 1886, Indian agents across Canada received their first batch of blank pass booklets. Any Indian who wanted to leave a reserve would first have to obtain an official pass specifying the purpose and duration of the absence, duly signed by an Indian agent.

Valid reasons for granting passes included to "get married" (ten days), "go hunting" (twenty-one days), or "visit a daughter at school" (fifteen days).[94] Sometimes passes were granted only "until sunset." In some places, Indians needed to submit a letter of recommendation from another federal official before an agent would authorize a pass.[95] Hayter Reed once described passes as a "privilege," revocable if "abused."[96] Anyone caught off the reserve without a pass was liable to be arrested for vagrancy or trespass and forcibly returned. The system transformed every unauthorized traveller into a fugitive and every reserve into a holding pen.

The pass system was used to limit contact between parents and children who were attending residential schools. Hayter Reed boasted in an annual report, "I must not forget to notice the success attained in preventing Indian visitors banging about the schools, and so unsettling the minds of the children, as well as too often insisting upon carrying them off for visits to their homes, from which they would only be recovered with much difficulty if at all."[97] Limiting passes for parents was a key tool for attaining this "success."

Pass issued in 1889 to John Constant so that he could travel "to see his children" who were attending an Indian residential school (PAS, S-E 19.35a)

In the decades to come, the cumulative effects of the pass system on Indigenous communities were devastating. It was a barrier to finding work, customers, or other opportunities off reserve. It also choked traditional education and culture by limiting opportunities to gather for ceremonies. By design, reserves became an archipelago of open-air prisons. A web of interconnected communities was cut into scattered threads.

Fears of another rebellion enabled the creation of the pass system, but other motives sustained it. Passes were justified on the dual grounds of protecting whites and civilizing Indians, though proponents of the system did not hesitate to obscure the true reasons behind false pretexts.

Canada was struggling to attract immigrants to settle the West, and Riel's uprising had given prospective settlers further pause. At the time, Indigenous Peoples constituted about half of the population of the North-West.[98] Indian hunters made farmers nervous about their cattle, if not their lives. The government hoped the new constraints on Indian movement would reassure settlers that their expansion would not be contested.

Keeping Indians on the reserves was also defended as a more effective means of reforming them. The Department of Indian Affairs wanted Indians to hunt less and farm more, and surely they would tend more to their crops on reserve if it was impossible for them to go anywhere else. Hayter adopted the paradoxical view that Indians had to be segregated before they could be integrated. He wanted Indians to become "imbued with the white man's spirit and impregnated by his ideas."[99] But first they had to remain physically separate for a little while longer: "It seems better to keep them together for the purpose of training them for mergence with the whites, than to disperse them unprotected among communities where they could not hold their own, and would speedily be downtrodden and debauched." Indians were apparently so vulnerable to corruption by white society's vices that they could not be trusted to travel freely. If they had a choice, Hayter thought, they would choose poorly, particularly when it came to alcohol.[100] Reserves were officially dry, and Hayter speculated that a further prohibition on movement was the best way to keep Indians sober. The pass system would keep Indians separate and, supposedly, protected.

INCREDIBLY, FROM THE very beginning, the architects of the pass system recognized its flagrant illegality. Even Indians were entitled to the freedom of movement. The treaties negotiated with Alexander Morris had explicitly guaranteed the right to hunt and trap off reserve.[101] Privately, the prime minister acknowledged as much.[102] Even Hayter Reed, an attorney, said the Indians had "the law on their side,"[103] though that fact did not seem to particularly bother him. "I am adopting the system of keeping the Indians on their respective Reserves and not allowing any leave them without passes," Hayter wrote. "I know this is hardly supportable by any legal enactment but we must do many things which can only be supported by common sense and by what may be for the general good."[104] Hayter penned those words on August 18, 1885. Only a few weeks before, he had been appointed a justice of the peace, tasked with upholding the law in the North-West Territories.

Many Indians "refused to tolerate the [pass] system and were often aggressive in demanding their rights," the scholar F. Laurie Barron writes.[105] As it happened, they had an unlikely ally in Lawrence Herchmer, who had risen from his position as Waywayseecappo's Indian agent to become the commissioner of the North-West Mounted Police. It was not the harshness of the pass system that disturbed Herchmer, a man who had previously said that starvation could do Indians some good. Rather, he was concerned that the system put his officers in an untenable position of enforcing a non-existent rule. As one police officer noted, Indians without passes were sent back to their reserves "on every possible occasion, but seeing that the Police have no right to do anything of the kind, it behooves one to be very careful."[106] In 1892, Herchmer sought advice from judges and government legal counsel, who told him that the pass system was unambiguously illegal. The next year, Herchmer ordered his officers to stop enforcing it.[107]

Hayter Reed, who had risen considerably in the government's hierarchy in the eight years since he had drafted the original memo proposing passes, expressed "extreme regret" in response to Herchmer's decision.[108] Hayter directed his Indian agents to keep enforcing the pass system anyway, notwithstanding the squeamishness of the Mounted Police. He acknowledged once again that "there has never been any legal authority for compelling Indians who leave their Reserve to return to them, but it has always been felt that it would be a great mistake for this matter to stand too strictly in the letter of the law. So long as this course is followed in the interests of the Indians themselves, a benefit rather than a wrong is done them. . . . All we can endeavor to do is to keep the true position from the Indians as long as possible."[109]

In the end, Hayter's view prevailed: the Mounted Police resumed enforcing the pass system in 1904, after Herchmer was no longer commissioner.[110] In certain places, the system was enforced until 1941, more than half a century after the first passes were issued.[111]

★ ★ ★

HAYTER MOVED TO Ottawa in 1893 after receiving yet another promotion; he was now deputy superintendent of Indians Affairs, the department's top bureaucrat. He had come a long way since his first encounter with "the Redman" at Lac Qu'Appelle as a young soldier two decades before. Gone were his musket and red coat and mutton chops—now Hayter wore ties and smoked cigars and signed memos. He had traded adventure on the plains for an office in the nation's capital, where it didn't take long for him to distinguish himself as "the crack polo player of Ottawa."[112]

Hayter Reed (McCord Museum of Canadian History, McGill University/11-10654, 1894)

At the age of forty-four, Hayter "Iron Heart" Reed married Kate Armour, a widow with a talent for interior design and an expansive social network in Ottawa. They built a magnificent stone house next to the Rideau River, within walking distance of Parliament Hill. Their hallway entrance featured the stuffed head of a buffalo.

7

"THE YOUNG NAPOLEON OF THE WEST"

A T THE END OF THE NINETEENTH CENTURY, WHILE MEN like Hayter Reed fulfilled their frontier fantasies, it was still far from clear whether Canada was a viable country. For decades, more people had been emigrating *from* Canada than were immigrating *to* Canada.[1] The colossus to the south, the United States, was pulling one family after another into its orbit. Canada had an abundance of arable land but a shortage of willing farmers. Then came the general election of 1896 and the Liberal government of Wilfrid Laurier, who promised more immigrants and put a thirty-five-year-old Manitoban named Clifford Sifton in charge of finding them.

Sifton arrived in Ottawa with a bushy moustache that was not altogether successful in conferring the air of a statesman on his youthful face. He was six feet tall, five inches taller than the average man of the time. The *Globe and Mail* described Sifton as "a Canadian of Canadians, a Liberal of the Liberals . . . a young man with every faculty at command in the full exercise of its powers, with a clean record, with high ideals and aspirations—what may not Canada reasonably expect from him?"[2] He would go on to redeem and betray such lofty expectations.

Clifford Sifton (Library and Archives Canada, "Hon. Clifford Sifton (Minister of the Interior)," Topley Studio fonds/a027943)

Sifton's grandparents were Irish Protestants who had crossed the Atlantic Ocean in the 1830s and settled in Ontario. His father was the first member of the family to head west after being awarded contracts to extend a telegraph line and railway tracks in Manitoba toward Saskatchewan. The contract for the telegraph line, which ran over a portion of Treaty 4 territory, was tendered less than a month after Chief Waywayseecappo signed with his "X."

When Sifton was a child, a bout of scarlet fever left him partially deaf. For the rest of his life he compensated by outworking his peers. He graduated at the top of his law class, though he didn't consider himself the best or the brightest of his cohort. Rather, "I worked harder than they did and I got the reward."[3]

For a time, Sifton had imagined his future might carry him away from Canada. A few months in England as a teenager had given him the ambition to join the British civil service and help administer India (where actual "Indians" lived). In the end, though, he opted to follow his father west after completing his legal training. In 1882, he and his brother moved to Brandon, a frontier town two hundred kilometres due west of Winnipeg that was booming because of a new railway connection. They established a law firm, Sifton & Sifton, where Clifford specialized in land and homestead law, which was the main preoccupation of new settlers. In his spare time, he excelled at lacrosse, a sport invented by the Iroquois and known at the time as Canada's national game.

During the Riel scare of 1885, Sifton joined a home guard militia scouring Brandon for rebels. He patrolled the streets for four nights in succession with a shotgun in his hands and a "6-shooter" handgun on his hip.[4] For all his ardour, he never found an occasion to shoot.

Three years later, at the age of twenty-seven, Sifton won his first election to the provincial legislature against a heavily favoured Conservative candidate. He prevailed by only forty-two votes. Sifton, a teetotaller and the son of a prohibitionist, brushed off accusations that he plied prospective voters with whiskey. The next election, he won again, and his Liberal Party captured a majority in the legislature. He earned the nickname "Young Napoleon of the West" for his tactical brilliance during electoral campaigns.[5] He later boasted that if you gave him the name of a voter in North Brandon, he could tell you the colour of that person's hair.[6] Sifton became Manitoba's attorney general in 1891 and developed a reputation as the finest orator in the legislature.

When Laurier became prime minister in 1896, he recruited Sifton to his cabinet as minister of the interior and gave him a wide mandate to settle the prairies. The mayor of Brandon hailed the appointment: "Mr. Sifton possessed within him abilities equaled by few and surpassed by none."[7] Sifton was now in charge of Canada's immigration policy, and he vowed to create a nation of farmers.

In a memo to the prime minister, Sifton said that "the object which is constantly kept in view" was "development of natural resources and the increase of production of wealth from these resources."[8] He was convinced that Canada would progress only through agriculture, which in turn depended on the recruitment of a hardier breed of settlers: "the possession of a preponderating rural population having the virtues and strength of character, bred only among those who follow agricultural life, is the only sure guarantee of our national future."[9] Unless Canada settled its vast territory and exploited its natural wealth, he argued, the country would not reach its full potential. Immigration would make Canada great.

The question was where to find more able bodies. Sifton opposed an influx of Asians on the supposed grounds that they made bad farmers, and he doubled the head tax on prospective Chinese immigrants. The agricultural prowess of Jews was similarly suspect. To lure Americans, Sifton sent samples of wheat to South Dakota and Indiana, "to prove to people there that it could be grown in Manitoba."[10] Still, there weren't enough Americans or Brits willing to give Canada a try—harsh winters were something of a deterrent. For a time, Sifton even considered banning the publication of the daily temperature in Manitoba.[11]

Sifton was looking for people "to fight the battle of the pioneer's life," which required "the toughest fibre that can be found."[12] He set his sights on eastern Europeans, particularly Ukrainians. That such people lived half a world away did not impede Sifton's ambition. He saw in Catholic Ukrainians singular talents for tireless farming and prolific babymaking. His ideal migrant was "a stalwart peasant in a sheep-skin coat, born on the soil, whose forefathers have been farmers for ten generations, with a stout wife and a half-dozen children."[13] Cheap, plentiful labour was what he wanted. "I do not care what language a man speaks, or what religion he professes," Sifton said. "If he will go on the land and make a living for himself and family, he is a desirable settler for the Dominion of Canada."[14] In time, he was confident that they would "assimilate with Canadians."[15]

IN EUROPE, THE Ukrainians were a conquered people, their territory carved up and controlled by Austria-Hungary and Russia. Landlords called Ukrainians pigs and shut down their schools. Ukrainian peasants had to bow when they came within one hundred metres of their landlord's mansion. They were not even allowed to marry without permission. Russia-controlled Ukraine had been renamed Little Russia, and the words "Ukraine" and "Ukrainians" were forbidden.[16] In 1863, Russia barred the use of the Ukrainian language altogether. Meanwhile, Russian authorities demanded crops for taxation and men for military service. Under such conditions, Ukrainians dulled their misery by consuming astounding amounts of hard liquor: twenty-six litres per year per person, if you included every man, woman, and child.[17]

When Ukrainians spoke of "land," the word was often married with another: "problem." For a growing family on a modest farm, the "land problem" meant that a family's property could be divided among grown children only so many times. Subsistence farms became too small, and then smaller still. In the late nineteenth century, the average Ukrainian family farm had only four acres.[18] For the children of such families, immigration was more an imperative than a choice. As the poet Alexander Kolessa-Khodovitsky later wrote:

Perhaps a river deep
We shall cross
But in our native land
We shall perish.[19]

Word spread that a country called Canada was doling out plots of 160 acres, for free! That fact alone made a strong case for migration, but Clifford Sifton also enlisted the power of profit and propaganda. He reached an agreement to pay a Hamburg-based shipping outfit, the North Atlantic Trading Company, for every Ukrainian peasant it brought to Canada: five dollars per male head of a family, plus two dollars for a wife and each additional child. Sifton also made sure his immigration agents were no longer paid on salary but instead received a commission, per migrant they recruited.

Sifton saw himself as a salesman, with the Canadian dream as his commodity. He dispatched thousands of agents to Europe to distribute hundreds of thousands of pamphlets, promising "Free land is waiting for you" and "Canada will give you land."[20] He authored a brochure claiming that the prairie soil was so rich it "stands more cropping without manure, than any other surface known to agriculture."[21] In August on the prairies, he wrote, "it is harvest time, and the wheat fields are like a sea of gold."[22] A 1904 pamphlet proclaimed that "there are no castes or classes in this country, all are equal," and that "all religious denominations, whether Christian or otherwise, enjoy equal rights." The schools were said to be "equal to any on the continent," and the prairie land was described as "the best poor man's country between the Atlantic and the Pacific oceans." Another pamphlet described Canada simply as the "land of promise."[23]

FREE FARMS

FOR MILLIONS.

✿ ✿ ✿

200 MILLION ACRES

Wheat and Grazing Lands for Settlement in Manitoba
and the Canadian North-West.

✿ ✿ ✿

Advertisement in the *Nor-West Farmer*, June 1897 (Archives of Manitoba/N11695)

Russian and Austria-Hungarian authorities became increasingly alarmed that emigration might deplete Ukraine's (exploited) labour force, and they took measures to stop it. In one case, a man named Iwan Pillipiw visited Manitoba to see for himself whether it was worth uprooting his family. He decided it was. When he returned home to sell his property and urge others to join him on the journey, he was arrested, charged with criminal propaganda, and sentenced to a month in jail.[24] After his release, he and his family promptly packed up and left for Canada.[25]

To stem the outflow of migrants, the authorities deployed more armed guards at the border. Ukrainian priests were ordered to preach against emigration and to emphasize the prospect of starvation in Canada.[26] Yet migrants sought and found ways out, in large and growing numbers. In 1896, 2,576 Ukrainians arrived in Canada. The following year, as Sifton's propaganda campaign was revving up, the number grew to 4,999,[27] and by 1902 it was 10,309. The next year, 17,418 more came. Many read the words of Ivan Drohomereski in his poem "Exodus From the Old Country":

> *I once was in my native land,*
> *And I often thought:*
> *Why should I be suffering*
> *In unhappiness?*
> *I shall go into the wide world,*
> *Where there's neither oppression nor lord*
> ....
> *Oh, to Canada I'll go,*
> *To the new land,*
> *And where, as they say,*
> *It is a free country.*[28]

Pushed by fear and pulled by hope, Ukrainians coming to Canada outnumbered the total number of American and British immigrants for the first time in 1899.[29] Among these Ukrainian migrants were Troy Luhowy's great-great-grandparents, Maksym and Dorota Yaskiw. They took their four children, who were between the ages of six and thirteen, and left the Ukrainian province of Galicia to journey across the Atlantic to Canada.

The trip took them a month. The train heading to Hamburg journeyed via the Austria border town Oswiecim (which later became infamous by its German name, "Auschwitz"). The fortunate travellers sat on narrow benches along the sides of the railcars; the rest perched crookedly on their bags in the aisles. At each stop, border agents, doctors, and merchants—along with plenty of scammers—did their best to extract whatever meagre savings the travellers had stashed in their luggage and underwear.

In Hamburg, then Europe's busiest port, Canadian agents were on the lookout for the right kind of immigrant. "If one should examine twenty people who turn up at Hamburg to emigrate," Sifton said, "he might find one escaped murderer, three or four wasters and ne'er-do-wells, some very poor shop-keepers, artisans or laborers and there might be one or two stout, hardy peasants in sheep-skin coats. Obviously the peasants are the men that are wanted here."[30] Sifton was content "letting the riff-raff go on to the United States and to South America."[31]

Maksym and Dorota were among the chosen ones. From Hamburg, the boat ride to Halifax on Canada's eastern shore took two weeks or so, depending on the whims of the ocean. The migrants stayed below water level in steerage, packed into bunk beds lining stuffy compartments. The seasick were plied with garlic and whiskey to calm stormy stomachs. The travellers whispered to one another about the *vilni zemli*, "free land," that awaited them.

Their boat, the coal-powered S.S. *Phoenicia*, carried 1,308 passengers. This ship was among the more comfortable vessels carrying migrants across the seas in those days, because it was actually designed to transport humans. Often, immigrants travelled on cargo ships that had carried cattle, pigs, or grain from North America to Europe. The passengers of such ships arrived in their new country smelling like the animals that had preceded them.

The Yaskiws landed in Halifax on May 21, 1899. The wooden dock was lined with sheds full to bursting with coal. After passing a medical screening, the family was ushered into a train, where they sat on bare wooden boards. Bold letters inscribed on the trains read "COLONIST CARS."[32] The words meant nothing to Maksym and Dorota, who didn't know a word of English. Thanks to Minister Sifton, there was no fare to pay.

The train rumbled westward. To farmers from the Ukraine, the rough terrain of western Ontario, with its never-ending parade of cliffs, rocks, and forests, hardly seemed like an agricultural paradise. A ripple of panic spread through the train—perhaps they had been dreaming a lie, after all.[33] But once they reached the unrelenting flatness of Manitoba, their worst fears receded. Then, after 3,500 kilometres by rail, their train pulled into Winnipeg's central station.

From there, the Yaskiws took yet another train, which took them north to the town of Shoal Lake, where they were handed tents, axes, pots, utensils, flour, and sugar. Then the family hitched a wagon to their final destination, some place called Rossburn. Later that summer, Maksym and Dorota completed paperwork to receive a 160-acre government-issued homestead for a mere ten dollars.

In 1896, the year Sifton became minister of the interior, the government granted 1,861 homesteads to newcomers. By 1904, that number had skyrocketed by almost twenty times, to 32,684.[34] Each one anchored a family determined to rewrite its destiny.

For some, the journey ended in tragedy. In the spring of 1899, an outbreak of scarlet fever engulfed a group of new arrivals to

Manitoba. Four hundred people were quarantined a few kilometres from Rossburn and housed in makeshift tents. In May, just weeks before Maksym and Dorota arrived, a freak spring snowstorm proved too much for the most vulnerable to endure. Three adults and forty-two children died.

However, the overwhelming majority of new arrivals settled safely and set about fulfilling Sifton's lofty expectations of productivity. While Sifton was minister, new immigrants helped triple the number of acres under cultivation in Canada, to more than three million, and production of wheat quadrupled.[35] Sifton exulted over such figures. In a speech in 1902, he boasted about the transformation of the prairies. Before, he said, the Canadian West had been described "as a land of large promise but somewhat slow and poor performance, as a land of illimitable possibility but limited realities, a land generally described, indeed, with a fine flow of rhetoric." But, thanks to the influx of settlers, Sifton said, "stagnation has given way to abounding activity . . . and the whole situation has undergone an alternation that is little short of phenomenal."[36]

Still, Sifton remained driven by an anxiety that "just as soon as you stop advertising and missionary work, the movement is going to stop."[37] He maintained a frenetic pace, habitually working fourteen to sixteen hours a day.[38] Even after plowing through mounds of paperwork late into the night, he was known to be back at the office before the rest of his staff arrived the next morning. "The burden of carrying the affairs of the West is a heavy one," he confided in a colleague.[39] "I am worked out," he wrote to another. "I wish some of the damn fools who are grumbling had my job for a week. They would quit it wiser and sadder men."[40]

During the summer of 1898, he collapsed from exhaustion.[41] After resting for a few weeks and regaining his strength, he resumed the same manic work habits as before, perfectly in keeping with his lifelong scorn for idleness. To Sifton, a wasted work hour in Ottawa was as unforgivable as an uncultivated acre in Manitoba.

The results of his dogged efforts were indisputable. On Sifton's watch, more than one million people came to Canada, boosting the country's population by about 20 percent.[42] Yet what Sifton viewed as a historic achievement did not immediately receive the rapturous praise he thought it deserved. "I find some ground for wonder," he told a friend in 1902, "in the lack of appreciation of what is going on in the West where we have turned dismal failure into magnificent success."[43]

On the contrary, the new wave of immigration had sparked a nativist backlash. The Ukrainians in particular, though they constituted only a fraction of the new arrivals, tended to attract the most malignant scrutiny from newspapers and Sifton's political opponents. The year of the Yaskiws' arrival, newspapers in nearby Brandon, the town Sifton represented in Parliament, labelled the incoming Ukrainians as "barbarians," "pampered paupers," and "ignorant and vicious foreign scum."[44] According to one editorial, "Importing such creatures into our country is about as sensible as deliberately bringing vermin into a new house." The premier of Manitoba, Sir Rodmond Roblin, called the immigrants "foreign trash."[45]

A newspaper in Winnipeg labelled Ukrainians as "probably the least promising material that could be selected for nation-building." The next year, the same paper wrote with even less subtlety: "It cannot be too emphatically repeated that the people of Manitoba want no such 'settlers' as these 'Galicians.'"[46] (Like the Yaskiws, many of the immigrants were from the province of Galicia.) The article continued: the "dumping of these filthy, penniless and ignorant foreigners into progressive and intelligent communities is a serious hardship to these communities....These people bring with them disease ... and dirty habits."Though the federal government welcomed the Ukrainians, evidently many Canadians did not.

When a Ukrainian was suspected of shooting and killing an Anglo-Saxon woman in Winnipeg in 1899, the *Winnipeg Telegram* ran a headline calling it "Another Siftonian Tragedy."[47] Shortly thereafter, an Anglo-Saxon woman named Hilda Blake confessed to the crime, though the reflex to scapegoat Ukrainians far outlived this particular incident. It was a time for scornful epithets: "European freaks and hoboes,"[48] "scum of Europe," "herds of half-civilized Galicians."[49] Established Euro-Canadians, usually Protestants, sneered at the Eastern Catholic strangers pouring into the countryside. Like Maksym and Dorota, the newcomers were often poor and poorly educated. Most were illiterate. Critics derided them as "Sifton's pets."[50]

Undeterred, Minister Sifton remained their bugle and their shield. In 1899, Conservative Party member Edward Prior attacked the new immigrants during a speech in Parliament. Prior called the Galicians a "menace to our well-being and prosperity." He added, "The worst of it is, that these men are not coming in solely of their own accord, but they are coming in with the assistance of the government."

Across the parliamentary chamber, Sifton rose and spoke, loudly and proudly, in defence of the strangers he had helped bring to Canada. "So far as the Galicians are concerned, the attacks that have been made upon them, in my judgment, are most unfair and most ungenerous. If we are ever going to have the North-west populated, we shall not succeed in doing it by standing on our boundary with a club or putting the microscope on every man who wishes to come into the country."[51] Sifton insisted that all Canadians would benefit from the industry of these hardy settlers who were willing to toil "from daylight to dark."[52] Across the aisle, Prior remained unconvinced, though he eventually conceded, "I have never been in company with . . . a Galician . . . that I know of, but I have heard a great deal about them."

In 1899, Sifton told a skeptical crowd in Winnipeg that he "was willing to stake his reputation as a member of Parliament and a minister of the Crown that in five years' time there would not be found a business man who would say that the policy pursued was not a wise one."[53]

Privately, Sifton was blunter. "The cry against the . . . Galicians is the most absolutely ignorant and absurd thing that I have ever known in political life," he told a friend. "There is simply no question in regard to the advantage of these people, and I do not think there is anyone in the North West who is so stupid as not to know it. . . . The policy adopted of exciting racial prejudice is the most contemptible possible policy because it is one that does not depend upon reason. . . . All you have to do is keep hammering away and appealing to their prejudices, and in the course of time you will work up an excitement, but a more ignorant and unpatriotic policy could not be imagined."[54]

Sifton faced opposition from both sides of the political aisle on this issue. A fellow Liberal member of Parliament, Frank Oliver, said "these people" would be "a drag on our civilization and our progress," even if they did contribute economically. He recognized they were adept at working the soil, but to be worthy of living in Canada "it is not enough to produce wheat out of the ground."[55] They were an "alien race" with "alien ideas," and their presence would deter immigrants "of a superior class."[56] Likewise,

Hugh John Macdonald, the leader of the Conservative Party and son of Sir John A., declared that he did "not want a mongrel breed" coming to Canada. Instead, he "wanted white men."[57] At this time in Canadian history, Maksym and Dorota, for all their pallor, did not qualify as white.

Yet Sifton never wavered. When the general election of 1900 rolled around, Sifton eagerly courted the votes of the new arrivals who had received their naturalization papers. He helped create and distribute a political pamphlet that described how Galicians had been "neglected and in a miserable condition and that immediately after I took office they were looked after and work found for them."[58] The Liberals won another majority, and Sifton remained at the helm of the Department of the Interior.

Immigrants kept coming by the tens of thousands, clearing land, enduring winters, and, over time, thriving. With his mission largely accomplished, Sifton resigned from his post in 1905, after nearly a decade in the job. He retired altogether from politics in 1911, having unalterably changed the course of his country. Some 180,000 Ukrainians made their way to Canada in the two decades between 1895 and 1914, by which point Ukrainians outnumbered Indigenous Peoples.

After his retirement, Sifton's legacy was widely celebrated. His critics had been proved wrong. Prime Minister Robert Borden said of Sifton, "He was inspired with a sincere patriotism, and no Canadian had a broader outlook or a higher optimism as to the future of our country."[59] The *London Advertiser* wrote, "A new Canada emerged with the twentieth century, and Clifford Sifton's name is written imperishably in this inspiring chapter of Canadian history."[60]

And yet there is another side, less well known and certainly less inspiring, to the story of Clifford Sifton.

★ ★ ★

DURING THE YEARS Sifton was minister of the interior, he was *also* the superintendent of Indian affairs. This put him in charge of both Canada's newest arrivals and its first inhabitants. His twin missions were to welcome immigrants and civilize Indians. The logic of this dual mandate was simple: clear the path for settlers.

When Sifton assumed the leadership of the Department of Indian Affairs, his top bureaucrat was Hayter "Iron Heart" Reed. The two men shared the basic view that Indians could not be trusted to govern their own lives. "Our position with reference to the Indians is this," Sifton said, speaking on behalf of the government. "We have them with us, and we have to deal with them as wards of the country."[61]

Sifton began his tenure with a promise to limit spending on Indians as much as possible. Over the course of his decade as superintendent, funding for the Department of Indian Affairs would increase by a relatively modest 30 percent.[62] During the same period, the overall budget of the Department of the Interior, of which Indian Affairs was a part, increased by 400 percent. "Immigration we must have," Clifford Sifton once told his top official stationed in Europe. "You will have all the money that may be necessary."[63] Indians were a far lower priority.

In the longer term, Sifton saw government-funded education as the most viable way "to bring the Indians into a state of civilization or comparative civilization," and to reduce "any chance of them becoming a disturbing factor in the community."[64] Which was not to say that he expected too much from them. "I have no hesitation in saying, we may as well be frank, that the Indian cannot go out from a school, making his own way and compete with the white man."[65] As compared to white Canadians, an Indian "has neither the physical, mental or moral get-up to compete. He cannot do it."

Under Sifton's leadership, the number of Indian children receiving a state-sponsored education rose to ten thousand. Meanwhile, he insisted that "the expenditure upon Indians, and particularly upon Indian education, has reached a high water mark, and we must now look to reducing rather than increasing it in any way."[66]

In order to trim the budget while still maintaining the project of civilizing Indians through education, Sifton approved a gradual shift away from attempts to teach them trades at so-called industrial schools. Rather, he proposed "a less elaborate system of what we call boarding schools where a larger number of children can for a shorter time be educated, more economically and generally more effectively."[67] In time, Canada would come to call these institutions residential schools. To Sifton, it was crucial that these schools would be far from reserves, so that Indian children would be "removed from the surroundings which tend to keep them in a state of more or less degradation."[68]

Along with Hayter Reed, Sifton had a direct hand in establishing the residential schools that Maureen's mother Linda and grandfather Michael later attended. In 1897, Hayter wrote a memo to Sifton recommending a per student grant of $110 to the Brandon Indian Residential School, to get the school up and running. Sifton approved.[69]

In 1904, after a fire destroyed the Qu'Appelle Indian Industrial School in Saskatchewan, Sifton personally intervened to have it rebuilt.[70] The new building was where Michael Twovoice learned to read and write, and where missionaries trumpeted the virtues of assimilation.

Tragically, during Sifton's time as superintendent of Indian affairs, some residential schools had mortality rates of *50 percent*. In 1907, a government-appointed inspector called the mistreatment of Indigenous children at these institutions a "national crime."[71] At the Brandon residential school alone, at least forty-one students died on Sifton's watch.[72]

In 1899, Sifton approved Treaty 8 to solidify government control over 850,000 square kilometres of land in parts of what are now Alberta, Saskatchewan, British Columbia, and the Northwest Territories. Like other treaties signed in the same era, Treaty 8 was a document riddled with arcane legal jargon, negotiated with people who could not read it and who left with a completely different understanding of what it meant. To Sifton, the purpose of the treaty was "to pacify and keep pacified the North-West territories" and to avoid "having an Indian trouble on our hands."[73] There was a gold rush under way in northern Canada, and Sifton wanted to make sure the Natives were no impediment.

As well, he oversaw the work of Indian agents across the country, who were vested with pervasive power over Indians on reserves. Yet Sifton insisted that Indian agents tread softly in at least one respect: "It is absolutely essential that Indian Agents should scrupulously refrain from interfering directly or indirectly with the Missionaries upon Indian Reserves."[74] Indians were wards; missionaries were untouchable.

Looking back on his record as a government minister, Sifton was proud of what he had accomplished. "I shall be content, when the history of this country shall be written, to have the history of the last eight or nine years, so far as western administration is concerned, entered opposite my name," he said.[75] To Sifton, his most important mission had been increasing immigration.[76] He viewed Indians, his "wards," as a liability to be managed and minimized.

Meanwhile, he celebrated immigrants, his "pets," as the guarantors of Canada's future prosperity. And since the material progress of new arrivals like Maksym and Dorota Yaskiw was the best advertisement for others to follow, Sifton did everything in his considerable power to ensure that they got the favourable start they needed. Compared to a place like Rossburn, Waywayseecappo was an afterthought.

Years later, an early Ukrainian settler to Rossburn wrote a poem that began,

> Many came from distant lands
> Unaware what the future held,
> To settle on unknown Canadian virgin lands
> A new life, in a new land to weld.[77]

Virgin land, but for those Indians across the Birdtail.

8

"ONE LOAD OF BARLEY"

I N 1889, 153 INDIANS LIVED ON THE WAYWAYSEECAPPO reserve. About half had been categorized by the government as "pagans," but the determined efforts of Christian missionaries had been steadily increasing the number of Roman Catholics and Presbyterians among them. There was also more farming on the reserve. A federal inspector with the Department of Indian Affairs noted with satisfaction that 182 acres of crops—wheat, oats, barley, rye, potatoes, turnips, carrots, and onions—had been sown in the reserve's heavy black loam soil, up from 50 acres the previous year. Slightly more than twenty of these acres were overseen by Otakaonan ("the Gambler"), now more than a decade removed from his speeches at Treaty 4 negotiations. "Some of the young men have begun farming for the first time this year," the inspector noted approvingly.[1] The federal government continued to profess that farming was the surest route to progress for Indians.

In October that year, after the fall harvest, the Department of Indian Affairs announced a radical new approach to agriculture on reserves. Henceforth, labour-saving machinery would be banned. Although farming technology was improving rapidly at the time, Indian agents would require farmers on reserves to seed by hand, harvest with scythes and hoes, and grind grain with hand mills. Furthermore, Indians would be required to manufacture these most basic of tools themselves. On some reserves, even nails were not permitted.[2] In other cases, Indian agents banned lanterns.[3] So at the same time the government was forcing Indians into agriculture in the name of productivity, it was banning the most productive tools.

The mastermind of this new policy was none other than Hayter Reed, avid proponent of the pass system. "The general principle," Hayter explained, "is not to allow machinery to save [Indians] work that they should do with hands available on Reserves."[4] Indians would have "to cut and sow their grain in the most crude manner possible."[5] With less technology and less efficiency, the thinking went, more Indians would work harder, and thereby experience the redemptive power of industry, thrift, and self-sufficiency. What's more, officials saw little point in letting Indians invest in technology they could not afford, because they were viewed as too feeble-minded to manage debt.[6] Bands that tried to pool their resources to buy expensive machinery were to be stopped.[7] "Great discretion has to be used relating to the kind of investments the Indian is allowed to make," Hayter wrote.[8]

Hayter believed new machinery could be justified only when manual labour was scarce, which he didn't think was the case on reserves. It did not seem to occur to him that coerced inefficiency was a powerful incentive to do less.

In 1893, a group of Cree and Ojibway Indians on Treaty 4 territory petitioned Parliament to permit them to purchase a mechanical binder, a machine that cut stalks of grain and bound them into bundles. An official in the Department of Indian Affairs, they wrote, had "objected to us buying a Binder as he said it would make the young men lazy. . . . This has completely discouraged us, as our old implements are worn out . . . [and] many of the fields we used to farm are now all grown over with grass."[9] Even some federal officials conceded how counterproductive the policy was. "Personally," one Indian agent observed, "I do not see how any band of Indians in this district can ever raise sufficient grain or cattle to become self-supporting as long as they have to work with sickles and scythes only."[10]

Meanwhile, farmers in Rossburn had collectively organized themselves to purchase a threshing machine.[11] Such a machine could do in one afternoon what ten men did by hand in two weeks. Surely people in Waywayseecappo were aware of this, and even Hayter acknowledged that Indians "see white men in the possession of self-binders and other costly inventions for saving labor" and "think that they should have such implements."[12] But he believed that the use of such tools by Indians would "leave them little more to do than to sit by and smoke their pipes, while work is being done for them without exertion on their part." Hayter embraced the racist idea, then prevalent, that races progressed in fixed, progressive stages, and, therefore, Indians should not be permitted to "emulate in a day what white men have become fitted for through the slow progress of generations." The Indians could have better technology when they were civilized enough to deserve it.

Under Hayter Reed's fastidious watch, the Department of Indian Affairs enforced these restrictions on farming technology from 1889 until 1897, the year Hayter retired from government. During that span, per capita acreage under cultivation on reserves across the prairies fell by about half.[13] Farmers on Waywayseecappo fared even worse. In 1889, they cultivated 182 acres, but nine years later, that number had fallen to a mere 8.[14]

In addition to restrictions on technology, Waywayseecappo also had to contend with what was known as the "permit system," created in 1882 by an amendment to the Indian Act. Without signed permission from an Indian agent, Indians living on reserves were not allowed to sell food they grew or animals they raised to anybody off reserve.[15] Unlike the pass system, which was enforced despite its manifest illegality, the permit system was spelled out in legislation that made it perfectly legal. In principle, the freedom of contract was sacrosanct in Canadian common law, but this liberty was suspended for Indians, whom the state accorded the legal status of children.

The federal government sought to justify the permit system on the basis that it would protect Indians from fraud. Without benevolent supervision, Hayter Reed explained, Indians would first "part with hay while their cattle were left to starve" and trade away "grain and roots which they require for sustenance," then "squander the proceeds" and ultimately "come on the Government for support."[16] Prime Minister John A. Macdonald made a similar assessment: "If the Indians had the power of unrestricted sale, they would dispose of their products to the first trader or whiskey dealer who came along, and the consequence would be that the Indians would be pensioners on the Government during the next winter."[17] The government argued that the permit system would instead promote self-sufficiency and thereby stave off future federal expenditures.

In practice, the permit system hamstrung farmers on reserves. As a group of Cree and Ojibway Indians on Treaty 4 territory noted in an 1893 petition: "Whenever we have a chance to sell anything and make some money the Agent or [Farming] Instructor steps in between us and the party who wants to buy, and says we have no power to sell: if this is to continue how will we be able to make a living and support ourselves? We are not even allowed to sell cattle that we raise ourselves."[18]

Even some settlers publicly condemned the unfairness of the permit system. The *Virden Chronicle*, a newspaper based in a small town a hundred kilometres south of Waywayseecappo, ran an article titled "Indian Grievances" on January 11, 1894. Indians on reserve were "very dissatisfied" with the permit system, the newspaper reported. "They farm their own land, work hard all summer, and through the obnoxious order are not allowed the full benefit of the fruit of their own labour. They are thus placed at a disadvantage in competition with their white and more highly civilized neighbours." Rather than celebrating this disadvantage, the *Virden Chronicle* heaped scorn upon it, because the permit system was creating grievances that could "assume serious proportions and we do not want another rebellion." Louis Riel's shadow still loomed.

Not only were Indians being restricted from selling their goods, the article explained, but Indian agents were fining or threatening white buyers for making purchases without permits. As a result, "The grain dealers have almost concluded not to purchase any more grain from the Indians, except at very low rate, as they are entirely at the mercy of the Indian Agent....An Indian's wheat is just as good as a white man's, but the dealers claim that if they are by purchasing it, making themselves liable to prosecution, they must protect their own interests." The *Virden Chronicle* demanded an investigation into Indian complaints and an end to the permit system.[19] Yet nothing changed, in Waywayseecappo or elsewhere.[20]

Between the technology restrictions and the permit system, Indians were not permitted to farm efficiently or to sell their products freely. Meanwhile, the arrival of a (heavily government subsidized) railway connection in Rossburn in 1905 gave Waywayseecappo's white neighbours the incalculable benefit of access to distant markets.

In short, the government repeatedly declared that it wanted Indians to farm in order to become more civilized, but it made it nearly impossible for farming on reserves to be successful.[21]

At best, federal policies for reserves were the result of disastrously misguided paternalism, though the historian Sarah Carter advances a more damning interpretation. She argues that the federal government was in fact trying to "protect and maintain the incomes of white farmers" by insulating them from on-reserve competition.[22] In 1888, for example, a group of settlers in Saskatchewan wrote to their member of Parliament to complain that "the Indians are raising so much grain and farm produce that they are taking away the market from the white settlers."[23]

Of course, it remained all too easy to attribute blame to Indians themselves. One of Waywayseecappo's Indian agents criticized the reserve's "not very good farmers" for being "easily discouraged."[24] A federal inspector described Waywayseecappo's inhabitants as "unprogressive, morose, and unwilling to be guided by officials. Their inordinate pride appears to be the greatest obstacle to their advancement."[25] Across the valley of the Birdtail, settlers in Rossburn looked on—and drew similar conclusions.

This was part of a broader pattern: the government orchestrated failure on reserves, then Indians who suffered the consequences got blamed.

★ ★ ★

THOUGH HAYTER REED'S technology restrictions stopped being enforced in 1897, the permit system lasted far longer. Half a century later, in February 1942, a federal official caught two men from Waywayseecappo selling wood at $1.50 per load to a white farmer without authorization. One of the men, Joe Mentuck, later told the RCMP, "I did not have a permit to sell, I know I should have one and meant to get one but left it too long."[26] Mentuck had hoped to exchange the wood for a dozen chickens, an overcoat, and a sweater. His family was hungry, and the winter was frigid.

The local Indian agent, A.G. Smith, was slated to review the incident in Rossburn on March 6, at which point he could lay formal charges for the violation of the Indian Act. (In such cases, Indian agents assumed the role of magistrates.) Smith was sufficiently troubled by the circumstances of the case to write his superior in Ottawa to ask whether he had discretion to waive fines, especially when he thought an Indian was not particularly blameworthy. The purchaser and seller were each subject to a $20 fine, even if the load of wood was worth only $1.50. "The white man can probably pay the fine with ease," Smith wrote, "but the Indian may have to deprive his family of some of the necessities of life to pay his fine, or go to prison."[27]

There is no surviving record of what Agent Smith ultimately decided.[28] Yet he and his successors would be tasked with enforcing the permit system for decades to come. As late as 1969, the Department of Indian Affairs and Northern Development issued a permit to allow the sale of a heifer.[29] And the provision of the Indian Act that made it illegal for Indians to sell to non-Indians was not repealed until 2014.[30]

★ ★ ★

ON THE MORNING of Sunday, October 17, 1943, the pews of Waywayseecappo's Presbyterian church were packed for an event about the ongoing World War. Seen from the outside, the white paint on the wooden building gave it a ghostly pallor among the sharpening colours of autumn. To ward off the chill, volunteers periodically shovelled coal into the basement furnace.

Waywayseecappo's Chief at the time was Prince Astakeesic, the grandson of Waywayseecappo, and he addressed the congregants first. He spoke in Ojibway, but a local translated into English. According to a report published in the *Rossburn Review*, the Chief "spoke very feelingly and patriotically of the young men and the cause for which they volunteered to work and fight. He spoke of the Blessing of Freedom and was convinced that the British would see the war through to a grand Victory and Freedom for all."

Chief Astakeesic concluded by unveiling the Honour Roll, a plaque listing the names of men from the reserve who had already signed up. The names were bordered by stylized maple leaves, painted green and yellow, alongside the flags of Great Britain and Canada. The name of the Chief's son, George Astakeesic, was printed near the top of the alphabetical list. George was deployed with the 1st Canadian Infantry Division, which was then facing off against German tanks in the deserts of North Africa.

Next, a recruiter from the Canadian military made his way to the podium. He praised "the splendid attitude of men coming forward and ready, if need be, to pay the supreme sacrifice, not only for loved ones at home and for country and Empire, but for the unfortunate peoples being so basely and cruelly treated in the War Zones."

The local Presbyterian missionary spoke last. He pointed to the Union Jack and marvelled at the way it was "honoured by peoples of all classes, colours, creeds and languages, and how, at the sound of distress and pain from Europe, the men had rallied together from Continents and Isles of the Sea." Thanks to so many brave men, "the oppressors were feeling the weight and power of the Soldiers of Truth and Righteousness."[31] The service concluded with the singing of the hymn "Onward, Christian Soldiers":

> *Like a mighty army*
> *Moves the Church of God:*
> *Brothers, we are treading*
> *Where the Saints have trod.*
> *We are not divided;*
> *All one body we:*
> *One in hope and doctrine,*
> *One in charity.*

Michael Twovoice, Maureen's grandfather, was among those listed on the Honour Roll, though he was never shipped overseas on account of his tuberculosis infection. Michael's friend Hugh McKay was also on the Honour Roll and had already been serving in Europe for months at the time of the October ceremony in the Presbyterian church. After basic training, Private McKay shipped overseas in December 1942 as a machine gunner in the Royal Canadian Artillery. He would go on to serve in the Army for forty-four months and was abroad for three years. A month after D-Day, he helped liberate the French town of Caen from Nazi control. Hugh fought in France, Belgium, Holland, and finally Germany, where he was wounded in combat.

McKay was discharged on February 19, 1946, six months after the Japanese joined the Germans in unconditional surrender. He received enough medals to crowd the left breast of his uniform, including the War Medal 1939–1945, the France and Germany Star, the Defence Medal, and the Canadian Volunteer Service Medal and clasp. His military records indicate he was five feet eight inches tall, with brown hair and black eyes. His complexion is listed as "dark."

Pte. Hugh McKay (Courtesy of Jim Cote)

After returning from Europe, McKay settled back home in Waywayseecappo. Soon after, he received a letter dated July 31, 1946, from the Department of National Defence. "This Certificate is forwarded you with the sincere congratulations of this Headquarters," a brigadier wrote. The document recognized McKay for his "bravery in action" and was signed by Canada's secretary of state for war "to record His Majesty's high appreciation" for McKay's "distinguished service." Hugh framed the certificate and hung it on his wall.

Like many veterans, McKay seldom talked about the war, even with his son Jim. But what he did share Jim remembers, including a story about a time McKay approached his commanding officer seeking deployment to the front lines. The officer liked the young private enough to discourage him from putting himself in even greater danger. "If you go to the front," he told McKay, "you will see things you'll never forget for the rest of your life, terrible things. And that's *if* you come back."

Driven by a sense of duty, McKay persisted, and got his wish. He later told his son, "That officer was right." For years after returning home, McKay experienced debilitating flashbacks when airplanes rumbled overhead or when storms popped and flashed. His wife would try to bring him back into the present by slapping him in the face and yelling, "Hugh! Hugh!"

While he was an active member of the Army, McKay had visited bars across Canada in uniform and was served without question. After he returned home in 1946 as a civilian, he visited the bar in the Rossburn Hotel, expecting nothing different. When he entered, though, the patrons turned their heads in unison. They looked like a group of cows distracted from their cud.

"Hey, you," the bartender said. "Get lost."

"I'm a veteran, I served," Hugh said.

"I don't care what you did, get the hell out."

In the Canada of 1946, the bartender was following the law. Beer parlours could not legally admit Indians, even those who had risked their lives fighting Nazis. "There was something patently ridiculous," the historian James Gray writes, "in a system which permitted an Indian to risk his life for his country but denied him access to a bottle of beer."[32] Like many thousands of other Native veterans, McKay had to confront the painful dissonance between Canada's wartime rhetoric about freedom and the harsh reality of his racist neighbours in a racist nation.

MCKAY NEVER FORGOT nor forgave his expulsion from the Rossburn Hotel and made a point of avoiding town as much as possible afterwards. (Years later, he would relish Waywayseecappo's establishment of its own separate school.) After the war, he worked to earn his living as a farmer. Still, he could not escape further indignities, including the demands of the permit system.

Permit to sell a load of barley (Courtesy of Jim Cote)

On November 25, 1947, McKay received permit no. 49539, which authorized him to sell "one load of barley" for $65.20. McKay was "permitted to sell" only because he and a buyer had first obtained the express permission of the local Indian agent. A freedom fighter abroad, Hugh McKay was still treated as a ward at home.

Jim recalls an occasion in the 1950s when his father tried to sell a cow. "I nursed that calf!" McKay yelled. "I pulled it out of its mother with my hands. I fed it, I raised it. It's my cow! I should be able to sell it."

His request for a permit had been denied.

9

"REASONABLE AMUSEMENT"

O N THE EVENING OF FEBRUARY 17, 1896, THE TEMPER-
ature in Ottawa plunged to minus thirty-five Celsius.
This did nothing to deter the guests of the Historical
Fancy Dress Ball, who kept warm under fur blankets as they
glided along Wellington Street in horse-drawn sleighs.

The ball was organized by the governor general's wife, Lady
Aberdeen, who was thrilled to have the chance to host a lavish
event for the rich and powerful of the nation's capital. "To tell the
honest truth," she confessed to her diary, "we started this idea of
having a Ball representing the outstanding periods of Canadian
history with the hope that it might lead young people to reading
up a bit & that it might divert Ottawa gossip at least into past
times, away from . . . the everlasting discussion of hockey and winter sports varied with Ottawa society scandal."[1] Among those to
receive a coveted party invitation was Hayter Reed, on account
of his wife Kate's friendship with Lady Aberdeen.

The Senate Chamber of Parliament was cleared of its chairs
and desks to make way for a temporary white pine dance floor.

Banners of blue silk garlanded the sixteen marble pillars lining the walls. With the seated galleries full and the chamber packed to standing-room capacity, one thousand people managed a snug fit.

At nine o'clock, the crowd hushed as an orchestra started playing "God Save the Queen." This was the cue for the governor general and Lady Aberdeen to enter in a procession through the middle of the chamber. Lady Aberdeen wore a purple satin dress featuring a bodice of darker velvet, along with a coronet of sparkling diamonds that held her veil in place. Her two youngest boys trailed immediately behind, wearing powdered wigs and carrying the train of their mother's dress. Once the viceregal couple reached the dais at the far end of the room, they sat down on a pair of thrones. Then Lady Aberdeen gave a nod, and trumpets announced the start of the first dance. "From the first moment," she later wrote, "one could not help feeling that the thing was 'going.'"

The Aberdeens' fancy dress ball in the Senate Chamber (Library and Archives Canada/Samuel J. Jarvis fonds/c010108)

The entertainment kicked off with a series of dance perform-ances representing nine periods in Canada's history, from Viking incursions around AD 1000 to the arrival of the Loyalists in 1779. From the galleries overlooking the chamber, the view was posi-tively kaleidoscopic. "The floor beneath resembled a mosaic, with men and women, garbed in vari-hued apparel, as the pieces that made up the whole," an onlooker noted. "Every conceivable tint was in evidence. . . . Wander as the eye might, it was always met by a spectacle of colored loveliness."[2]

After the final dance performance, the guests briefly resumed their mix-and-mingle before they were interrupted by a series of lurid whoops and cries. A group of people dressed up as Indians sprang from the four corners of the room, pantomiming toma-hawk chops in their best impressions of noble savages. They soon converged in front of the governor general and Lady Aberdeen. The group's leader wore a wig with braided ponytails, along with a feathered headdress that hung from his head to his heels. He carried an eight-foot-long wooden staff adorned with feathers. His fringed buckskin and shirt were a haphazard mix of Cree and Blackfoot styles.

Kate Armour Reed was among the few to recognize the man in the costume: it was her husband, Hayter, thoroughly enjoying himself, his pale face smudged with reddish-brown paint. He was joined by his stepson Jack, also dressed up for the occasion. Hayter had provided many of the outfits for the performance from cloth-ing he had collected during his fifteen years with the Department of Indian Affairs. (Hayter's collection was so extensive that he had loaned many items from it a few years earlier for an exhibition at the Chicago World's Fair.) "Their striking costumes added a pic-turesque effect to the brilliant scene," *Lounger Magazine* reported. "They would have delighted the heart of a genuine son of the forest if he could have seen them."[3] Of course, there was no actual Indian present at the party to test that proposition.

Hayter Reed and his stepson Jack (Library and Archives Canada, Topley Studio fonds/a139841)

"Tenth Historic Group: Indian Group," with Hayter standing fourth from the right (Library and Archives Canada, Mrs. K. Stephen collection/ICON14103)

167

Hayter was playing the character of Donnacona, an Iroquois Chief whom French explorer Jacques Cartier had encountered on his first transatlantic trip, in 1534. When Cartier first set foot in North America, he declared possession of the territory and planted a thirty-foot cross with an engraving in French: "Vive le roi de France." But Donnacona objected. According to Cartier, the Chief approached in a canoe, "then he pointed to the land all around us, as if to say that all the land was his, and that we should not have planted the cross without his leave."[4] To avoid a confrontation, Cartier pretended that the cross was innocuous, a mere navigational landmark. The following year, when Cartier returned, he kidnapped Donnacona and took him to France, where the Iroquois Chief was paraded before the French king as exotic proof of the New World. Donnacona ended up dying in France, far from home.

Now, three and a half centuries later, Hayter was addressing the governor general and Lady Aberdeen in broken Cree, doing his best Donnacona impression in the wrong language.[5] He expressed the "love of his Indians" for Canada's head of state.[6] As Hayter spoke, the other members of his party whooped and grunted in approval. Then, after Hayter finished his address, he presented the governor general and Lady Aberdeen with a peace pipe. As absurd as this whole display was, the audience found it utterly compelling. Here in Ottawa, Hayter was the undisputed voice of Native peoples.

Hayter and his band of ersatz Indians had stolen the show. "The whole proceeding was well managed," a historian later wrote, "and certainly unique in the Senate chamber, which has never before been invaded by the Indian aborigines, in real or mimic guise."[7] After the performances, dinner was served in the cavernous rotunda of the main Parliament building, where guests "chatted in the gay and happy spirit characteristic of the evening," one observer said.[8] A member of Hayter's group felt sufficiently emboldened to (falsely) boast to partygoers that he was wearing moccasins made with human scalps.

"The history of our own country is too little known," a journalist noted, "and the historical pageant had the effect of bringing it before the society of the capital in a most striking and effective manner."[9] The event forced even "the careless student of our history to recognize its great charm and varied interest," another wrote, "and to feel a deeper pride in this 'Canada of ours.'"[10]

The glowing reviews delighted Lady Aberdeen. She had only one regret, which she expressed repeatedly over the course of the evening: if only she had thought to request an Indian war dance.[11]

MEANWHILE, IN WAYWAYSEECAPPO, federal agents were intensifying their long-standing efforts to suppress Native dancing ceremonies, which the government viewed as obstacles to the civilizing process. Hayter Reed himself had long championed these draconian restrictions.

Back in 1884, Parliament amended the Indian Act to criminalize "giveaways," rituals involving gifts, which were a common feature of many Indigenous ceremonies.[12] Hayter supported banning this "very objectionable" practice because it was "occasion for an interchange of presents and the giving away of property, even to outsiders. In many instances Indians are known to have dispossessed themselves of everything they owned."[13] Hayter described Indians on the plains as "the only perfect socialist in the world."[14] In time, the government hoped to transform them into straight-thinking individualists.[15]

After Hayter became the top bureaucrat in the Department

of Indian Affairs, he supported a further legislative amendment in 1895 that prohibited any ceremony involving "wounding or mutilation."[16] This amendment aimed to suppress the Sun Dance, widely practised in the prairies, which involved feats of physical endurance, including, in some cases, skin piercing.

Technically, only events involving "giveaways," "wounding," or "mutilation" were illegal—but, just as with the pass system, Indian agents were encouraged to operate beyond the strict letter of the law. Claiming legislative authority, agents worked to quash all sorts of ceremonies nationwide. Those who defied the prohibition faced the prospect of months in jail.

In Waywayseecappo, the annual Sun Dance was the community's most sacred traditional ceremony, and participants from other reserves travelled long distances to attend. The dance took place in an encampment formed of teepees arranged in a circle, with a round ceremonial lodge at its centre. The circular shape affirmed a sense of coming together and unity. Inside the central lodge, there was singing, drumming, and dancing. Those who had pledged to dance continued intermittently for multiple days and nights, during which time they neither ate nor drank. "The dancing was a fulfilment of personal vows," Waywayseecappo Elder Jim Cote says. "It was dancing for the wellness of all family members and the community. That's what those dances were for."[17]

A Sun Dance ceremony often lasted four days, but it could go on for as long as eight. The Sun Dance was a time to feast, to pray, to give thanks, to renew bonds within and between communities. It was a place where traditional teachings were passed along from one generation to the next. Elders led the proceedings, while the young watched, listened, and learned. Inside the circle, participants feasted together on soup, meat, berries, and bannock. Many gifts were exchanged, including clothing and blankets and even horses and wagons. These were ways to affirm the importance of caring for each other and sharing the bounty of the land.

"It is these annual acts of renewal and spiritual and community refurbishment," Harold Cardinal and Walter Hildebrandt write, "that enabled . . . First Nations to retain their inner strength, cohesion, and spiritual integrity."[18] And it was precisely because of the immense cultural importance of these Sun Dances that the Canadian government was so hostile to them.

In Rossburn, the annual Sun Dance in Waywayseecappo was a source of terror. One Rossburn family, the McKees, recalled watching with trepidation every summer as "tribes gathered from all over the country." Rhythmic booms from the steady drumming cascaded through the valley. "The noise of the tom-toms was terrifying," the McKees said. It came as a great relief when another settler "warned the government and these things were stopped."[19]

In 1896, the Indian agent overseeing the Waywayseecappo reserve was J.A. Markle, whom Minister Clifford Sifton later described as "one of the best Agents in our service and a man of sound judgment and high character."[20] His office was in the town of Birtle, some thirty kilometres from the Waywayseecappo reserve. In June, about four months after Hayter and his pantomiming Indians dazzled the Historical Ball in Ottawa, Agent Markle received a tip about an impending Sun Dance in Waywayseecappo. Markle promptly summoned the Chief for a meeting in Birtle. At this time, the Chief was Waywayseecappo's son, Astakeesic—"Sky Is Crossing" in Ojibway—who was described in a government report as "temperate but not at all enterprising [and] is too influenced by his old father who still clings to pagan customs."[21]

According to Markle's account of his conversation with Chief Astakeesic, Markle read out loud the dancing provisions in the Indian Act and said he was prepared to enforce the law as necessary, but "appealed to [Astakeesic] not to jeopardize our present friendly relationship after he had been kindly and fairly warned." Markle reported that Astakeesic "could not at first see how it would be possible to cancel the dance and ask the invited friends to return home." Eventually, though, the Chief promised that if any dancing occurred, it would be kept short, and would not have a "torture, give away or fasting feature." He also assured Markle that he would turn back any visitors from other communities.

In the same report, Markle also described a subsequent meeting with a group of Indians from the Crooked Lake reserve who were travelling to attend Waywayseecappo's Sun Dance. Markle warned them that if they participated in a dance, "I certainly would give them trouble." According to Markle, "after a long talk," the group's leader eventually "promised to return home, and that he would not take part in any dance on the Waywayseecappo's Reserve." For his part, Markle "consented to allow him to visit the Reserve and camp one night to see his friends." The pass system made that consent necessary.

Three days later, Markle filed a follow-up report. He noted that visitors from three other reserves had indeed converged in Waywayseecappo, but they had quickly dispersed without dancing. "I am glad to be able to report that I persuaded the Indians not to hold a Sun Dance," he wrote. Then he added, "All the Indians present are unquestionably a sorrowful lot, and gave up the dance very reluctantly, but they did it without one angry word being spoken on either side."[22]

It is hard to imagine that angry words were not spoken once Markle left.

★ ★ ★

IN 1898, THE Department of Indian Affairs' most senior official in the prairies, Commissioner Amédée Forget, advised an Indian agent that a given dance could technically not be stopped if the specific banned features were not present. Forget warned against "ascribing to the [Indian] Act a scope which it does not possess."[23] Even so, agents were encouraged to use other methods at their disposal: namely, withdrawing rations from those who participated in dancing and refusing travel passes to Indians who wanted to attend dances on other reserves.

That year, eighty-two-year-old Cree Chief Piapot was arrested, convicted, and imprisoned for taking part in a Sun Dance. Fifteen years earlier, faced with the starvation tactics of Hayter Reed, Piapot had joined Big Bear in leading the dignified procession of thousands who decamped from the Cypress Hills. Now Forget invited Chief Piapot to his office to discourage him from supporting dancing in his community. A translator named Peter Hourie mediated the conversation, which reportedly went as follows:

FORGET: *Ask him, Peter, why, when he knew that it was contrary to the policy of the Department, he allowed a Sun Dance to be held.*

PIAPOT: *When the Commissioner gets up in the morning he has many varieties of food placed before him, and if he doesn't like what is in one dish, he has a number of others from which to choose. He does not know what it is to have an empty belly. My people, however, are often hungry and when they cannot get food, they pray to God to give it, and their way of praying is to make a Sun Dance.*

FORGET: *He has an argument there. Tell him, Peter, that we are two big chiefs here together. I ask him as one big chief speaking to another, not to make any more Sun Dances.*

PIAPOT: *Very well, I will agree not to pray to my God in my way, if you will promise not to pray to your God . . . in your way.*

FORGET: *By Jove, he has me there. The old rascal should have been a lawyer.*[24]

Banter aside, the government made no concessions, opting instead to invoke powers under the Indian Act to unilaterally remove Piapot as his community's Chief.

Across Canada, federal restrictions on traditional ceremonies continued to provoke deep resentment among Indians. In British Columbia, intense opposition convinced the provincial government to formally appeal to Minister Sifton in 1898 to ease restrictions affecting the potlatch, a ritual involving so-called giveaways. The potlatch occurs in a feast hall and is the principal meeting place among the West Coast tribes featuring gift giving, feasting, and dancing. It is a time to celebrate marriages, confer names, confirm social status, settle land disputes, and gather clans for collective decision-making.

Sifton rejected the request on the grounds that such ceremonies had a "most demoralizing effect upon the Indians who participate."[25] (By "demoralizing," he was referring to a supposed negative effect on morality, not on morale.) Sifton added that "the repeal of the law now . . . would be viewed by the Indians as an evidence on the part of the Government of weakness and vacillation and would produce disrespect and want of confidence in the source from which it emanates." Sifton stayed the course, as did his successors, who went on to legislate yet more restrictions.

In 1902, eighty-six-year-old Piapot met with the governor general, Lord Minto, and persuaded him that the limitations on dancing were misguided. Yet Minto, in turn, could not persuade the government to change its approach.[26]

Decades passed. Still, the Indians danced.

In 1913, Duncan Campbell Scott became the head bureaucrat in the Department of Indian Affairs, a position he held for nearly twenty years. Scott exhibited a singular disdain for what he called the "senseless drumming and dancing" of the Indians.[27] On December 15, 1921, he circulated a letter to his agents across the country:

Sir,--

It is observed with alarm that the holding of dances by the Indians on their reserves is on the increase. . . .

I have, therefore, to direct you to use your utmost to dissuade the Indians from excessive indulgence in the practice of dancing. You should suppress any dance which cause waste of time, interfere with the occupations of the Indians, unsettle them for serious work, injure their health or encourage them in sloth and idleness. You should also dissuade, and, if possible, prevent them from leaving their reserves for the purpose of attending fairs, exhibitions, etc., when their absence would result in their own farming and other interests being neglected. It is realized that reasonable amusement and recreation should be enjoyed by Indians, but they should not be allowed to dissipate their energies and abandon themselves to demoralizing amusements. By the use of tact and firmness you can obtain control and keep it, and this obstacle to continued progress will then disappear.[28]

In 1925, Percy Lazenby was the Indian agent for the Rolling River, Swan Lake, and Waywayseecappo reserves. In one of his reports about Waywayseecappo, Lazenby described the "moral status" of its Indians as "deplorable."[29]

In June of that year, after Lazenby refused to allow a Sun Dance to be held at Rolling River, he received a letter from a lawyer representing the residents of that reserve. "As far as I can see," the lawyer wrote, "the holding of the sun dance is not contrary to the law."[30] He was referring to the fact that the Indian Act did not ban all dancing, but only criminalized dances if they contained the prohibited features.

A few days later, another lawyer, this time representing the Swan Lake reserve, wrote a similar letter to Lazenby. This lawyer contended that his clients should be allowed to hold a Sun Dance in a form that did not break the law. Swan Lake even invited a Christian missionary, an Indian agent, and a Mounted Policeman—the ultimate trifecta of officialdom—to witness their dance and verify that nothing unlawful transpired. "Everyone has a celebration of some sort," the lawyer wrote, and Canada's "earliest inhabitants should be entitled to their own, particularly when they are not doing anyone any harm."[31] The Indians of Swan Lake, their lawyer wrote, "would be pleased to know if the Ottawa authorities in whose fairness they have great faith will . . . allow them to hold this Sun Dance."

This faith was sorely misplaced. Earlier that year, the most senior Indian Affairs official in the prairies, Indian Commissioner W.M. Graham, had instructed Agent Lazenby that "even though the dances might not actually be illegal, they should be discouraged."[32] Agent Lazenby subsequently received explicit instructions from his superiors to prevent Rolling River's proposed Sun Dance, in any form.[33]

Lazenby knew full well that he was acting beyond the scope of the law—incredibly, he acknowledged as much in one of his own reports: "I realise that if the Indians refrain from doing anything forbidden in . . . the Indian Act, they cannot legally be stopped from having a dance." And yet he still stopped them, as instructed. "We met the Chief on the road just outside of the reserve, and talked with him about the dance, and told him that instructions had been received from the Commissioner's office, that the dance must not be put on." Before signing off, Lazenby added, "I am expecting that the Waywayseecappo Indians will be requesting permission to hold a Sun Dance shorn of it's [sic] illegal aspects, and I would be glad if the Department would advise me just what attitude to take when these requests are made."[34]

As it happened, Waywayseecappo was planning a Medicine Dance, not a Sun Dance, [35] but the dances all looked the same to settlers, who had come to fear the sound of Indian drums. Agent Lazenby dutifully called a Mounted Policeman, Sergeant Mann, to help break it up. Mann rushed to meet Lazenby in Rossburn, and together the men headed across the Birdtail River. They found that the Medicine Lodge, the epicentre of the ceremony, had already been dismantled in response to an order by another official from the Department of Indian Affairs that the dance be stopped. "Although the Indians acted and spoke in a very respectful manner to us," Sergeant Mann later reported, "I could see that there was an undercurrent of feeling amongst them, as it appears that they cannot understand why the Dept. would not let them hold the dance as they had broken no law in so doing, but that as they had received orders to stop, they had stopped."[36] Once again, there is no record of the Indian point of view.

Sergeant Mann was sufficiently troubled by the incident that he filed a separate, "Confidential" report to his commanding officer, outlining his concerns:

1. *There are only two dances that are unlawful. The Sun Dance with the old mutilation and wounding included, and the "Give Away Dance."* . . .

2. *It is becoming apparent that many of the Indians are aware of the above fact.*

3. *It is becoming apparent that the Indians especially the oldtimers cannot see why at their annual reunions that they cannot hold and take part in some of the oldtime ceremonies, of course leaving out the objectionable portions. In connection with this they know that religious thought both Christian and heathen is a personal matter and not restricted by law.*

That summer, Sergeant Mann wrote, he had been called upon to stop "dances which were according to the [Indian] Act quite legal"—first at Rolling River, and now at Waywayseecappo. In the future, he expected trouble if officers had to enforce rules that both police and Indians knew did not exist.[37]

Around the same time, the two most senior officials in the Department of Indian Affairs—Deputy Superintendent Scott and Commissioner Graham—were discussing the best way to address the ongoing scourge of Native dancing. Their exchange had been provoked by the two lawyers who had the audacity to insist that their Indian clients could lawfully dance.

"The matter of these aboriginal dances and celebrations of the Indians is a vexed question," Scott wrote. "So much valuable time is squandered that ought to be devoted to farm work, that the department has set its face against them. At the same time we do not wish to deprive the Indians of reasonable amusements." In the end Scott concluded, "The time has gone by for the sun dance."[38]

For his part, Commissioner Graham wrote that "nothing in the nature of aboriginal dances will be tolerated." He fretted that even graduates of residential schools "dress up like old time Indians and are the laughing stock of the white community around." Graham thought the continued dancing made the work of converting Indians into farmers more difficult. "Unless a firm stand is taken by the Department," Graham concluded, "we are not going to get far."[39]

Two years later, in 1927, the Indian Act was amended to make it nearly impossible for Indians to hire lawyers. It became a crime for lawyers to receive payment in pursuit of a legal claim "for the benefit" of an "Indian tribe or band"—unless, that is, the federal government gave its written permission.[40]

ON SEPTEMBER 21, 1936, Canada's governor general, Lord Tweedsmuir, travelled to the town of Fraserwood, Manitoba, 250 kilometres due east of Rossburn. He was there to address a crowd of 1,500 Ukrainian Canadians, "from babes in arms to aged patriarchs," according to a report by the *Winnipeg Free Press*.

A local Ukrainian Canadian politician spoke first (in Ukrainian, but translated to English). He praised Canada for having welcomed so many of his kin as immigrants: "Here they have found liberty, freedom of thought and speech and great opportunities for themselves and their children."[41]

The governor general spoke next. "The Ukrainian element is a very valuable contribution to our new Canada," he said, articulating an early version of what later came to be called multiculturalism. "I wish to say one thing to you. You have accepted the duties and loyalties as you have acquired the privileges of Canadians citizens, but I want you also to remember your old Ukrainian traditions—

your beautiful handicrafts, your folksongs and dances and your folk legends. I do not believe that any people can be strong unless they remember and keep in touch with all their past. Your traditions are all valuable contributions toward our Canadian culture which cannot be a copy of any old thing—it must be a new thing created by the contributions of all the elements."[42]

A troupe of Ukrainian youth celebrated Tweedsmuir's visit with a series of performances in "richly-colored native costumes." A photographer from the *Winnipeg Tribune* took a picture of the governor general watching the ceremony. The caption in the newspaper reads, "His Excellency smiles with evident pleasure as he watches tiny tots mincing through their folk dances."[43]

It would remain illegal for Indigenous Peoples to dance and hold ceremonies in Canada for another fifteen years.

THERE IS NO better embodiment of the dissonance between the federal government's embrace of immigrants and oppression of Indians than the career of Clifford Sifton, the Young Napoleon of the West. If Hayter Reed is the undisputed villain of this story, Clifford Sifton is its greatest hypocrite.

"I have an almost fanatical opposition to any legislation which interferes with contractual rights," Sifton once said.[44] Yet he didn't seem to mind that the Indian Act placed onerous restrictions on a simple contract for a load of barley. As minister of the interior, he sponsored the global journey of downtrodden immigrants, but as superintendent of Indian affairs, he presided over unlawful confinement of Indians to reserves. Sifton helped tens of thousands of settlers receive 160-acre plots for a pittance, but the Indian Act made Indians ineligible for homesteads.[45] Canada made room for Catholic Ukrainians, but not for "pagan" Indians. There was never such a thing as the Ukrainian Act.

In 1927, Sifton gave a graduation speech at Queen's University, which was awarding him an honorary doctorate. He was sixty-five years old, long retired from politics, and just two years away from a heart attack that would end his life. "Few, I think, have had occasion to see more of Canada and Canadian conditions than I have," he told the graduating students.

"You are Canadians. What does that call to your mind? That you are one of nine million people to whom Providence has committed perhaps the greatest heritage that has ever been given to an equal number of people." Sifton paused, then added, "Nine millions of white people."

Sifton argued that Canada was particularly blessed because it did not have to contend with the usual litany of obstacles facing other countries. "No negro problem; no yellow problem; no slum problem, because our climate does not favour, and in fact, does not permit the existence of large slum populations." (He did not even bother mentioning the "Indian problem," as some of his peers did.) "You are part of these nine million people," he continued, knowing his audience, "and by your academic training and your intellectual equipment, you are called upon to lead them. The resources of Canada are before you. It is the part of these nine million to determine how these resources shall be employed—in short, to make or mar Canada. Do your part, and the future of the country will take care of itself."[46]

Sifton himself had already done as much as anyone, both making and marring Canada.

PART III

"SIFTON'S PETS"

"NEVER FORGET"

I T DIDN'T TAKE LONG, AFTER CLIFFORD SIFTON'S RETIRE-
ment from politics in 1911, for Canada to turn on the immigrants he had fought so hard to welcome. Many Canadians
continued to view the recent arrivals as unwelcome strangers
despite their undeniable usefulness. In wartime, they came to be
seen as a threat.

In 1914, the assassination of the archduke of Austria in
Sarajevo set off a cascade of ever-larger dominoes that ultimately
provoked the First World War. Canada, still an appendage of the
British Empire, was dragged into the fighting. This, in turn, set off
another destructive chain of events at home.

In Rossburn, an effigy of the German kaiser Wilhelm II was
set alight on Main Street.[1] Suspicions grew about the Ukrainian
immigrants who had formerly lived in the Austro-Hungarian
Empire, now among Canada's avowed enemies. The federal government required immigrants who had not yet received Canadian
citizenship to register as "enemy aliens" and regularly report their
whereabouts. Parliament also passed the Wartime Elections Act,

which stripped the right to vote from Ukrainian Canadians who had been naturalized as citizens after 1902. "Sifton's pets" no longer had a powerful guardian.

The RCMP attempted to assuage unfounded fears. The Ukrainians caused "little trouble" despite "wild rumours," the RCMP insisted. "No fear need be entertained."[2]

"Enemy aliens" behind barbed wire near Vernon, British Columbia (Image E-06412 courtesy of the Royal BC Museum)

Incredibly, even though the "enemy aliens" who had come to Canada from the Ukraine were formally barred from enlisting in the Canadian armed forces, thousands did so anyway by lying about their birthplaces. Yet such displays of fealty did not quell widespread suspicions of treachery. Employers caved to popular pressure to fire their Ukrainian employees. Thousands lost their jobs. Before long, municipalities resented the growing burden imposed by the recently unemployed, many of whom were young Ukrainian men. To avoid the expense of covering their basic welfare needs, municipalities encouraged the federal government to arrest and detain them.[3] In time, as many as 5,954 Ukrainians were detained in makeshift penal camps. Of 950 internees held at a squalid detention centre in the town of Brandon in 1915, for example, the overwhelming majority (820) were Ukrainian.[4] The men were forced into hard manual labour and paid twenty-five cents a day, a fraction of the prevailing market wage.

A prisoner inside an internment camp in British Columbia, Mr. N. Olynyk, wrote a letter to his family in which he said, "We are not getting enough to eat—we are hungry as dogs . . . and we are very weak. Things are not good. . . . We get up at 5 o'clock in the morning and work until 10 o'clock at night. Such conditions we have here in Canada, I will never forget."[5]

In Alberta, detainees built much of the infrastructure of Banff National Park. Among them was seventeen-year-old John Kondro, otherwise known as "Prisoner of War 224."[6] On February 8, 1916, his father, Jacob, wrote a letter to the government seeking his release: "I did not think that Canada would take their own people and put them in prison in an internment camp. I am naturalized as a citizen of the Dominion of Canada. Please let him go." It seems that even citizenship was an inadequate defence against wartime xenophobia.

In Parliament, a few lonely voices dissented from the government's heavy-handed measures. Wilfrid Laurier, who had once stood shoulder to shoulder with his trusted minister Clifford Sifton, was no longer prime minister and his Liberal Party was out of power. But he was still a member of Parliament, and he used a speech in the House of Commons in 1917 to denounce the treatment of immigrants: "Do you believe that when Canadian immigration agents will go . . . among [eastern Europeans], that these different races will be disposed to come to this country when they know that Canada has not kept its pledges and promises to the people from foreign countries who have settled in our midst? . . . I believe we shall be judged some day by our actions here."[7]

By the end of 1917, most Ukrainian detainees had been released, though not on account of Laurier's advocacy. Rather, the war had caused an acute shortage of manpower in the private sector, and, with most other able-bodied men fighting abroad, employers needed Ukrainians to fill the gap. Ironically, they then earned higher than normal wages because of ongoing labour scarcity. This, in turn, triggered yet more resentment. A bitter observer wrote in 1918: "You can see the country being cleaned out of our fine, Anglo-Saxon stock and the alien left to fatten on war prosperity."[8] The war came to an end later that year, but antagonism between Ukrainians and Anglo-Saxons would endure for a long time to come.

VLADIMIR YASKIW, TROY Luhowy's great-grandfather, was eleven years old when he accompanied his parents Maksym and Dorota on their trip from the Ukraine to Canada in 1899.[9] It wasn't long before Vladimir changed his name to Dick, and as soon as he became eligible for his own homestead at the age of eighteen, he applied for one just south of his father's.

The First World War broke out when Dick was twenty-six, but he was among the lucky ones who managed to avoid internment. Instead, he found decent-paying jobs laying railway tracks and drilling oil wells. In 1919, he became the first Ukrainian settler in Manitoba to own a Ford Model T. Nevertheless, his growing family remained in an economically precarious position. Dick and his wife, Lucia, bought their first house with the help of a bank loan, but they soon fell on harder times and were evicted after missing a series of payments. By 1925, Dick and Lucia were raising ten children in a two-room house made of mud and brick. There was so little space and warmth that the smaller children slept at the foot of each bed, perpendicular to the others. Then Lucia gave birth to twins. On the most frigid days of winter, the children were forced to skip school because they didn't have adequate clothing.

In the early decades of the twentieth century, the "pioneer" years, resilience was the most highly prized virtue. Parents told their children a proverb from the old country: "*De nema boliu tam nema i zhyttia*" (Without pain, there is no life). Hectare by hectare, they cleared the land: adults chopped trees, horses uprooted stumps, toddlers picked pebbles. For many, home was a building called a *budda*: a cramped, tent-shaped structure made of mud and hay with a thatched roof, built in the Old World style. The floor was of packed earth, and children often kept warm by sleeping on top of mud stoves. In the evening, families sang folk songs:

We toiled and we suffered
That better times should come
That others may prosper.

In the meantime, children found fun where they could. Wrapping from store purchases became colouring paper; whittled willow branches made the best slingshots; horse turds became passable hockey pucks.

In those days, the town of Rossburn was populated mostly by Anglo-Saxons, and Ukrainians lived on farms in the surrounding countryside. Outside of planting and harvesting seasons, Ukrainians sought wages wherever they could, and Anglo-Saxons were all too happy to have cheap labour to clean their houses and staff their businesses. As a sympathetic poet in Rossburn wrote:

These sturdy peasants from o'er the sea,
in silence and in pain
Slaved at all the menial jobs,
a piece of bread to gain[10]

Parents wanted better for their children, yet lack of access to quality education remained a major barrier to economic advancement. The rural schools attended by Ukrainian children rarely attracted qualified teachers, who were loath to venture into "foreign" districts that were considered backwards.

"Hardship was a way of life," said Troy's great-grandfather Bill Derlago, who arrived in Rossburn as a child in 1906. "It took a great deal of courage and tenacity to survive. . . . But I sincerely believe that the hardships we endured made us strong, endowed us with a capacity for endurance which sustained us to this day, and I'm sure will sustain us in the days ahead." This sentiment was typical of the pioneer mentality, seared into one generation after the next.

TROY'S FATHER, NELSON Luhowy, was born in 1943. When he was three years old, a young sociologist from Toronto named P.J. Giffen spent a few weeks in Rossburn. This is how he described a Saturday night on Main Street:

Throngs of people come and go on the street and from the lighted
cafés and stores. Several vans with steaming horses stand in the
street, and a large number without horses are lined up in front
of the livery stable. The sound of music comes from the large
community hall where a dance is being held. . . . The atmosphere
is one of the rough hustle and bustle of a frontier community.[11]

To Giffen, the most striking thing about Rossburn was "the existence side by side of two social systems." There was, he wrote, an "almost complete cleavage between the two groups at the level of informal interaction." They did not share tables at Rossburn's café, let alone eat dinner in one another's homes. Local dances were widely attended but even under the cover of music and merriment there was little mixing. A man from Rossburn said, "Their men are jealous as anything if one of their girls" crossed the dance floor, which made them "get mad and want to start a fight."[12] Intermarriage was almost unheard of. Giffen could identify only a single couple that had dared.

The fact that the two groups lived apart, one in town and the other in "the bush," increased the social disconnect. "I don't like . . . the way they always stick to themselves," complained a Rossburn resident. "They don't seem to want to mix, no matter how hard you try to make them welcome." Another said, "They still live like pigs with their huge families," "always jabbering away in their own language."[13]

"They just don't live like white people," a Rossburn resident said. Another added, "They're great ones for making bootleg liquor," and a typical wedding was "a real drunken brawl."[14]

These were descriptions of Ukrainians, not Indians. By the 1940s, the fair-skinned immigrants still weren't considered white enough by Anglo-Saxons, and deep antagonism against the newcomers remained.

The business of hiring, buying, and selling did bring the Anglo-Saxons and Ukrainians into regular and close contact, though there was often a stark imbalance in economic power. "As is usual in the case where two antagonistic groups live side by side," Giffen observed, "a modus vivendi has been achieved which enables the community to function with a minimum of overt conflict."[15] Yet the way people treated one another during such "necessary contacts" gave "no clue to the bitterness that would be expressed to the sympathetic listener in private conversation by members of either group."[16]

In response to feeling discriminated against, many Ukrainians wished to live and thrive separately. "English people won't accept us as equals," one Ukrainian said, "so if we lose our culture we are nothing." Another told Giffen, "The British people made it plain they thought they were better than Ukrainians and didn't want us, so [we] said 'to hell with you, we can get on by ourselves.'"[17] Decades later, leaders in Waywayseecappo would strike similar notes when they withdrew their students from Rossburn.

As Giffen surveyed the situation in Rossburn in 1946, he was skeptical that the Ukrainians could resist assimilation over time. American ballroom dance was replacing traditional Ukrainian dances. Daughters were not learning from their mothers the painstaking craftwork that had been practised for generations. "Loss of the ethnic culture appears to be inevitable in the long run," Giffen concluded.[18] "Assimilation is taking place," slowly, surely—just as Clifford Sifton had once hoped.[19]

NELSON LUHOWY GREW up on a farm fifteen kilometres south of Rossburn. He was the fifth boy of six—Clifford Sifton would have approved of Mrs. Luhowy's brood of a half-dozen.

When Nelson was born, the municipality was three-quarters Ukrainian and their proportion was still growing. Anglo-Saxons resented what they called an "invasion."[20] Still, Rossburn itself remained largely Anglo-Saxon, with Ukrainian families like Nelson's mostly living on homesteads outside of town.

Nelson's childhood fit squarely within the pioneer narrative of struggle and overcoming—even more so, perhaps, than most. One day, when Nelson was six years old, he developed a severe headache during a trip with his parents to Rossburn's grocery store. By the time they returned home, he was flushed with fever and dripping sweat. His mother gently placed cold cabbage leaves on his forehead while he lay down. He felt himself go limp, from boy to abandoned marionette. He lost feeling in his arms and legs. A doctor confirmed the worst: Nelson had polio.

Nelson Luhowy *(front row, right)* (Courtesy of Nelson Luhowy)

His parents took him by train to Winnipeg, where he was admitted into a children's hospital. Doctors stuck long needles into his legs and nurses placed hot yellow towels on his arms. He remained in hospital for six months, fearing the periodic jabs from giant needles. He was kept in a big ward with fifty or sixty other children afflicted with polio, each confined to a single bed with white sheets.

When Nelson was eventually discharged, the hospital refused to send him away with crutches. Walking would be hard, the staff said, but he needed to grow stronger. At home, though, a sympathetic older brother could not bear the sight of Nelson wincing and wobbling, so he made him a pair of crutches out of plywood two-by-fours. When the crutches broke a few months later, Nelson pleaded for another pair. This time his brother was less merciful. "No," he told Nelson, "you have to start walking on your own."

At the dinner table, Nelson's parents grumbled about the arrogance of the "English," who looked down on Ukrainians. But the Luhowys were going to make it, whatever it took. Industriousness and thrift were both mantra and necessity. Every child constantly had to earn his keep; even polio was no excuse for idleness. In harvest season, while his brothers baled hay, Nelson made himself useful by driving the tractor, swinging his whole body to change gears with the stick shift. Many of the nearby farms hired Indians to help out during the harvest, but Nelson's parents were able to make do with the help of their sons. Nelson did get a pass from milking the cows, even though the family relied on weekly income from selling cans of cream. If a cow stood up and kicked, he wasn't agile enough to get out of the way.

The only way for the boys to get pocket change of their own was trapping muskrat, mink, and beaver and selling the fur. Nelson was put in charge of the skinning in the barn. Somehow there was never quite as much blood as he expected. After making a few incisions down to the bone, he held the hind legs with one hand and with the other tugged the skin away from his chest. It was like pulling off a sock.

For as many years as he could get away with it, Nelson leaned on his mother when they walked together, arms linked at the elbow. Eventually, mostly thanks to hours of biking around the farm, his legs strengthened enough for him to play sports with his friends. Hockey was his favourite game, and Maurice "Rocket" Richard of the Montreal Canadiens was his favourite player. The Rocket didn't back down from anything. Nelson listened to Habs games on the radio, and on Saturday nights in the 1950s he visited an uncle's house to watch *Hockey Night in Canada* on the black-and-white TV. Though he liked to imagine himself scoring just like the Rocket, he never quite managed to skate. His ankles just weren't strong enough. He settled for playing goalie in boots.

Baseball became Nelson's second-favourite sport, even though he wasn't able to run. When he hit a pitch, another boy would bolt toward first base in his place. It was on the way to a baseball game in the nearby town of Birtle that Nelson saw an Indian residential school for the first time. The large building was visible from the road, just outside the town. His parents told him it was the school for the Indians. As far as Nelson could tell, the Indians seemed to have a comfortable place to live and sleep, and he was sure they were getting a better education than he was. At the time, Nelson's school had only a single room, which all the students in Grades 1 through 8 shared. "When I looked at the big building there, I didn't say: 'Look at that awful place,'" he recalls. "I never thought people were being mistreated. I thought they were lucky to have that big building, to have that yard and garden. It looked state-of-the-art. Compared to their school, mine was nothing." The sight of the residential school actually made Nelson jealous.

Nelson's ideas about Indians developed in the absence of any direct contact with them. He can't remember having a single conversation with an Indian while he was growing up, though he used to see some from time to time near his family's farm. They trapped muskrats in the sloughs along the roads. Indians also came up in conversation at home. On occasions when Nelson neglected his clothing or didn't do a chore, his parents would say, "You're just like an Indian." Because Indians, he was made to understand, were careless, lazy, and reliant on constant handouts—in short, the opposite of hardened, industrious pioneers.

Nelson's dad warned him early on to be wary of Indians. The message stuck after an incident involving one of Nelson's older brothers. One day, an Indian walking down the road bordering the farm asked the brother for help: he was stranded and his car had run out of gas—could he borrow some? He promised he'd pay it back. Nelson's brother agreed to help, but after borrowing the gas, the visitor never returned. *Of course*, scoffed Nelson's father when he found out that his son had been had. "You can't trust Indians."

On Saturdays, the whole family would drive into town to collect their mail, shop for groceries, and visit friends. Businesses stayed open until ten, and Rossburn's Main Street swelled with cars. Nelson's favourite place in town was the movie theatre. A quarter from his parents was enough to buy french fries, a drink, and a movie ticket. In those days, many of the movies had to do with cowboys and Indians. "The Indians lost in every movie," Nelson remembers. "Their Chief would be killed in battle, and we'd get the land. They were always losers." Sometimes Nelson would spot a real-life Indian in the theatre with him. He didn't object but he was surprised. He expected them to be too intimidated to sit with everyone else.

Nelson recalls seeing drunken men from Waywayseecappo staggering along Rossburn's sidewalks. (It wasn't until much later that he came to understand that Indians were drinking in alleys because they weren't allowed to enter the bar.) A few times, Nelson witnessed brawls among them. Whenever fights broke out, groups of passersby gathered to gawk and sneer. Nothing Nelson saw or heard in Rossburn challenged his assumption that Indians belonged on the lowest social rung. Ukrainians might not have been rich, but they took comfort in not being Indian. "The English looked at us the way we looked at Wayway," Nelson says.

NELSON, HIS PARENTS' fifth son, was the first in the family to graduate from high school. His four older brothers had all dropped out to work, but Nelson's physical disability gave him more leeway to stay in school. Then, with encouragement from one of his teachers, he decided to train to become a teacher himself. He only needed one year at teachers' college, which he completed in Winnipeg before starting his teaching career in 1964. The school was in the town of Solsgirth, thirty-five kilometres from Rossburn.

Within a few years, Nelson married a fellow Ukrainian Canadian, Anne Kozun, and, after saving up a down payment, the young couple bought a two-storey house in Rossburn. The only way Nelson and Anne could afford the house was with the help of a twenty-five-year mortgage. Getting the loan from a bank didn't seem like a particularly remarkable thing to Nelson—this was what most people buying houses did. This is what his parents had once done and, before that, what his grandparents Dick and

Dorota Yaskiw had done. It would have surprised Nelson to learn that it was nearly impossible for anyone in Waywayseecappo to get a bank loan, whether to purchase a home or to start a business. This was because banks were not allowed to seize property on reserves, as a consequence of the unique legal status of reserve land, and, therefore, Indians living on reserve had no access to the collateral necessary to obtain loans. As far as Nelson was concerned, "The Ukrainians got 160 acres and that was it." In reality, this land *also* gave them access to capital, which made all the difference between economic progress and stagnation.

To help make ends meet, Anne landed a job at the local credit union. Whereas Nelson had a half-hour drive to work, Anne just had to walk down the street. Their new home was located on Main Street, two blocks down from Pioneer Avenue.

PEOPLE LIKE NELSON Luhowy were raised to see themselves as part of a heroic story, which went something like this: Ukrainian immigrants arrived in Canada without English, without education, without wealth. But they strived and endured and, over time, prospered. Because the Ukrainians escaped poverty and withstood racism, they knew it was possible. "We had to make it on our own," Nelson says. "We struggled, but we all worked. There was never too much work." For a Ukrainian who went from a childhood in a mud house to having grandchildren comfortably in the middle class, it was hard not to conclude that the Ukrainian immigrants earned and deserved their success. And they *had* worked hard. Who could deny it?

The Indians across the Birdtail started poor, just like the Ukrainians, but they stayed poor. "They were given land, too," Nelson says, "but they didn't make anything of it." Looking at this situation, many Ukrainian Canadians concluded: We are doing something right, and the Indians must be doing something wrong. If we succeeded and they failed, surely people were getting what they deserved.

And what was it, exactly, that was holding the Indians back? Laziness, surely! Meanwhile, the federal government was trying so hard, spending so much, decade after decade, to fix Waywayseecappo's problems. And everyone knew the Indians on the reserves were paying lower taxes. They had it easier yet somehow still did worse ... or at least that's how it looked from across the valley.

This story, built on stereotypes, is the kind of story that explains *and* justifies. For someone like Nelson, the inequality between the two sides of the Birdtail, stark and long-standing, was a fact of life. The Indians' poverty was expected. It was normal. Just being Indian explained the poverty.

Nelson did what most people instinctively do when confronted with a disparity between groups: he blamed individuals. The decades of government policies that had held reserves back were largely invisible to outsiders, while the shortcomings of particular Indians were on clear display. As Ibram Kendi, a scholar of racism, observes, "Racial inequity is a problem of bad policy, not bad people."[21] Yet too often we conclude the opposite. The stereotyping that Ukrainians had themselves endured did not inoculate them against the same kind of thinking. Ironically, their own bitter experiences with racism tended to further distance them from Indians. After all, Ukrainians had overcome their challenges, so why couldn't the Indians?

During Clifford Sifton's tenure and well beyond, the federal government had constricted technology, goods, and people on reserves, with disastrous and enduring results. The effects of these policies compounded over time, year after year, generation by generation. Meanwhile, people in Rossburn largely saw their neighbours as the authors of their own misfortune.

We might call this racism. We might also call it intimate familiarity with only one side of a long and tragic story.

FACEOFF

WHEN TROY LUHOWY WAS A TODDLER, HIS FATHER, Nelson, put a hockey stick into his hands and insisted that he treat it henceforth like an appendage. Troy's childhood orbited the town's indoor hockey rink, just a few minutes' walk from his home. This was where Nelson came to fetch him most winter nights before bedtime. Troy loved skating so much that the only way his dad could get his son off the ice was by shutting off all the lights.

Troy's modest size didn't stop him from becoming the star of his Eight and Under team. In one game, as Troy streaked down the ice on yet another breakaway, a man stood up in the stands and shouted, "Kill the little bastard!" During hockey season, Troy's heroics were featured in almost every issue of the *Rossburn Review*. His mom diligently scissored out each story and stored them in a blue binder. On December 10, 1979, the paper reported that Troy's team had managed a 4–4 tie against the nearby town of Shoal Lake: "Scoring for Rossburn was Troy Luhowy, with all 4 goals." The following week, the team beat archnemesis Birtle

11–6. "Scoring for Rossburn was Troy Luhowy, with 10 goals and one assist." And so on, game after game, with the news clippings slowly filling up the two-inch binder.

Troy Luhowy, aged eight (Courtesy of Troy Luhowy)

Troy attended Rossburn Elementary, which had never bothered to change its name to include "Waywayseecappo." The school offered second-language classes in French and Ukrainian, but not Ojibway. By the time Troy started Grade 1, in 1976, the school had been racially integrated for fifteen years. This seemed normal to Troy, whose hockey team included two players from Waywayseecappo.

The one downside to having teammates from the reserve was their erratic attendance. Troy remembers hearing adults asking, in the minutes before games started, "Think the Indians will show?" The main obstacle was that families in Waywayseecappo often didn't own cars, which made reliable transport difficult, and parents from Rossburn rarely offered rides to make up for this. Troy's dad certainly didn't.

At school, Troy's small size left him vulnerable to enemies that he made with his big mouth. Luckily for him, he also became friends with a boy from Waywayseecappo who sat immediately behind him in class. As Troy recalls it, on the very first day of Grade 4, Lionel leaned forward and offered a warm hello. As time went on and they became closer friends, Lionel made a point of checking whether anyone was bothering Troy—if so, he would gladly straighten it out. Lionel had long black hair and wore a jean jacket with studs, a good look for intimidating the people who might give Troy a hard time. This worked well for Troy, except that Lionel was showing up to school only a couple of times a week. During his absences, assignments piled up on his desk. When he did attend class, Troy helped him sort through the stack. "Don't worry about this one," Troy would say. "And this one is just some busywork you don't have to hand in. But try this one, and that one." Still, Lionel ended up further and further behind.

Two girls from Waywayseecappo, Joyce Shingoose and Belina Oudie, also took a liking to Troy. They were both a bit older and, by Grade 5, about a foot taller. One time, Troy bragged a tad too gleefully about some of his hockey heroics, which drew unwanted attention from two bullies from Rossburn—"heavies," as Troy later described them. But then Joyce and Belina material-ized, inserting themselves between Troy and his assailants. "Leave him alone," Belina said. And just like that, the heavies backed off. "If someone tried to bother any of the non-Natives and they were our friends," Belina recalls, "Joyce and I would stick up for them. Troy was friendly, easy to get along with, and every once in a while I think I asked him for a bit of help with a math question."

When Troy started school, he hadn't noticed anything par-ticularly different about students from Waywayseecappo. "They weren't the Wayway kids to me," he recalls. "They were just kids." As time passed, though, he noticed that teachers weren't investing quite as much time in students from Waywayseecappo and that more and more of them were being held back to repeat grades. The older students were often "quite a bit bigger than the rest of us," Troy says. Lionel was among them, and Troy could tell how uncomfortable this made him. He recalls Lionel asking him, "What do I have to do to pass?" Troy wasn't sure what to say. He didn't develop any real understanding of why Lionel and other students from Waywayseecappo had such irregular attendance, or what might be holding them back. "I just assumed everyone had a house like mine," he says. "I assumed they all had parents like I did, a mom and dad who would help with schoolwork."

Troy had more contact with students from Waywayseecappo than most Rossburn kids had, but he rarely saw them outside of school and hockey. He never once visited the home of a friend on the reserve, which made it easier for him to maintain his assumptions. "I never said, 'Hey, you want to come over?' and they didn't say, 'Hey, do you want to come over?'" Troy recalls. "Back then, nobody really did that." Besides, Troy's dad would not have allowed it. Nelson pictured his only child going into a decrepit house on the reserve, creeping with mice and who knows what diseases, and being fed a sandwich with mouldy bread—no way.

In the summer of 1982, Waywayseecappo withdrew all its students from Rossburn. When Troy returned to start Grade 6 after the summer vacation, Joyce, Belina, and Lionel were gone, along with the rest of the students from the reserve. For Troy, the change was most obvious during recess. "I didn't have my muscle anymore," he recalls, "so I learned pretty quickly to keep my mouth shut." The era of integration with Waywayseecappo had come to an abrupt end.

Troy lost touch with friends from Waywayseecappo—the relationships were too shallow to survive separation. Still, he kept seeing people from Waywayseecappo in town. The reserve had relatively few shops of its own and did not permit the sale of alcohol, so people came to Rossburn for restaurants, shopping, and drinking. Troy could tell the hotel bar was busy when he spotted unaccompanied children from Waywayseecappo hanging around nearby, waiting for adults to take them home. The racial dynamic that he witnessed in town was similar to what his father had seen a generation earlier.

Every now and then, Troy would run into a former classmate from the reserve, such as the time he was bicycling past the hotel and noticed a dark-haired boy named Derek sitting in a parked car. The window was down. Derek looked bored. Troy slowed down and waved.

"Hi, Troy," Derek said.

"Hi, Derek," Troy replied, before pedalling away.

Neither had anything more to say.

★ ★ ★

HOCKEY WAS THE axis of Troy's adolescence. He was a solid student, but he only really tested his limits on the ice. He relished being the smaller guy who worked harder. More often than not, he was chosen to be team captain. Coaches trusted him during crunch time, to nurse leads or kill penalties. Troy spent a lot of time in the "dirtier" areas on the ice, places that more delicate and sane players avoided, like the corners, where he charged in heedlessly to fetch pucks, his opponents trailing by inches, or near the net, where he wormed and slashed to hold his ground against thicker defencemen. Troy never topped 160 pounds in high school, and his game relied to a worrisome degree on his kamikaze certainty that he was the kinetic equal of two-hundred-pound opponents.

When Troy was fifteen years old, he was recruited by Rossburn's adult hockey team, which travelled around the province for games. His job was to prolong the glory days of beer-bellied veterans in their thirties and forties. That year, the Rossburn team made it to the league finals, a best-of-seven series. The opposing team was from the Sioux Valley reserve, an hour's drive south of Rossburn. One game in particular stands out in Troy's memory. It was late in the series, on neutral territory, and featured four or five hundred fans in the stands—two-thirds Native, one-third white, many drunk. Bad blood had been brewing between the teams from the start of the series.

A behemoth defenceman named Frank was the most feared player on the Sioux Valley team. He was so big that he didn't even bother with shoulder pads. During warm-ups, Frank skated over to one of Troy's teammates, Kevin, who was stretching on the ice. Frank pointed his stick at Kevin's head and said, "I'm going to tear out your fucking eyeballs tonight." Kevin kept stretching for a few more moments, thinking it over, and then he returned to the locker room to take off his uniform. He had decided to sit out the game. "You know," he said to his teammates, "this is senior hockey. It's just not worth it."

Rossburn's coach then had the brilliant idea of pairing Troy with Frank during the game, an assignment Troy embraced. He had to wear a full face mask because he was a minor—as far as he was concerned, this made him invincible.

At faceoff, Troy lined up opposite Frank and looked over at a man more than twice his age. Frank was chewing gum. Sweat dripped off his stubbly chin, and his jersey tightened over the beginnings of a gut. Frank glared back at fresh-faced Troy, with his full mask, and stopped chewing.

"Get out of your cage, Tweety Bird!" Frank said.

"Fuck you, Indian!" Troy replied.

Troy had known Frank's name, but in that moment he reached for a cruder instrument. "I wasn't thinking," he says, decades later. "It just came out. At the time, that's what I heard in the dressing room, that's what I heard on the bench—'fucking Indians.' The older guys, they didn't say, 'You shouldn't be saying stuff like that.' More like: 'Right on, give it to them!' My dad was no different. I heard what he and others were yelling in the stands."

Rossburn went on to lose the game. In the stands, heated arguments broke out along racial lines. It seemed like worse was still to come, so someone decided to call the police. Troy was taken aback when two squads of RCMP officers entered the locker room to escort his team out of the arena. They took the fire exit, just in case the national pastime degenerated into something more akin to civil war.

The next year, while Troy was in Grade 11, he joined a regional team with players his own age in the Manitoba Midget "AAA" Hockey League. Troy was the team's second-highest scorer that season, with twenty-nine goals and thirty-six assists. The team was called the Yellowhead Chiefs, and its logo was a ripoff from the Chicago Blackhawks: a stereotypical Indian in profile, with feathers in his hair.

There was not a single Native player on the team.

TROY SUSPECTED HE wouldn't make it as a pro hockey player but he kept striving anyway. He proved good enough on the ice and clever enough in the classroom to get offered an athletic scholarship to attend Brown University, an Ivy League school in the United States. It wasn't the NHL, but it was still a ticket to a wider world. Unfortunately for Troy, in a game he played shortly after receiving the offer from Brown, his right skate got stuck in a rut at precisely the wrong split second, long enough for a player from the opposing team to collide with him. Troy heard ligaments in his knee pop. It sounded like wet wood in a fire.

Troy told Brown's hockey coach about the injury but insisted that he could recover in time to play for the university. He completed every step of the recommended rehab and counted the days until he could play again. In his first game back, nine months and two days after his injury, he wore a knee brace, just in case. Back on the ice, he felt like he had wings again. Then, just a few shifts in, an opposing player blindsided Troy. He felt the exact same ligaments snap.

Disconsolate, he called Brown's hockey coach and said, "It happened again. I tore everything again." Troy's competitive hockey career was over, along with any dreams of the Ivy League. There would be no more news clippings for his mom's blue binder.

In time, Troy settled on a new plan. After a miserable summer laying highway asphalt, he decided to become a teacher, just like his dad. He studied physical education at the University of Manitoba in Winnipeg, then moved to Brandon in the fall of 1994 to study for his teacher's certification at Brandon University.

DURING TROY'S FIRST autumn in Brandon, Halloween fell on a Sunday. Troy started the night at a house party, drinking Coors Light with a group of classmates. Normally they would have gone to a bar, but bars were closed on Sundays. Someone suggested a trip to "the old Indian school," the closest thing Brandon had to a haunted house. Troy and a few others had heard that students had died out there a long time ago, but no one knew how or why. "If there are any ghosts," one of Troy's friends said, half-drunk, half-joking, "this is, like, the perfect time to check it out." *Yeah,* Troy thought, *let's do it.*

They piled into two trucks and drove west from the city, along Grand Valley Road, and before long they spotted the silhouette of the abandoned school at the top of a hill. It looked just as spooky as they had hoped. The trucks followed a bumpy gravel driveway that led to the rear of the main building. They arrived around midnight, with a generous slice of moon overhead.

Troy and his companions headed for the main entrance. They were far from the first visitors to the derelict school, which was surrounded by broken beer bottles. Previous revellers had long since kicked down the flimsy plywood that had once sealed off the entrance. Troy ambled in with a can of beer in his right hand and a second can bulging in his jacket pocket.

Inside, bits of plaster and chunks of concrete littered the floor. Each step crunched. "There was a lot of damage in there, a lot of smashed walls, a lot of smashed windows," Troy recalls. Moonlight illuminated parts of the building, but otherwise he and his friends found their way using lighters, the flames casting dancing shadows. As they explored, some of the guys started telling scary stories. "I heard someone died in *this* room," one said, eyeing a small, windowless chamber. "And the basement, that's where they put the morgue. That's where they kept the dead bodies."

The group decided to split up and then try to scare each other. Troy headed off alone, squinting as he slowly picked his way through the debris. He paused when he found a room with a gaping hole in the wall, which seemed like a perfect place to stage an ambush. He picked up a piece of concrete from the ground and waited, sipping his beer. When he finally heard a few of his friends approaching, he selected just the right moment to toss his projectile toward them through the hole. The concrete landed with a crash, and his friends yelped like puppies.

The rooms and hallways Troy wandered that night were the same rooms and hallways where Principal Strapp locked Clifford Shepherd without clothes, where Jim Cote plotted his escape, where Linda Jandrew lined up without her shoes. To Troy, though, it was just a creepy old building, a place that time and everyone else had forgotten. With the past muted, all he heard was the crunching underfoot and the occasional screams and peals of laughter when one friend sprung out and shouted, "Boo!"

Troy cannot recall the topic of residential schools ever coming up during the two years he spent at Brandon University's teachers' college. The year he graduated, 1996, was the same year that the last Indian residential school in Canada closed.

BLOODVEIN

I N THE FALL OF 1999, TROY'S FIRST FULL-TIME TEACHING job brought him to the Bloodvein First Nation reserve, in northern Manitoba. He had never heard of the place. "It's only 236 kilometres from Winnipeg!" the man recruiting Troy exclaimed. "There are lots of young teachers up here. It's good!" Troy would fill the shoes of a gym teacher who was leaving partway through the school year. He planned on getting some experience on a reserve up north, as many new teachers did, then moving on to a "normal" job in a provincial public school.

The Bloodvein reserve spans sixteen square kilometres, but most of its roughly one thousand inhabitants live near the shore of the mighty Bloodvein River, which flows into Lake Winnipeg. The river was reportedly named by Christian missionaries in the aftermath of a battle between Ojibway bands in the eighteenth century, when gore stained the water pink. Troy didn't hear that story until later, so at first he thought the name came from the crimson streaks on the stones that lined the riverbanks. The bright lines looked like arteries.

In warmer months, the trip to the reserve required a ferry or an airplane to cross Lake Winnipeg.[1] Since Troy was arriving in early March, though, he was told he could make it all the way in his truck, as long as he was willing to brave a stretch of winter road over the frozen lake. On his drive in, he was distressed to find himself going through occasional patches of slush. He wondered, *What the hell am I doing here?*

Like the other teachers who were not from the community, Troy lived in a compound of apartments called the teacherage, which, as a bastion of relative affluence, was the target of frequent break-ins. The windows were smashed often enough by thieves that the teachers eventually boarded them up with plywood and sacrificed sunlight for safety. The lock on Troy's door made him think of a bank safe. It took a forceful heave of an arm to move the heavy steel bolt, which turned with a thunk.

Most teachers didn't last long in Bloodvein. Some were there only a few months, and almost nobody stayed more than a few years. They found the reserve too remote, the work too hard, the pay too low. And there were always the ones who came thinking that by teaching on a reserve they were going to save the world. Troy got to know the type. They didn't last either. "They gave it their all for two months, then they left," he says. "They couldn't handle the place. They got frustrated. They thought they weren't making a difference. They saw no hope for the kids, basically."

As far as Troy was concerned, though, teaching gym was a blast. His abiding mission was to keep all his students engaged for the entire class. Nothing irked Troy like a kid who never got off the bench. But ordering a student to just get out there and play was not his style. Instead, he invented games that involved everyone, including those who didn't like sports. Since most of his students spoke Ojibway as their first language, he looked for fun ways to build their English vocabulary. To win a game, a team might have to bounce a ball, score a basket, and complete ten jumping jacks, but also spell a challenging word, like "December," or write down, say, two rules of soccer. "The kids who could read well would be embraced because each team needed them, too," Troy says. "Maybe they couldn't kick a ball, but they could spell." He estimates that three-quarters of his Grade 7 students could not compose full grammatical sentences in English.

Sometimes Troy insisted that a goal would not count unless a team member solved a multiplication problem. On a chalkboard along the wall, he would write out something like "$5 \times 6 = ?$" That might stump half the Grade 7 class, Troy recalls. Other times, he opted for an impressive-looking subtraction, something like "$12,687,249 - 6 = ?$" "One of those would just blow them away," he says. No more than a few could figure it out. Troy was aware that this was not normal, this was not good, but he tried not to dwell on it.

Troy was facing the same challenges as the other teachers, of course. Students who arrived at school with empty stomachs were irritable. Those without running water at home were seldom clean. Over time, Troy was astonished to learn how many children from the community were living with foster parents. "But I didn't feel sorry for the kids or anything," he recalls. "They were just kids. A lot of them, when you see what they have going on in their families and at home, you're amazed by how resilient they are."

Troy's students especially appreciated that he would come back to the school at night to open up the gym for a few hours, just to give them an indoor space to play in. It wasn't long before the students started calling him "Coach" instead of "Mr. Luhowy." That's when he knew he was in.

Within a few months of his arrival, Troy received an invitation from community members to go moose hunting. Troy knew a little about shooting but nothing about hunting. "You'll learn," people told him. After a few hours of trekking on foot into the bush, Troy spotted a moose within firing range. He aimed his rifle at the massive animal. "I can get him," he said excitedly. "Wait," his companions urged. "Not yet."

But Troy had a clear shot, so he pulled the trigger. The butt of the rifle slammed into his shoulder. Up ahead, the moose recoiled, shuddered for two heartbeats, and collapsed with a wet thud. Troy's companions scolded him. "Good luck carrying that out by yourself," they said. The plan, which everyone but Troy had understood, had been to kill a moose closer to the river, so the dead animal could be floated home. Instead, Troy was forced to carry the awful weight of the moose's severed, bloody haunches. "I couldn't carry it all, but they made me carry the most," he recalls. "So I learned."

BACK IN ROSSBURN, Nelson officially retired in 2001, two years after Troy moved to Bloodvein. He was fifty-eight years old and had been teaching in provincial public schools for almost four decades. That summer, Waywayseecappo happened to be looking for an instructor to teach mature students working toward their high school diplomas. Nelson received an unexpected call: Would he consider teaching in Waywayseecappo for a few months? "It was the last thing in the world I figured I'd do," he recalls. But his wife was still working full-time as a bank teller, and he didn't have anything else to keep himself busy. After checking whether taking the job would affect his pension (it would not), he decided he had no excuse. He was willing to give it a try.

Classes were held at the old hockey rink that had been converted into a school in 1982. (A new kindergarten to Grade 8 school, the one Maureen Twovoice would later attend, was built in 1992.) The building was run down, Nelson recalls, with peeling plaster and broken urinals. None of this really bothered him, although he did struggle with the staircase he had to walk up every day to get to his classroom. He used a cane and leaned heavily on the railing. "Once I got up there," Nelson says, "I didn't go down until the end of the day."

At this point, Nelson knew nothing about treaties, nor why reserves existed. He had never heard about anything bad happening at Indian residential schools, which he still regarded as superior to the schools he had attended as a child. Because of where he had taught during his thirty-eight years in the provincial school system, he'd had only a handful of Native students, all of them living with white adoptive families. After spending virtually his entire life within a few kilometres of a reserve, Nelson had never developed a real friendship with an Indigenous person. Of course, this had not prevented him from forming judgments based on the little he had seen and heard. His whole life, he'd been hearing family and friends saying things like "they're not paying taxes," "they're on welfare," "their houses are built for them."

Nelson wasn't quite sure what to expect in his new job, but he arrived with his guard up and his expectations low. Some of his students would be fresh out of prison, sent to his classroom by court order. Others would be grandparents who were older than he was. But since this was a paying job, and a job he had agreed to do, he resolved to teach to the best of his ability. Going in, Nelson says, "I didn't know if I could trust them. Not that I had any experience—I never had anything to do with them."

Before long, one student in particular came to stand out.

Her name was Elizabeth Shingoose, and she went by Tizz. When Nelson met her, she was in her early thirties. Nelson later learned that she had dropped out of high school after getting pregnant when she was in Grade 10. On Nelson's route to work, he sometimes noticed Tizz walking up a steep hill that led to the school. Even as fall turned to winter, with snow piling up deeper and deeper at the side of the road, Tizz kept walking to school up that hill and always showed up on time. One week, she got sick with a bad cold, but that didn't stop her from coming to class. She arrived wearing a face mask, to protect others from getting sick. Nelson was impressed.

Tizz also happened to be exceptionally bright. When Nelson asked a question of the class, she was usually the first to volunteer an answer. She had grown up mostly in the city of Brandon and attended provincial public schools. She once joked to her classmates that she knew all the answers because "I didn't go to the Wayway school."

"Well," another student shot back, "if you're so smart, how come you never graduated?"

Tizz paused, searching for the right comeback. "Because I fell in love!"

Sometimes Nelson asked Tizz to translate words into Ojibway for the benefit of the class. He joked, "Tizz, those aren't swear words, are they?" She laughed and said, "I wouldn't do that to you, Mr. Luhowy."

Nelson had been apprehensive when he started the job, but it wasn't long before that feeling "went away completely," he recalls. "They were so dedicated. They wanted to learn. Before I would have said, 'they didn't want to work.'"

Nelson was getting occasional glimpses into the lives of his students, often from reading personal essays he assigned for homework. "One wrote about looking forward to the night when she could have a warm shower and sleep in clean sheets," he says. "Quite a few wrote about growing up with kokum. I didn't even know what a kokum was—eventually I figured out they were talking about a grandmother, because their parents had been out of action."

He noticed that many of his students were showing up to class hungry, or kept wearing the same jacket even as the seasons changed. Some couldn't afford to pitch in five dollars a month toward a shared coffee supply. If a student broke or misplaced their glasses, it was usually months before they managed to get a new pair. "In the meantime," Nelson says, "the only way they could read was by putting the paper two inches from their face."

At lunchtime, Nelson ate at his desk, and he liked to chat with students who came by to say hello. Bit by bit, these conversations helped him gain a better understanding of what it took for them just to attend classes. "There are so many issues that you don't realize unless you are there," Nelson says. "No food, no job, no car, no gas for the car, family issues, medical issues. It takes a lot of courage on their part to keep going and be successful. I could see them struggling, but they try and try."

THE JANITOR OF Bloodvein's school, Leslie, took a special liking to Troy. Leslie had grown up on the reserve and had lived there most of his life. It wasn't long before he introduced Troy to mackerel fishing along the Bloodvein River, which they explored together on Leslie's sixteen-foot boat. He taught Troy how to navigate the powerful currents by reading subtle wrinkles on the water's surface. Leslie had enormous, callused hands, and Troy marvelled at how deftly he tied and baited hooks.

Pictographs along the Bloodvein River (Courtesy of Hidehiro Otake)

Leslie spoke to Troy in Ojibway, teaching him one word at a time. He would point at objects or animals they could see from the boat. "*Ziibi*." River. "*Migizi*." Bald eagle. "*Makwa*." Bear. In time, Troy's Ojibway outpaced his limited Ukrainian. He was feeling a deep need to adapt himself to his surroundings, in a way he never had before.

Mostly Leslie and Troy fished in silence, but every now and then Leslie would ask Troy a question.

"*Troy, aandi ezhaayan?*" ("Troy, where are you going?")

"Uh, I'm going fishing."

"No . . . I mean, where are you going? In life?"

"I don't know," a puzzled Troy said. "I'm here."

Leslie gave him a severe look. "I'm trying to teach you something here, Troy. Think about it. You have to know where you're headed."

Troy didn't have much of a plan, really. He had already been in Bloodvein far longer than most teachers and hadn't made any plans to leave. He had fallen in love with a redhead from Brandon named Michelle, whom he had gotten to know during weekends away from the reserve, and he had managed to persuade her to try living with him in Bloodvein ("It's only 236 kilometres from Winnipeg!" he found himself exclaiming.) "I think Leslie knew I wasn't going to be in Bloodvein forever," Troy says. "I think he had seen a lot of teachers go through there. I think his point was, 'As much as you like it, you're not from Bloodvein, you're far from your family.'" And there were practical matters, too—Troy wouldn't be able to have his own house in Bloodvein, since he wasn't a member of the First Nation. "I don't think he wanted me to get out of there. He just wanted me to think about what I would do, where I would be, later on."

ONE DAY, NELSON noticed that Tizz wasn't her usual gregarious self. She was quiet, brooding. Nelson invited her over to his desk during the lunch break and asked her what was wrong. "I'm pregnant," Tizz said. "And I'm not sure if I can keep coming to class."

Tizz was starting to put on weight from the pregnancy, and the walk to the school was becoming too demanding. She also had two other children to look after.

"I don't see you as a quitter," Nelson said.

"How can you tell?" Tizz asked.

"It's just the personality that comes out of you, your determination to get things done," Nelson told her. "How about I make a plan to pick you up and drive you to school?" It wasn't much of a detour from his regular route, and he recalled his own dad or brothers driving him to school every day. (It wasn't until later that he thought about all the times Troy's teammates from Waywayseecappo missed games because no one was willing to pick them up.)

Tizz said a ride would make a big difference, actually. She offered to pay Nelson him for the trouble, but he rejected the offer. "I don't want your money," he said. "I want you to graduate."

And so Nelson started picking up Tizz every morning at 8:45 a.m. sharp. This arrangement continued for months, until shortly before Tizz gave birth to a baby girl in a hospital in Brandon. By that time, she had reluctantly reached the conclusion that she wouldn't be able to keep attending school while she cared for her newborn.

Nelson decided to pay Tizz a visit in the hospital. He had caught wind of her plan to put her studies on hold and wanted to see how she was doing. As Tizz recalls it, when Nelson arrived unannounced in her hospital room, she was lying on the bed, cradling her daughter in her arms. Nelson looked at the baby and smiled. "Such a cute little sweetheart," he said. Still smiling, he looked at Tizz and deadpanned, "So, I hear you're going to quit!"

They both allowed themselves a laugh. Then Tizz admitted that, yes, she had real doubts about whether she could carry on with school. Nelson said, "Well, I'm sure we can work something out." He suggested that he could arrange a small room adjacent to the classroom with a computer, space for a cradle, and enough privacy for her to feel comfortable breastfeeding.

Tizz was surprised—shocked, really. She had never had a teacher support and encourage her like this. Her eyes filled with tears. "Okay," she said. "When I'm out of hospital, I'll come talk to you. I'm going to keep going."

About five months after Tizz returned to class, she received her high school diploma. Nelson arranged for a special graduation cap to be made for her daughter, complete with its own little tassel.

Nelson, flicking Tizz's tassel for good luck (Courtesy of Elizabeth Shingoose)

After the ceremony, Tizz gave Nelson a hug. "I thanked him for not giving up on me," she recalls, "and for not letting me give up on myself." Now it was Nelson's turn to cry.

Nelson had been hired to teach in Waywayseecappo for one year, but he decided to stick around. "People were taking courses to help get a job, to better themselves," he recalls. "Many were there to encourage their children or grandchildren, to show that education was important. It was a surprise to me. Before, I didn't know they cared so much. Their dedication made me want to try harder, too. It made me feel different toward them. I thought, if they can learn, maybe I can learn."

★ ★ ★

THE SPRING OF 2006, Troy and Michelle made plans to leave Bloodvein. Troy had taught there for seven years, far longer than outsiders usually stayed. The community held a ceremony to thank him for all his work, though Troy didn't think he had done anything special. "I just kept coming back," he says. If it weren't for falling in love with Michelle, he probably would have stayed longer. But now they wanted to start a family, and being closer to home would make that easier. Troy had heard about a job teaching gym in Waywayseecappo and applied. He got the job, at least partly because of the respect his dad had earned as a teacher there. Soon, both father and son would be teaching in Waywayseecappo.

At the end of the school year in Bloodvein, the time came to say goodbye. As Troy packed up his things, one of his students came by to ask: "Coach, is it true you're not coming back next year?" Before long, a group of current and former students assembled to help carry boxes to his truck. "Are you going to visit?" one asked. "Yeah, yeah, I'll come back," Troy said. He meant it, but he also wasn't sure what else to say.

Troy and Michelle drove to the main dock, where they would catch the ferry that could accommodate their car on its deck. A group of friends and students had gathered to send them off, Leslie among them. He shook Troy's hand, then they hugged. "I'll see you again," Troy said. "Yeah," Leslie replied, "I'll see you when you visit."

As the ferry left the shore, Troy waved to all those who had come to say farewell. He would miss them.

He regrets not returning since.

I 3

"THE WAY IT WORKS"

W HEN TROY LUHOWY BECAME WAYWAYSEECAPPO'S gym teacher, in 2006, he taught every grade, from kindergarten all the way to Grade 8. He was probably the only teacher who knew the name of every single student in the school. Most of his classes had more than thirty students. Some had as many as thirty-five. On the worst days, teaching felt like crowd control, but even then Troy liked his job. He got to play with kids all day.

Perhaps a third of Troy's students had been required to repeat grades; a lot of Grade 7 or 8 students were old enough to be in Grade 9 or 10. The wide age range in classes posed a challenge for the school's teachers, but it didn't take long for Troy to spot an opportunity. As he saw it, students with a few extra years of puberty were poised to become dominant athletes. Though reserve schools were not officially part of the regular sports leagues for provincial schools, Troy threw his considerable energy into organizing matches and joining tournaments in towns near and far.

For starters, he stacked a middle school soccer team with a lineup of "big boys," as he called them. They didn't have cleats or shin pads—neither the school nor their families could afford them—but they kept winning anyway. The Waywayseecappo team was so dominant, in fact, that it became hard for Troy to find anyone willing to play goalie. On this superteam, the goalie was little more than a spectator without a seat. In preparation for one regional tournament, Troy hoped to recruit a Waywayseecappo student named Darwin, a cherubic boy of questionable athletic ability. "Okay, boys," Troy told the team, "you have to be really nice to Darwin. We need him." Of course, nothing was to be said to Darwin about the position he would play. "Let's get him on the bus," Troy advised. "Don't say anything about goalie until we start rolling." Everything went according to plan: Darwin signed up to join the team. Then, safely aboard and en route to the tournament, Darwin took a long look at the hulks surrounding him and, the realization finally dawning on him, said, "I'm going to end up in net, won't I?"

During the entire tournament, Darwin didn't allow any goals. It helped that he didn't face a single shot.

Troy developed a knack for producing champions. Once, he spotted a Grade 8 student named Everett who had what it took to become a track-and-field star. The only real barrier to glory was Everett's choppy school attendance. Before a competition, Troy would remind him, "Everett, no matter how late you get to bed, or whatever, you're coming to this race. No matter what!" If Everett still didn't show up on time, Troy would commandeer the school van and go to his house to get him.

In one track-and-field competition for their provincial school division, Troy signed Everett up for every possible event: 100 metres, 200 metres, 400 metres, 1500 metres, long jump, high jump—you name it. By the end of the meet, Everett was pea-cocking for photographs, his chest festooned with blue first-place ribbons. Troy looked on, grinning as widely as Everett.

"I wanted kids that maybe weren't the best students to have something they could excel at," Troy says. "My goal was to give them a little bit of a boost. It was also for all the students in Wayway, to make them feel, 'We can do this, we're as good as the other schools.'"

The competition was less thrilled, and Troy got the feeling that other schools took a special dislike to losing to Waywayseecappo. The following year, the provincial schools started insisting on new age limits for athletic competitions, and the brief era of Troy's superstars came to a close.

TROY ENJOYED TEACHING in Waywayseecappo, just as he had in Bloodvein, but he wasn't particularly surprised when col-leagues didn't stick around. Of twenty or so teachers on staff, a third to half left every year. A central reason was money: Waywayseecappo's teachers received far less than their peers in nearby provincial schools—as much as $20,000 less, depending on seniority. On top of that, the teachers in Waywayseecappo had to deal with packed classrooms and an especially large share of students with special needs of one sort or another. During one particularly bad year, a Grade 4 class cycled through four separate teachers.

A general lack of resources also made teaching at Wayway-seecappo challenging. When Troy started, the school had long since given up on providing textbooks to each student. Instead, teachers handed out photocopies or just used overhead projectors. There was also a regular shortage of basics like pens, pencils, crayons, glue, and markers—items the school tried to provide because so many parents couldn't afford them. Veteran teachers knew that the week before the school year started was the best time to visit the supply room and stock up; supplies usually ran out well before the end of the year. On at least one occasion, the principal called a staff meeting to remind teachers to take only what they absolutely needed from the supply room. According to Jim Cote's niece, Marellia Cote, who had grown up in Waywayseecappo and been working at the school since 1997, the most committed teachers came to accept that paying for some basic materials was part of the job.

Recruiting qualified staff to Waywayseecappo was an annual nightmare, and the school often had no choice but to hire less-than-stellar candidates. The school mostly hired inexperienced teachers fresh out of university or retired provincial school teachers looking for extra income. The school would commonly find itself without a full roster of qualified teachers in the last week of August, right before classes started. "By that time, you're really scraping the bottom of the barrel," a senior administrator recalls. If a teacher didn't have a job by then, there was often a good reason for their unemployment.

The truth is, Troy didn't plan on sticking around long term either. After two years in Waywayseecappo, he applied for a position at Rossburn High School, which was looking for someone to teach physical education and basic computer programming. The job paid $12,000 more than what he made on the reserve. Troy and Michelle had just welcomed their first child and they were planning on a second. Their two-bedroom mobile home was only sixteen feet wide. With the extra money, they could find a bigger place. The only hitch was that Troy knew approximately nothing about computer programming, so he wasn't shocked when he didn't get called back. But he knew there would be more openings. It was just a matter of time.

DURING TROY'S FIRST four years teaching in Waywayseecappo, the school churned through three principals. The third one didn't even last a summer: she quit without notice or explanation the day before classes were set to begin in September 2010. That left the school even more desperate than usual. Still, Troy was surprised to be asked to take the reins as principal. His first thought was: *I like the gym, leave me alone.* On reflection, though, he decided to give it his best shot. He was pretty sure he could do no worse than the previous principal. Plus, there were ten new teachers that year. "I figured they wouldn't really be able to tell if I didn't know what the hell I was doing," he says.

His first order of business as principal was to take a close look at the school's budget. Jackie McKee, the school's no-nonsense finance director, walked him through a series of grim spreadsheets. She told him money was so tight that the school was chronically late on its electricity bill.

"Jackie," Troy said, "how are we supposed to make this work?"

"We have to make it work. This is what we get."

Jackie explained that Waywayseecappo's band council received about $7,300 per student from the federal government to cover education expenses. By comparison, she told him, the public school in Rossburn, just down the road, received about $10,500 per student from the Manitoba government—over 40 percent more.

"That's crazy," Troy said.

"Well, that's the way it is."

"But it makes no sense."

"That's how it works, Troy. We do the best we can."

By this time, Troy had been working at reserve schools for more than a decade. He knew that these schools were funded by the federal government and that regular public schools were funded by provincial governments. He also knew that he had always been paid less than his counterparts in provincial public schools, even though many people in Rossburn assumed he was paid more. But this was the first time it had really dawned on him that, year after year, reserve schools across the country were receiving far less money than provincial schools. "They were all getting funded like that," Troy says. "I had been in First Nations education for a long time, ten years, and I had no clue. I was naive."

Then Jackie explained another crucial, unpleasant fact about students from Waywayseecappo who were attending school off reserve. Waywayseecappo's school went up only to Grade 8, so students had to leave the reserve for high school. When a student like Maureen Twovoice crossed the Birdtail to attend Grade 9 in Rossburn, the federal government continued to provide $7,300 to the Waywayseecappo band council to cover the cost of educating that student. But—and here was the rub—the Rossburn school board charged Waywayseecappo $10,500, the annual cost of educating the student in its provincial school. The $3,200 difference had to come from somewhere, and Waywayseecappo had no choice but to siphon funding from its own school. Even though fewer than a quarter of Waywayseecappo's students were studying in provincial high schools in Rossburn and nearby Russell, those students were consuming more than a third of Waywayseecappo's overall education budget. So the amount of money actually available to spend on a student at the reserve school was not even the comparatively low $7,300, but closer to $6,300.

This diversion of resources from on-reserve education budgets to provincial schools was a common problem. In Ontario, according to an analysis by the federal parliamentary budget officer, federal funding for the education of students living on reserves increased by 1 percent per year between 2004 and 2015, but virtually all of that funding increase went toward paying provincial school tuition for students studying off reserve.[1] In other words, overall funding was modestly increasing, but support for schools on reserves was stagnant.

After his conversation with Jackie, Troy retreated to his office, where he sat in stunned silence. He pulled out a cheap solar calculator and subtracted 7,300 from 10,500, then multiplied that by 314, which was how many students he had in kindergarten through Grade 8. *Holy shit*, he thought, *that's a lot of money—* more than a million dollars. He could now see why the teachers were underpaid, why the classes were so big, why there never seemed to be enough crayons by April. He also knew what most people in Rossburn thought, which was that Waywayseecappo was receiving plenty of money from the federal government, as usual, but just wasn't using it right. Troy looked at his calculator again. It made no sense to him. If he tried to explain this back in town, he thought, people wouldn't believe him.

"There are so many people who automatically think that those reserve kids get more but never learn," Troy says. "People just don't know. They don't get it." And neither, for a long time, had Troy. "I just fit in with that perspective that they have all this money but they were blowing it. But they didn't, and they never did."

During Troy's drive home, down and up the valley, he thought of his son Reid, who would soon start Grade 1 in Rossburn. *What if Reid was the one being sent to a school that always got less?*

Over dinner with Michelle, Troy shared what he had learned that day. He said, "We're cheating these kids." He did not expect to play some heroic role in fixing the problem, but promised himself to do the best he could.

A few months later, Troy received the results of a reading test that had been given to Waywayseecappo's students. Of thirty students in Grade 4, only one was reading at grade level. In Grades 1, 2 and 3, none were.

Of course, people in Waywayseecappo with a knowledge of history found all of this less surprising than Troy did. In an interview with the *Winnipeg Free Press*, community Elder Bryan Cloud said, "Apartheid is alive and well in Canada."[2]

PART IV

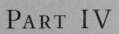

PARTNERSHIP

"STARK AND OBVIOUS"

MAUREEN TWOVOICE STARTED HER DAILY COMMUTE
across the Birdtail River in 2006, the same year Troy
began teaching in Waywayseecappo. Maureen would
later say of her time attending high school in Rossburn, "Damn,
it was so hard."

By the time students from Waywayseecappo started Grade 9
in Rossburn, most were years behind the provincial curriculum.
Many were stuck at what educators call a "frustrational reading
level," which means: you are so far behind, and it is so obvious,
that you'd rather slam your desk than turn the page. The principal at the time, Tammy McCullough, saw how many students
from Waywayseecappo struggled to adapt to the "big shocker" of
transitioning to a provincial high school. "I cared about all my
students," McCullough says, "and it's heartbreaking to see where
there's that gap. The opportunities just hadn't been there for them.
It's sad. They just get gobbled up."

McCullough had been Maureen's Grade 5 teacher on the
reserve before she accepted a teaching job in Rossburn, in part

because the move bumped up her salary by $11,000. Now, as principal, McCullough watched her former star pupil struggle. Maureen "had probably fallen behind a bit every year," she says. "Her spark was still in her, but it was not quite as bright."

In class, Maureen felt lost, disoriented. Beyond the challenge of schoolwork, she had to adapt to classrooms where most students weren't Indigenous and all her teachers were white. "I felt like there were less people on my side if anything were to happen," she says. In the beginning, math class was the only place where she ever raised her hand to ask a question, partly because math class was where she had the most friends from Waywayseecappo.

After years of hearing her mom tell dispiriting stories about attending school in Rossburn, Maureen came in expecting similar treatment. "It was almost like the negative experiences my mother had were mine too," she says. "I had this standoffish behaviour. If something was bothering me, I would just shut down instead of saying anything."

Still, she tried her best to focus on schoolwork. She realized how close she had come to dropping out altogether the year before, and she was not going to waste her second chance. "When I got the opportunity to get to Grade 9, there was no way I was messing it up," she says. "I wasn't interested in high school drama or making friends. I was just there to catch up and get out of there."

To her surprise, she started noticing that a number of her teachers seemed genuinely to care about her. Bit by bit, she warmed to them, and as the months went by she developed a habit of going to see these teachers after class. By the end of Grade 9, she was regularly raising her hand in all her classes.

Maureen caught up, and then she pulled ahead. In Grade 10, she made the honour roll. In report cards, her English teacher praised her as "an exceptional student showing determination and intelligence." Her science teacher described her as "a wonderful, dedicated and conscientious student." Her math teacher said she was "a joy to have in class." She hadn't received report cards like this in years.

During this time, Maureen didn't make a single close friend from Rossburn. She never endured racist taunts as her mother had, but there was always a social barrier that kept students from Rossburn and Waywayseecappo apart. "We exchanged words here and there, but not to create friendship," Maureen says. Bob Ploshynsky, the principal who succeeded Tammy McCullough, recalls that "prejudice was palpable in the building." Maureen tried not to dwell on it.

One incident, though, pierced her armour. It happened during a class in which Maureen happened to be the only student from Waywayseecappo. A teacher was talking about the early history of Manitoba when a boy with blond hair and blue eyes blurted out, "We were here first!" By "we," he meant Ukrainians. Maureen could not tell if he was joking. She thought, *Um, no you weren't*, but she wasn't quite sure how to respond. "I knew that what he said bothered me," she recalls, "but I felt like I didn't know enough of my own history to argue back without sounding like I was making it up." Instead, she stayed quiet, and her face flushed red with frustration.

Though this moment lingered with her, Maureen knew it wasn't much compared with what her mom had put up with. While Maureen was in Grade 11, Prime Minister Stephen Harper delivered a formal apology in the House of Commons for Canada's treatment of Indigenous children at residential schools. Maureen came across a printed copy of the speech and decided to take it home to show her mom. Linda took the document to her room to read it alone. "To the approximately 80,000 living former students and all family members and communities," the prime minister said,

> the Government of Canada now recognizes that it was wrong to forcibly remove children from their homes, and we apologize for having done this. We now recognize that it was wrong to separate children from rich and vibrant cultures and traditions, that it created a void in many lives and communities, and we apologize for having done this. We now recognize that in separating children from their families, we undermined the ability of many to adequately parent their own children and sowed the seeds for generations to follow, and we apologize for having done this. We now recognize that far too often these institutions gave rise to abuse or neglect and were inadequately controlled, and we apologize for failing to protect you. . . .
>
> The Government of Canada sincerely apologizes and asks the forgiveness of the aboriginal peoples of this country for failing them so profoundly.[1]

After Linda finished reading, she crumpled the paper and flung it into the hallway. "This won't bring back the hearing in my ear," she said.

THE FOLLOWING YEAR, 2009, Maureen graduated from high school.

On the morning of the ceremony, her younger sister, Samantha, devoted more than an hour to curling Maureen's wavy hair. "Oh my god," Samantha said, "I can't believe you did it!" Maureen put on a sky-blue dress she had picked for the occasion. The dress exposed her shoulders, which, to Maureen's annoyance, were spotted with acne. She solved the problem by using an elegant white scarf as a shawl. A pair of matching white sandals pinched her toes but completed the outfit perfectly. Maureen felt beautiful.

Of the ten other students from Waywayseecappo that had started high school in Rossburn with Maureen, only three were graduating with her. As Maureen watched her classmates being called up to receive their diplomas, she thought of her grandfather Michael, who had received his high school diploma almost sixty years before. Maureen had never met him—Michael died four years before she was born—but she had seen old pictures of him and grown up hearing stories about his way with words. One time, she had a particularly vivid dream in which she found herself walking into a home that was bubbling with voices and laughter. She saw her grandfather inside—all dressed up, with greased hair and a spiffy suit. He seemed to be hosting the event, some kind of community feast, and all of a sudden Maureen found herself seated near him at a table. He was talking to her animatedly. When Maureen woke up, she could still see her grandfather's face. But though she tried and tried she could not remember his words.

Twovoice was the last name called at the graduation ceremony. By that time, Maureen's curls had reverted to waves. She didn't really care—this was a moment she had been imagining for a long time, and here it was. As she headed up the aisle to collect her diploma, she made sure to locate her mom's face in the crowd. "Just her being there was a big thing," Maureen recalls. "Even after all the times we hadn't gotten along, she was there to experience the accomplishment with me." Linda was smiling, her face streaked with tears. Maureen felt a lump growing in her throat, and kept walking toward the stage.

★ ★ ★

Maureen Twovoice beat the odds. Between 2011 and 2016, only a quarter of students living on reserves in Canada graduated from high school in four years.[2] Most never do. The consequences of the staggering dropout rate are well documented: lower employment and higher incarceration; less political engagement and worse health; shorter lifespans and deeper poverty.

Today, some 120,000 school-age children live on reserves across Canada. All too often, their families are racked by high rates of intergenerational trauma, financial hardship, substance abuse, youth suicide, and sexual violence: aftershocks of Canada's legacy of residential schools and structural inequities. *In addition* to these imposing hurdles, the schools these children attend have been chronically underfunded, just like Maureen's school in Waywayseecappo.

Ninety percent of Canadians are educated in public schools that are funded and regulated by provinces. A signature feature of the provincial public education system is that it invests more, not less, in schools that have higher costs and greater needs: notably, schools that are geographically remote, or that have more low-income students or second-language learners. The rationale is to give every student, no matter where or who they are, a fair chance at success. Yet federally funded schools on reserves—which often have a disproportionately high number of students with acute needs—have systematically received less. For decades.

After communities such as Waywayseecappo recoiled from provincial public schools and established control over their own schools on reserve—a shift that began in the 1970s and was the norm by the 1980s[3]—it became ever clearer that the federal government was not matching the level of funding that provincial schools received. In 1984, teachers at the Waywayseecappo school wrote letters to Ottawa as part of a campaign for additional resources. "My children are the hope for the future in this reserve," teacher Lorana Chandler wrote. "I am not asking for the world, I am asking for the essentials that are enjoyed in *every* provincial school." Another teacher, Duncan Allen, wrote, "Is there a high school in the Public School system which does not have a library facility? Is there a high school in the Public School system in which science has to be taught without laboratory facilities? The answer to both these questions is obviously 'NO.' Why then I ask you, should the pupils at Waywayseecappo Community School be subjected to these unreasonable and unnecessary barriers to their education?"[4]

Waywayseecappo's appeals for fairer education funding continued after Brian Mulroney replaced Pierre Trudeau as prime minister in 1984. In response to a query about funding for education on reserves, the minister of Indian and northern affairs, David Crombie, wrote in 1986, "My department is concerned that funding for Indian schools should be equivalent to that provided by the provinces, and is making every effort to ensure that this will take place."[5] And yet, equivalent funding did not materialize.

On the contrary, by the late 1980s, the inequality was "stark and obvious," according to Harry Swain, the deputy minister of Indian and northern affairs (as the department was then called) between 1987 and 1992. Swain was the most senior bureaucrat in the department, nearly a hundred years after Hayter Reed occupied the same post with a different title. He recalls that the official department policy was to provide equal services on reserves.[6] In principle, that meant that students living on reserves were supposed to receive a quality of education comparable to what was available to a similarly situated non-Native community. "Reaching parity was our aspirational goal," Swain says, but the government did not invest enough to make it a reality. "By our calculations, we were spending fifteen to twenty-five percent less per capita than what provincial governments were spending, which led to predictably worse outcomes. Parity would have taken a hell of a lot more resources than we had."

The gap appalled Swain. Every year he was deputy minister, he says, he pushed for a bigger budget to improve services on reserves. One of his main arguments was that Canada was violating the constitutional guarantee, in section 15 of the Charter of Rights and Freedoms, to "equal protection and equal benefit of the law without discrimination." When Swain faced off against officials trying to slash budgets, he told them that the failure to provide equal services on reserves was an open invitation to a discrimination lawsuit. He says he used to warn his government colleagues, "We're going to get our asses sued off and we're going to lose."[7] In the end, Swain thinks his efforts had some effect—not in achieving equal funding, but in staving off an even bigger gap.

Meanwhile, Waywayseecappo and communities like it suffered the consequences. In January 1991, five members of the Waywayseecappo Education Authority wrote to the federal government about yet another dispute over funding:

> *Why is it always nearly impossible for us native people to get what we need, when other races of people have no problem whatsoever in getting their needs fulfilled? Is it what we think it is, because if it is let us remind you that this is the 90's. The needs, aspirations and goals of our native children are the same as their neighbours just over the reserve boundaries.*[8]

One of the authors of this letter was Jim Cote, Hugh McKay's son.

★ ★ ★

JEAN CHRÉTIEN WAS elected prime minister in 1993, more than two decades after he had belatedly acknowledged the failings of integrated education "of the whitewash variety." Chrétien inherited a federal government sinking into a quicksand of debt. His finance minister, Paul Martin, promised to tame the deficit come "hell or high water." As part of Martin's plan, a 2 percent cap was placed on annual spending increases for services on reserves, including education, even though a 2 percent annual increase was manifestly insufficient to keep up with the rates of inflation and population growth. The measure was said to be temporary, and other departments faced outright cuts to their budgets.

The deputy minister of Indian affairs at the time, Scott Serson, recalls calling Phil Fontaine, the national Chief of the Assembly of First Nations, to assure him that the spending cap would be removed as soon as the deficit was under control. In time, Serson became ashamed of that phone call. By 1998, the government was back to running budget surpluses, yet the 2 percent spending cap would remain in place for almost two more decades, until 2016. Michael Wernick, who served as deputy minister of Indian affairs between 2006 and 2014, observes, "Every single year, for close to twenty years, ministers of finance from the Chrétien government, the Martin government, and the Harper government had an opportunity to change it, but they didn't." Spending less was a *choice* that was made repeatedly, year after year.

At the time the cap was implemented, Scott Serson says he thought it was "about defeating the deficit, not holding a group of Canadian citizens at an insufficient level for 22 years." He went on to write that "it is only reasonable to conclude that the deliberate, but unstated, policy of the Canadian government is to maintain the vast majority of First Nations in poverty."[9] In a 2012 interview, Paul Martin said, "The cap was a mistake and there's no excuse for it."[10]

Meanwhile, Manitoba and other provinces ramped up their education spending. Between 1996 and 2015, provinces increased funding for public schools about twice as fast as the federal government increased funding for on-reserve education.[11] Over time, the two funding curves diverged, at first by a bit, eventually by a lot, until one day in 2010, Troy Luhowy looked at the numbers on his calculator and wondered how things had gone so terribly wrong. A gap had become a chasm.

The inequality between the two sides of the Birdtail was not an aberration. It was not some unfortunate, isolated case. It was, rather, perfectly in keeping with the norm for the five hundred schools on reserves across Canada. In 2012, Saskatchewan's minister of education, Russ Marchuk, estimated that in his province students on reserves were receiving as much as 40 percent less funding than students in public schools. "You observe the effects of a lack of resources first-hand," he said. "Lower graduation rates, children not school-ready, lower employment rates. These are the results of a lack of funding."[12] Yet again, Canada was making a mockery of Alexander Morris's assurance, all those years ago, that the Queen "always cared for her red children as much as for her white."

The disparity in funding has been mirrored by a disparity in outcomes. Canada's auditor general, the government's most credible number-cruncher, calculated in 1996 that the outcomes gap between Indigenous students living on reserves and the Canadian student population as a whole would close by 2019. But as time passed, things progressively worsened. In 2000, the auditor general estimated that the gap would persist until 2023.

In 2004, the projection extended to 2032. In 2011, the auditor general said it might take even longer than that, but declined to specify a date.[13]

Treaty 4, like other treaties, includes a promise from the government to maintain a school on each community's reserve ("Her Majesty agrees to maintain a school in the reserve"), but Indigenous communities have paid a steep price for invoking this right. Canada's underfunding has ensured that these separate schools would be unequal. Knowing this, Waywayseecappo and almost every other reserve community *still* chose to retain their own schools. That's how deep the wound was from residential and integrated schools. That's how deep the need was to have a meaningful say in the education of their children.

In 2012, politicians in Ottawa were sufficiently roused by activists and media scrutiny to formally recognize that there was a problem. The following non-binding resolution received unanimous support in the House of Commons: "That, in the opinion of the House, the government should" be "providing funding that will put reserve schools on par with non-reserve provincial schools."[14] After the resolution passed—once parliamentarians from all parties had uttered many fine words and patted one another on the back in a rare display of righteous unanimity—nothing much changed. Parliament had committed itself to an aspirational goal and then failed to implement a plan to make it a reality.[15] In 2016, the national funding gap between reserve schools and provincial public schools was reported to be approximately 30 percent, which amounted to a staggering shortfall of $665 million in that year alone.[16]

Beyond all the material constraints the chronic financial shortfall imposed, it also suggested to hundreds of thousands of Indigenous students that maybe they didn't really deserve any better. It was as though Canada was telling them, "You get less because you'll never amount to anything anyway."

"It's always been that way," says Waywayseecappo's long-time elected Chief, Murray Clearsky. "They don't want to educate the Indian, to put it mildly."

Which prompts the question: *Why?* Why did Canada underfund education on reserves for so long? This is the query that first brought us to Waywayseecappo and Rossburn, to the valley they share and the river between them. If Canada is to meaningfully address this long-standing problem, we need a clear diagnosis of its causes.

15

"PEOPLE SAY WE'RE RACISTS"

IN CANADA'S EARLY YEARS, THE LIKES OF HAYTER REED and Clifford Sifton assumed that Indigenous Peoples were inherently inferior to whites, and said so openly. It is comforting to think that state-sanctioned racism is a thing of the distant past, perpetrated by villains in black-and-white photographs. And yet, *after* embracing a Charter of Rights and Freedoms in 1982 and formally apologizing for abuses at residential schools in 2008, modern Canada continued to systematically underfund students like Maureen Twovoice on reserves like Waywayseecappo. Successive federal governments, Liberal and Conservative, sustained this underfunding, with the tacit support of Canadians who elected them. Indeed, the contemporary mistreatment of Indigenous students is consistent with the broader historical pattern.[1] We have just replaced evil masterminds with cruel neglect. The villains today might be less readily identifiable, but Canada is still guilty.

Part of the explanation is the long half-life of racism, which endures in ever more insidious forms. Indigenous lives remain widely devalued—in our policies, in our politics, in our minds. The underfunding of Indigenous schools could continue because too few Canadians noticed, and, of those who did, too few cared. The fact of grossly unequal services on reserves may have been "stark and obvious" by the late 1980s, but by then Canadians had grown accustomed to the idea of failing Indigenous communities, failing reserve schools, failing Indigenous students. Too many Canadians came to see obviously worse outcomes on reserves as normal and Indigenous Peoples themselves as responsible. This explanation had the added attraction of skirting the ways settlers had benefited from the dispossession of Indigenous Peoples. Racism is a filter that renders the obvious invisible.

From the very outset, reserves were especially vulnerable to unequal treatment because they were separate from the rest of the country. This separation is not merely geographic—there are also constitutional and administrative dimensions. The document that accompanied Canada's birth as a confederation, the British North America Act of 1867, put provinces in charge of education and the federal government in charge of "Indians and lands reserved for the Indians." This original division of power is the reason why Manitoba is responsible for funding public schools in Rossburn and the federal government is responsible for funding Waywayseecappo's school just across the valley. As the anthropologist Harry Hawthorn once put it, reserves are "isolated federal islands surrounded by provincial territory."[2] This jurisdictional Swiss cheese enabled what followed: separate became, then remained, unequal.

People living on reserves constitute only about 1 percent of Canada's overall population, and, therefore, have extremely limited electoral clout. But to be few is one thing—to be few *and* separate raises further challenges. When a province alters funding to public schools, which over 90 percent of students attend, almost all students in the provincial system are affected. If funding decreases, everyone suffers; if funding increases, everyone benefits. Either way, there is a common outcome for most people, and, therefore, a common cause. But the situation is altogether different for students on reserves. Their schools do not benefit from increased provincial spending and, conversely, no child in provincial schools is affected by the underfunding of reserve schools. Non-Indigenous parents never have to contemplate the possibility that their own children could attend a chronically underfunded school, let alone a school on a reserve.

The geographic separateness of reserves only further accentuates their political isolation. Most Canadians have never set foot on a reserve, many of which are distant from urban centres and some of which are not even accessible by road. This makes it even easier for most voters and the politicians they elect to ignore reserve communities.

To make matters worse, the federal government did not feel bound by law to deliver basic services on reserves comparable to services provided by provinces (and still doesn't). Worse, starting in 2007, it engaged in slow and expensive litigation to defend the government's right to use its discretion to provide less.[3]

The issue is not simply that reserves are too easily overlooked—they are also widely *resented*. Ask Nelson Luhowy; he'll tell you. The prevailing view in Rossburn is that reserves like Waywayseecappo receive *too much* government money, not too little. Polling data show that many, if not most, Canadians agree with this sentiment.[4] Nelson hears about it all the time at the Rossburn Hotel over lunch. Whenever Waywayseecappo comes up, Nelson hears the same old stuff. Namely, that people on the reserve do not pay their fair share of taxes.

"Oh," Nelson says, "are people ever sore about the question of taxes." For purchases made in Waywayseecappo, as on other reserves, people who are officially recognized by the federal government as "Status Indians" do not pay federal or provincial sales taxes.[5] In addition, income earned on reserve by Status Indians is sometimes not subject to income tax. In Rossburn, as elsewhere, this seems wrong, unfair, a basic violation of the social contract.

"If I go to a store and I pay a dollar, then you pay a dollar and thirteen cents, that would bother you, wouldn't it?" Nelson says. "That communicates to people that it's not fair." When the federal government funds anything in Waywayseecappo, Nelson says, the first reaction over lunch in Rossburn is often, "Oh, guess that's more of our money going in to pay for it." *Our* money: Nelson hears a lot of that. As in, *our* tax dollars, to which *they* don't contribute. The fact that a disproportionate number of people in Waywayseecappo rely on government assistance only hardens the sense of grievance in Rossburn. "We're paying their welfare," Nelson hears at lunch. "They're getting a free ride." Despite support—or, many suspect, *because* of it—Waywayseecappo doesn't get its act together.

Federal politicians have long been aware of widespread hostility to government spending on reserves, and acted accordingly. "Putting it as bluntly as possible, no government ever won votes by spending money on Indians," long-time member of Parliament Charlie Angus writes.[6] In recent decades, whenever a federal politician in the governing party was asked a question about unequal services on reserves, the stock answer avoided the issue of inequality and instead emphasized how much the federal government was already spending. This sent a clear message to the (non-Indigenous) majority of voters: All this money we're spending, all those billions, that's *your* money—doesn't it sound like enough? As one Rossburn resident put it over lunch, "What is the Indian Affairs budget? It's, you know, billions of dollars. Where does that money come from? Even a dummy can figure that out. And yet, somehow, we're the assholes."

Beyond the taxation bugbear, many Canadians are also generally disinclined to support greater funding on reserves because of opposition to federal programs that seem to provide special benefits to Status Indians. For example, in Waywayseecappo, as on other reserves, Status Indians receive extended coverage for dental care and prescription drugs. To many, the existence of such programs undercuts claims that other services, such as primary and secondary education, are underfunded.

Brian Brown, who served as the mayor of Rossburn between 2014 and 2018, is the kind of person who prides himself on saying out loud what others only think. He is among the many who firmly believe that Status Indians should not receive any benefits not available to Rossburn's non-Native population. "I have a granddaughter," Brian said while he was still mayor. "How do I explain to her that when she goes to university, it will cost her twenty grand a year, but when her friend from the reserve goes, it will cost her absolutely nothing? To me, it's not right, and most of my constituents feel the same way. People say we're racists. I don't think I'm racist. I'd call it resentment. I just want everyone to be treated the same."

Like a majority of Canadians, Brown doesn't think that Indigenous Canadians should have any kind of special status.[7] This position is akin to the long-standing and widespread view that Quebec wrongly enjoys an exalted status among supposedly equal provinces. Brown is among the many who would still gladly embrace the approach Pierre Trudeau and Jean Chrétien once attempted with the White Paper of 1969: abolish Indian status and Indian reserves, along with any differential treatment that comes with them.

Brown's views stem in part from the conviction that Ukrainian Canadians never benefited from special treatment. "A lot of people here," he said, "their grandparents were immigrants. They know how rough it was." Yet people in Rossburn feel that they are being held responsible for Waywayseecappo's failures. "If something bad happens, we're the bad guy. Somehow it's our fault. I think they associate every white person with the past." And yet, Brian notes, he didn't have anything to do with residential schools.

Brown is also inherently suspicious, as many are, of anything that looks like an affirmative action program based on race rather than on economic need. "You and I may be different, with different nationalities, from different parts of the country, but in everything else we should be equal," Brown said. "But the reserve population is not." By which he means: the reserve population is treated differently, sometimes even preferentially. That so many people on reserves live in abject poverty does not seem to alter the enduring perception that Indians are receiving undeserved advantages.

BEFORE RESPONDING TO such views, as we must, it is important to recognize how widespread they are, and to take them seriously. We should not simply label the citizens of Rossburn as racist and then stop listening to what they have to say. We would do well, as a country, to linger with Nelson and Brian on Main Street, so that we may seek to understand, to reflect on where they are coming from. And empathize.

If we imagine ourselves in their shoes and hear the story they tell themselves, it is easier to recognize how utterly compelling it is. Rossburn's posture toward Waywayseecappo is inextricably linked to a larger story about immigrants who have struggled and endured, all the while feeling that the government has never done them any favours. The pioneer narrative of resilience, hard work, and self-reliance continues to inspire and enthrall.

Meanwhile, economic anxiety gnaws at rural communities like Rossburn. Wages are largely stagnant. As the town's population continues to fall, the tax base shrinks. The roof on the ice rink is leaking, and repairs will cost $50,000. There is also an unfinished, unkempt baseball diamond at the edge of town, still without a pitcher's mound. It has been that way for years, providing a daily reminder of decline.

It should not be surprising that many of the town's residents resent the reserve across the valley, which is seen to be benefiting from favourable tax rules and the federal government's largesse. Indeed, this phenomenon is not unique to Canada. Many American conservatives, as sociologist Arlie Hochschild notes, perceive a "rift between deserving taxpayers and undeserving tax money takers."[8] These conservatives, particularly in rural areas, profoundly resent that the government is "taking money from the workers and giving it to the idle," "taking from people of good character and giving to people of bad character." Those who benefit from the redistribution are seen to be "violating rules of fairness." Or, as Troy Luhowy often heard while he was growing up: Indians were "getting everything for nothing."

So the resentment is real, and it is deeply felt. Yet it is mostly anchored in assumptions and stereotypes that simply do not reflect reality. When it comes to taxation, for example, the views commonly heard in Rossburn are almost completely wrong.

There is a widely held misconception that Indigenous Peoples in Canada pay no taxes.[9] But this is patently false. Off reserve, Indians pay income tax, sales tax, property tax, provincial sales tax, federal sales tax, gas taxes, taxes levied on cigarettes and gasoline and alcohol—in other words, all the same taxes as non-Indians.

It is true that neither federal nor provincial sales tax is collected on goods purchased and used on reserves, but most reserve communities don't have enough retail merchants for the exemption to have much impact. Status Indians who work for their community are indeed exempt from paying income tax, but this exemption does not extend to commercial or non-governmental employment. And, because of this exemption, band councils often pay on-reserve employees 75 percent of what an off-reserve employee would earn doing the same job, reasoning that since the take-home pay will be roughly the same, no one should complain, and mostly no one does.

A virtually unusable sales tax exemption and an income tax exemption offset by low salaries are, at day's end, very slender benefits, if they are benefits at all.

There is nothing new in any of this. To the narrow extent that they exist, tax exemptions on "Indian lands" date back to before Confederation. In 1850, legislation in Upper and Lower Canada exempted reserves from taxation, and so did the first Indian Act of 1869.[10] During at least some treaty negotiations, the government seems to have promised that a treaty would "not open the way to the imposition of any tax."[11] As recently as 1990, the Supreme Court reviewed tax exemptions on reserves and held that they were still very much legal and legitimate.[12] People such as Brian Brown "don't understand the deal we had with the Queen," says Waywayseecappo's Chief Clearsky.

What's more, a high percentage of people on reserves are poor, which means, practically speaking, that most would not pay income taxes even if they were subjected to the exact same rules as everyone else. Reserves are simply not dragon dens where riches are hoarded to the detriment of Canada and the citizens of Rossburn. The average family in Waywayseecappo lives below the poverty line.

It is true that many First Nations communities invest in post-secondary education, providing tuition funds and sometimes living expenses for community members. But it is important to understand this arrangement for what it is: a local government choosing to invest in post-secondary education at the cost of using that same money to pay for other things such as road maintenance. Rather than asking why Indigenous communities do this, a better question might be why cities and towns focus on potholes and police rather than providing university tuition for their residents.

It is also true that the Indian Act lays out distinctive rules for Status Indians. This raises suspicions among those who equate equality with identical rules for all. Yet since its inception the Indian Act has been used to oppress Indigenous Peoples, not to privilege them. Any honest look at the history of the Department of Indian Affairs makes this clear.

And yet the idea that Indians have received and continue to receive unfair advantages persists. It is an idea rooted in ignorance and maintained by resentment. Only when people such as Nelson begin to spend time in reserve communities do they hear the stories, not of easy money, but of hard challenges and intergenerational trauma the likes of which they had never imagined.

Given Canada's wealth and Waywayseecappo's poverty, it is incredibly frustrating for people on the reserve—and Indigenous Canadians, generally—to hear about all the unfair benefits they are imagined to receive. Indeed, complaints by non-Indigenous Canadians about taxes and preferential treatment seem to altogether ignore Canada's long history of questionable dealings with Indigenous Peoples, particularly with respect to land. Whatever modest benefits Status Indians receive are tiny compared to the immense wealth Canada has extracted, and continues to extract, from Traditional Indigenous Territory — such as the $230 million the Province of Manitoba collected in 2019 from royalties on mineral mining, to pick but one example.

"Sure, we'll gladly pay more taxes," more than a few Indigenous Canadians have joked, "if you give us our land back."

AS MANY IN Waywayseecappo thought it was unfair for its primary and secondary students to receive lower government funding for education, so did many in Rossburn think it was unfair for Waywayseecappo to pay less tax or receive subsidized medications at the pharmacy. Canadians on either side of such arguments rarely convince each other. Mayor Brian Brown and Chief Murray Clearsky certainly haven't. Both sides invoke equality, but there is no basic agreement on what equality means or what fairness entails.

And this, it seems, is where Canada has been stuck for a long time. The resistance among non-Indigenous Canadians to further spending on reserves has never been specifically directed at the funding of primary and secondary education, nor at Native students themselves. Yet young people such as Maureen Twovoice have long been the collateral damage of deeper misunderstandings and disagreements between Indigenous and non-Indigenous Canadians.

For generations, Rossburn and Waywayseecappo were as stuck in this rut as any two communities could be. But then— incredibly, improbably—they found a way forward. In 2010, just a few months after Troy Luhowy became principal of the Waywayseecappo school, everything changed.

16

"KIDS ARE KIDS"

WAYWAYSEECAPPO AND ROSSBURN REMAINED emblematic of the national funding gap between Indigenous and non-Indigenous students until November 29, 2010. On that frigid day, which reached minus twenty-two Celsius with wind chill, something miraculous happened: a deal was reached to ensure that every student in Waywayseecappo would receive the exact same funding as a student in Rossburn. All of a sudden—literally, overnight—the federal government would match the provincial standard, dollar for dollar. With over three hundred students living on the reserve, that meant an infusion of more than a million dollars into Waywayseecappo's annual education budget.[1]

At this point, Troy Luhowy had been principal of the Waywayseecappo school for only three months and he had not been involved in the negotiations. Still, he could appreciate the significance of the moment. "After being behind all these years, now they were on a level playing field," he says. "It's amazing how difficult it was to get people to see the problem."

The new agreement was the product of more than two years of negotiations between representatives of Waywayseecappo, the federal government, the government of Manitoba, and the local provincial school division. It became known simply as "the partnership," and it launched a unique experiment to discover what would happen when students on a reserve received the same funding and services as students in provincial schools. Canada had never bothered to ask or answer that question.

THE AGREEMENT THAT equalized funding for Waywayseecappo began, as many changes do, with a person wondering: Why not?

In this case, that person was Colleen Clearsky, Waywayseecappo's long-time director of education. For years, she had been hearing about the "education gap" between Indigenous and non-Indigenous students. "Every time I went to a meeting someone mentioned it," she says. "My main goal was to try to close that gap, to do something for our students, but it was getting larger and larger." She and others in Waywayseecappo had been trying as best they could, with the limited resources the band council could offer, to "cover up all the cracks" that students were falling through. Colleen helped establish the adult education program for those who wanted another shot at a high school diploma, for which Nelson Luhowy would go on to teach; an "off-campus transition" program for teenagers, such as Maureen Twovoice, who were not coping with the regular classroom; and a kindergarten program, which first operated only for half days, and later was expanded to full days, five days a week.

All the while, Colleen was acutely aware of how much less the federal government was funding Waywayseecappo's students compared with students in provincial schools. "I looked at the funding we were getting here, and I looked at what they were getting in the provincial system, and I wanted to know: Why can't we just get the same funding as they were getting?"

Together with her colleague Jackie McKee, and with support from Waywayseecappo's elected leadership, Colleen started looking to partner with Park West School Division, the group of fourteen nearby provincial schools that included Rossburn's elementary and secondary schools. But what incentive might a group of provincial schools have to work more closely with a reserve school?

Stephen David was the assistant superintendent of Park West School Division when the partnership was launched, and he is the superintendent today. To hear David tell it, the partnership arose from a moment of moral reckoning. Before 2010, he says, "We had a school with 340 kids six kilometres from Rossburn, and so much disparity in terms of educational outcomes. The reality, when you coalesced it, is that it was about funding. You may hear people say it's not just about the money. Well, a lot of it was."

David insists that he and others felt a "moral imperative" to help close the funding gap—and, more importantly, the gap in outcomes—between students from Waywayseecappo and the rest of the students in his school division. He imagined his own daughter being sent to a chronically under-resourced school. "Of course I wouldn't want that, and neither would anyone else who could avoid it," he says. "There is no way to justify the way things were. I think if you try to think logically and rationally, there was no way to make sense of it. It was totally illogical, totally irrational. Beyond that—it was appalling. We have an obligation to people down the road. Kids are kids. They want to learn."

The man who became Park West's superintendent in 2012, Tim Mendel, emphasized other considerations in an interview with the *Winnipeg Free Press*. "It is in Park West's best interests that [the partnership] does well," Mendel said, because students from Waywayseecappo "will eventually come to our high schools."[2]

Yet even this kind of thinking, persuasive as it might seem in retrospect, did not capture the full extent of Park West's motivations. After all, students from Waywayseecappo had been under-performing in provincial high schools for generations, and this had not catalyzed any major changes before. Rather, the sense of urgency in 2010 came from another source: enrolment in the provincial school division had been steadily declining. For years, fewer students had been entering Grade 1 than were leaving Grade 12. This reflected the slow and steady depopulating of rural Manitoba: farms were increasingly larger and more mechanized, which meant fewer actual farmers with children to send to schools. Park West School Division's administrators had been watching the downward enrolment trend with alarm and increasing desperation.

If enrolment kept dropping, programs for students would be cut, teachers would lose their jobs, schools would close. Kids are kids, but they are also, from the perspective of school administrators, sources of revenue. And this is where Waywayseecappo, with its rapidly increasing population of school-age children, entered the equation. If Waywayseecappo's students could somehow be counted as part of the provincial school division, then Park West could solve its enrolment problem.

Colleen Clearsky had no illusions about why the provincial schools were suddenly eager to move forward with the partnership. "Their school population was declining, ours was rising. They needed our students, and we needed the funding. It went hand in hand. We both knew what we were doing, and why." Under the proposed terms of a partnership, every student at the Waywayseecappo school would be considered part of the provincial school division, and, crucially for Park West, Waywayseecappo would be required to use a portion of its increased federal funding to contribute to shared services. In this way, the partnership would directly benefit both Waywayseecappo *and* all the neighbouring public schools.

The partnership hinged, of course, on the federal government agreeing to dramatically increase Waywayseecappo's funding, for which the motivation is harder to explain. Didn't the provision of equal funding for Waywayseecappo represent a tacit admission of unequal funding for so many other communities? In the most bureaucratic way possible, an internal government memo conceded as much: "Although this arrangement would cost approximately $1 million more annually than the Waywayseecappo First Nation's current education-related funding, it would provide rapid alignment of First Nation and provincial school standards."[3] The very rationale for the partnership was an indictment of the federal approach to many other communities.

For years, the government of Stephen Harper had seemed strongly disinclined to spend a large amount of additional money on reserves. One of Harper's first acts as prime minister was to renege on a commitment by his predecessor, Paul Martin, to spend an additional $5 billion over five years to improve services on reserves. Harper reportedly told a senior aide, "If I had $5 billion to give away, I would give it to the farmers."[4] Reserves were simply not a political priority, and the government was generally skeptical that more money could improve outcomes without deeper (and controversial) reforms. However, Harper had delivered a seemingly heartfelt apology in 2008 for the federal government's role in supporting residential schools, which had the effect of bringing increased public attention to the deplorable educational outcomes for Indigenous students. According to Michael

Wernick, who was then the top civil servant in the Department of Indian and Northern Affairs, the Harper government was open to supporting locally driven initiatives that could make a strong case for improving results. The proposed Waywayseecappo partnership was exactly this kind of initiative.

Crucially, it was not particularly expensive for the federal government. As Wernick says: "You can find a million dollars in a seven-billion-dollar department. But if you had to find fifty million, that wouldn't have been possible. It was the small scale, the granularity, that made it possible."

Federal funding sealed the deal, but at its heart the partnership resulted from local actors seeing that investing more in students from the reserve was in everyone's best interests.

Canada as a whole was still failing to reach a similar conclusion.

AFTER RECEIVING THE new infusion of money, the first thing Waywayseecappo did was hire six more teachers. This nearly halved the average class size, to fewer than twenty students. Teachers also received raises to bring their salaries in line with those of their peers in Rossburn—for most, this meant an annual increase of between $13,000 and $18,000. And the school made long-deferred investments in textbooks and its library.

In exchange for additional funding, the federal government insisted on regular testing of students to track whether the partnership affected outcomes over time. Baseline results from 2010 showed that among all the school's Grade 1 to 4 students, only a single student was reading at grade level—one child out of 122. Six years later, half of students in Grades 1 to 4 were reading at grade level.[5]

"Half is still not acceptable," Troy said, "but we've come a long way. Things have gotten better in a hurry."

There were other signs of improvement, too. Overall student attendance improved, rising to 90 percent from 80 percent. Incident reports, which are written when a student does something sufficiently bad to warrant a trip to the principal's office, decreased 65 percent, from more than 2,500 a year to fewer than 900. In other words, students were doing a lot less fighting with each other or swearing at teachers.

It used to be common for the school to lose a third or more of its teachers every year. After the partnership began, though, turnover plummeted. By the 2016–17 academic year, Waywayseecappo had better teacher retention than the fourteen provincial schools in the division. "When a provincial school could offer teachers $15,000 more and classrooms that didn't have thirty-five kids, teachers left our school," Troy said. "Now, our students actually expect teachers to come back." A teaching vacancy at the Waywayseecappo school used to attract perhaps two or three applicants, and hardly the pick of the litter. These days, each opening receives hundreds of qualified applicants. In 2015, an experienced teacher from a provincial public school actually asked that she be transferred to Waywayseecappo. "I can guarantee you that never would have happened before," Troy said.

After a few spins around a virtuous circle, teachers and students allowed themselves higher expectations. Teachers started assigning more reading to be completed at home because they trusted that the students would actually do it and that loaned books would be returned. A 2015 survey of Waywayseecappo's Grade 8 students showed that 72 percent of them hoped to attend university, at a time the national high school graduation rate for students living on reserves was only about 40 percent.

Hope is not just a start—it is a necessary first step.

★ ★ ★

THE TANTALIZING TURNAROUND of Waywayseecappo's school can be attributed to equal access to services as much as equal money. With Waywayseecappo paying its share, the provincial school division began treating the school as a full member. That meant Waywayseecappo could take advantage of all the services available to the school division, including teacher training, student counselling, a speech pathologist, the latest teaching materials and curricula, maintenance crews, computer technicians, and all the sports leagues. (For Troy, there was no greater glory than the girls' basketball team winning the 2016 divisional championship.) At the same time, the Waywayseecappo school retained control over its hiring and curriculum, including the ability to teach culturally relevant subjects such as Ojibway language. Waywayseecappo has found a way to retain its autonomy while still benefiting from the economies of scale that came with being part of a larger unit. "I am not giving up much authority for the amount of good education we are getting," said Chief Murray Clearsky. "With more resources, the kids are already doing better."[6]

As part of the partnership, students from Rossburn now go to the Waywayseecappo school for opportunities that are not available in town, such as woodworking classes, where they churn out benches and shelves, and a cosmetology program, where budding hairstylists beautify their first clients. Sending provincial school students to attend any kind of class on a reserve was unheard of. For years, Waywayseecappo's students had crossed the valley to attend high school in Rossburn—now the flow of students runs both ways. As Colleen Clearsky says, "We wanted to give non-Aboriginal students a chance to see how it was when they came to our school. It was always us going out—why couldn't it be them coming to our school?"

Not all parents in Rossburn embraced the partnership. A member of Troy's extended family refused to allow his child to participate in the cosmetology program. "There's no way my daughter is going to school on the reserve," he allegedly told the Rossburn High School principal. But this kind of outspoken opposition was rare. There seemed to be a growing recognition that there might be things to learn on both sides of the Birdtail.

"Before, we were here, but it was like we were living on an island," said Marellia Cote, who grew up in Waywayseecappo and has taught at its school since 1997. "Now we are building bridges between the communities. We see each other more as people now."[7] For Chief Clearsky, this is a welcome development. "For so long our children never really mingled with off-reserve kids," he said. "I like seeing more of that. I don't want them to be assimilated, but in today's society we all have to get along." And Colleen Clearsky, who did so much to get the partnership under way, said it has resulted in a constant process of mutual learning. "They're teaching us and we're teaching them." She hoped that Waywayseecappo's students would learn to "walk in both worlds," as she put it. "I want them to be able to know where they come from, and to be comfortable in their own skin. And I want them to feel that way on the outside, off reserve, too."

The partnership also presented an opportunity for nearby provincial schools to adapt their practices to show a greater respect for Indigenous cultures—something the federal official J.R. Wright had advised, fruitlessly, half a century earlier, as had countless parents since. In 2017, Park West School Division advertised a position for an Indigenous coordinator to help infuse a

Native perspective into its schools. They hired a twenty-six-year-old by the name of Maureen Twovoice.

After high school, Maureen attended the University of Winnipeg, where she studied the history of Indigenous Peoples in Canada. There, for the first time, she read widely about Indian residential schools.

During one class, as she sat in the third row listening to a professor talk about intergenerational trauma, it finally struck her: *So this is why my family is the way it is.* Picturing her mom at the Brandon residential school made Maureen feel sick to her stomach. She thought of all the times she had gotten mad at her mom for drinking, all the times she wished her mom would just get over it. *Maybe,* Maureen now thought, *maybe it's not really the kind of thing people get over.* Maureen's hands grew sweaty. *Breathe,* she told herself. *Breathe.* She hoped her professor wouldn't ask her a question, because she was sure she would burst into tears before she could utter a single word. Her panic continued to rise, until she decided to escape from the classroom. In the hallway, she found a water fountain, drank deeply, and paced.

In a paper she went on to write about residential schools, Maureen explored the ways "intergenerational effects continue to control Indigenous people's daily lives" by looking at her own family. "Both my mother and father attended Indian Residential Schools," an experience that "has taken a toll on them both, especially in terms of parenting." Maureen wrote, "My mother also suffers from alcoholism. . . . When you look into her eyes you can almost feel the pain and adversity she has overcome in her life. She is willing to share with anyone who cares enough to ask."

Maureen described her father as "smart, humorous and generous," though he did suffer from alcoholism for a long period in his life. He had not shown up to her high school graduation ceremony, an absence that had wounded her. But, in time, she had learned to let it go. "My father was not present all the time throughout my life," she wrote. "I did not blame him after learning and understanding where he was coming from as an Indigenous man who had been a part of Canada's cultural genocide."

Maureen graduated in 2016 with a bachelor of arts in Indigenous studies and history, then enrolled in a master's degree in Indigenous governance. She began to research the way Indigenous leaders had understood Treaty 4 when they signed it. By this time, she had also fallen in love and, after four years together, Maureen and her partner decided they wanted to start a family. At the age of twenty-seven, Maureen gave birth to a girl, Teagan. She promised to try to be the kind of person for her daughter that she herself had needed as a child. "I wanted to break the cycle," she says.

When Maureen heard about the job opening for an Indigenous coordinator with Park West, she thought it might be a good fit. She had always hoped to return to Waywayseecappo in a role connected to education. This was her chance, and she seized it.

By the time she was hired, in 2017, the education partnership had been in place for seven years. Maureen was excited that Waywayseecappo students were finally getting the same resources as students in Rossburn. At the same time, it angered her to think of all the years they hadn't. She thought of her friends who didn't make it through high school. "Looking back," Maureen says, "I am upset for those who didn't make it. The government gave us the bare minimum. Did they not believe we could succeed? We all can."

As part of her job, Maureen organized workshops in provincial public schools about Indigenous history and culture. She also spent a lot of time with students from Waywayseecappo who were attending high school in Rossburn or Russell. Every now and then, a student would glance knowingly at the scars on her arms. "I've been there," Maureen would tell them. "I know how it feels. You can do this."

Maureen's work took her to every school in the division, but her office was in the Waywayseecappo school. Troy's office was two doors down.

17

"BURY THE HATCHET"

T HE BRANDON INDIAN RESIDENTIAL SCHOOL WAS demolished in 2000—forty-seven years after Jim Cote's escape, thirty-one years after Linda's discharge, seven years after Troy's trespass. A vacant lot now occupies the top of the hill from which the school used to loom. All that remains of the old building are a few half-buried bits of brick and concrete. On a warm summer day, the air smells of sage. Yellow butterflies abound, applauding with their wings. You might describe the place as serene if you didn't know its sordid history.

Troy Luhowy didn't know. Linda Jandrew can't forget.

In recent years, former students have held annual meetings at the old school site to share stories and try to come to terms with their experiences. Linda has never attended any of these gatherings. She wants nothing to do with the place.

As part of a 2006 legal settlement with the federal government, former residential school students received financial compensation for harms they suffered at these institutions. Those who had spent a year at a residential school were entitled to $10,000 in damages, plus $3,000 per additional year in attendance. Linda was among eighty thousand people who received this monetary payment—a crude and modest remedy for lasting wounds.

Students who were victims of serious physical or sexual abuse were also eligible for more financial compensation if they successfully presented their case to a special tribunal. Linda reluctantly joined thirty-eight thousand others who took this additional step. The first part of the process to quantify damages involved a chart that awarded "points" for various types of abuse, according to severity. Fondling or kissing by school staff was worth five to ten points, while "repeated, persistent incidents of anal or vaginal intercourse" or "penetration with an object" counted for between forty-five and sixty points. Adjudicators were required to "draw out the full story from witnesses . . . and test the evidence," including by cross-examination. Despite efforts to make the process less adversarial than a courtroom trial, historian J.R. Miller concludes that "for most survivors . . . the experience was trying, and for some traumatic."[1]

Linda's hearing was held on July 20, 2009, a few weeks after Maureen graduated from high school. During the questioning, she broke down in tears. "You did a good job by crying," Linda recalls her lawyer telling her afterwards, as if she had staged it. The adjudicator, Helen Semaganis, went on to approve Linda's claim. Semaganis wrote, "I found Linda Jandrew to be a truthful person. She did not exaggerate the details of her abuse." Semaganis added that it had been "an honour and privilege" to meet Linda, who had shown "courage" and "inner strength" during the proceedings.

Linda Jandrew (Courtesy of Maureen Twovoice)

Linda received a typed transcript of what was said during her hearing. During a spring cleaning a few years later, she threw the papers into the garbage, for the same reason Maureen had once burned her diaries. She didn't want the reminder. "But the memories," she says, "I can't get rid of them."

JIM COTE, HUGH McKay's son, is now one of Waywayseecappo's most respected Elders and refers to himself as "a young dinosaur." It has been more than six decades since he ran 120 kilometres from the Brandon residential school to his home in Waywayseecappo. He is a grandfather now, cherished for his wisdom and wit. Though he owns a truck, he jokes that he is still a "horse and buggy man." Like his father, Jim served many years as an elected representative on Waywayseecappo's band council.

Jim Cote (Courtesy of Jim Cote)

For decades after Jim's time at residential school, the mere sight of white people summoned images of his former torment-ors. "I would walk around Rossburn and see the faces of my old teachers who hit me for speaking my language or hugging my sister," Jim says. "It was something that was stuck in the back of my head. I had to fight it. As time went by, I tried to learn to black it out, to let it go."

These days, Jim is hopeful that relations between Waywayseecappo and Rossburn can improve. "We've never really had a buddy-buddy relationship," he says. "They used us—we spent our money there. But we always stayed in our own corners. I've always thought that wasn't right. If I was ever going to chair a meeting with people from Waywayseecappo and Rossburn, I would tell people to mingle." Jim still believes it is important and necessary for Waywayseecappo to have its own school, but he also tries to encourage young people on the reserve to be friendly when they're in town.

"When are we going to bury the hatchet?" Jim asks.[2] "And not in each other's backs."

ROSSBURN'S POPULATION HAS been declining since 1980. In April 1993, town residents chipped in $2,080 to buy full-page advertisements in Toronto newspapers that proclaimed "Lots for $1." A century had passed since Clifford Sifton lured faraway immigrants to the area with a promise of free land, and now Rossburn was desperately trying to recapture some of the old magic. A headline in the ad described Rossburn as a "GREAT PLACE TO LIVE!" Further exclamation marks followed in quick succession: "Clean air! Low crime rate! Wildlife!" For a time, at least, the gambit had the desired effect: the aggressive advertising and free lots attracted forty new residents within months. Yet it wasn't long before the town's population resumed its slow, inexorable decline.

In 2016, only 512 people lived in Rossburn, down 7 percent from five years before. In the same period, Waywayseecappo's population increased 12 percent, to 1,365.[3] The average age in Waywayseecappo today is twenty-six; in Rossburn, it is fifty. Rossburn's remaining businesses increasingly rely on customers from Waywayseecappo to survive, a fact that has shifted the perceived balance of power between the communities. "We need them," Nelson Luhowy says. "We'd be gone without them."

On July 10, 2018, after an incident at the laundromat in Rossburn, Jim Cote's niece, Gabrielle Cote, posted the following message on Facebook:

> Old bastards in Rossburn, telling my sister "Wayway should have their own laundromat" . . . your town would DIE without WAYWAY, this is OUR laundromat lol!!! We shop here, WE

have more people that spend here. THIS IS WAYWAY TOO 😊 😊 😊 *fuck sakes pissed off.*

Gabrielle's friends posted thirty-one comments, including:

"Shame on them!"

"Boycott 😊 *"*

"Just ignorance is all"

"Everyone keep your heads up we are strong"

"we're not like that, we're welcoming to any stranger that enters our area! . . . WELCOME TO WAYWAY!"

Now, as ever, both communities continue to debate the merits of separation and cooperation. Divisions, real and imagined, still run deep.

In October 2019, one year after Brian Brown lost his bid for a second term as Rossburn's mayor, he published a letter in a local newspaper. The letter was prompted by a story about an Indigenous hockey player who had been called racial epithets, and Brian seized the opportunity to unload his opinions about racism, reserves, reconciliation, and residential schools.

"The racism card seems to be getting played on a regular basis," he wrote. "It seems that it is not racism unless it is directed by a white person toward a non-white person." Brown recognized there were sexual crimes committed at Indian residential schools, but he saw the bulk of the other physical abuse as resembling the severe discipline all children of that era endured. Brian suggested that the history of residential schools was being used as an excuse for contemporary problems on reserves and that Indigenous leadership was too corrupt to make necessary reforms: "What are they doing to get their people off welfare, off booze and off drugs?" he wrote. "Obviously not very much when you look at the living conditions on most reserves." Brown concluded with his grim assessment of the future: "Unfortunately for the rest of the people in Canada, we have a prime minister who would rather reconcile (pay them what they want) than make an attempt to change the status quo."[4]

Brown's letter disheartened Waywayseecappo Chief Murray Clearsky, who responded by publishing a letter of his own the following week. "This opinion, written by the former mayor of Rossburn no less, contained nothing but racist stereotyping, false equivalence, ignorance and misinformation." Chief Clearsky expressed hope that Brown's letter did not reflect widely held views in Rossburn, but acknowledged that the relationship in Canada between Indigenous Peoples and non-Indigenous peoples remained broken. He rejected the comparison between what generations of Indigenous children endured in residential schools to standard, old-fashioned discipline, writing, "Genocide was in fact Canadian policy." In response to the trope of corrupt Indigenous politicians, Chief Clearsky noted that "First Nations governments are not any more corrupt than other levels of government, whose scandals also become public, but never a stereotype." (He might have invoked the staggering levels of corruption in Quebec uncovered by the 2011 Charbonneau Commission, but he tactfully declined to point fingers.)

In conclusion, Clearsky wrote: "We are not weak. We are not lawless. We will not apologize for struggling to overcome what has been done to us, and we certainly recognize that there are those among us who are struggling profoundly. What certainly doesn't help are non-Aboriginal Canadians airing their uninformed, racist beliefs and opinions about our lives and communities."[5]

Rossburn's elected leadership joined Chief Clearsky in repudiating Brown's comments, and the town councillors committed themselves "to move forward in partnership with [Indigenous Peoples] in a spirit of reconciliation and collaboration."[6]

WHEN NELSON LUHOWY began teaching adult ed in Waywayseecappo, in 2001, he thought it would be a temporary gig. He ended up staying for eighteen years. In that span, some seven hundred students passed through his classroom. About 160 received their high school diplomas. Even though most didn't complete the program, Nelson saw how hard they tried. "Lots of them were so dedicated. They wanted to better themselves, one way or another. That's the most important thing I saw," Nelson says. "And they treated me well."

Some of Nelson's favourite moments as a teacher involve students who were older than sixty-five. "They wanted to impress their grandkids, to show that education was important, that it can be done."

In Nelson's final two years teaching in Waywayseecappo, one of his students was Linda Shingoose, the mother of his former student Tizz. "Nelson seemed different from other people from Rossburn," Linda Shingoose says. "It was like he didn't think of me as Native— he thought of me as a person. And that's how he treated a lot of people I knew. If I had a problem, he would listen and not interrupt. He said I was pretty smart. I said, 'Me, smart?' 'Yes, you are,' he said. 'And you'll be graduating next year.' I didn't believe him, but he was right." Seventeen years after her daughter completed the same program, Linda Shingoose, at the age of sixty-six, received her diploma in June 2019, just as Nelson was retiring. The following year, Tizz's daughter, Tori—who was born while Tizz was pursuing her diploma with Nelson—also graduated from high school.

It has now been two decades since Tizz met Nelson. "He's white and I'm Native," she says. "Our reserve and Rossburn are usually racist against each other. But he didn't treat us like that. He had confidence we could complete Grade 12. He's the best instructor I ever had, a very awesome guy. I'm glad I had him and still have him in my life."

At Waywayseecappo's annual summer feast later that summer, Nelson was honoured for his many years of teaching. Chief Clearsky presented him with a locally quilted star blanket, a rare honour and a sign of both acceptance and respect.

Nelson receiving a star blanket, with Verna Wilson (*left*), Evelyn Seaton, and Chief Murray Clearsky (Courtesy of Troy Luhowy)

The ceremony prompted Nelson to reflect on what he had learned during his years teaching on the reserve. "My opinions changed," he says. "I learned to have more patience, more tolerance, more understanding." If Nelson could, he would try to talk to his younger self. "I'd try to change the old Nelson. I would try

275

to convince myself. I'd say, 'You know, give them a chance. Don't think they're all bad. They're as good as we are.'"

Nelson pauses, then adds: "Would I have listened? I don't think so. I was a racist. I likely still am."

AT THE WAYWAYSEECAPPO Community School, the day officially starts at 9:00 a.m., when a voice on the intercom announces, "Please stand for 'O Canada.'" By 9:03, the students have been reminded to *stannnnd on guarrrd* for their country.

The fall of 2019 marked Troy's tenth year as principal. On a wall in his office, he has pinned a printed message from one of his teachers: "Keep Calm and Let Troy Handle It." On the same wall there are pictures of his two kids, Addison and Reid, in full hockey gear, alongside another portrait of the whole family outfitted in Montreal Canadiens jerseys.

Troy and Michelle, with their children Reid and Addison
(Courtesy of Troy Luhowy)

It is still too soon to tell whether the partnership with Waywayseecappo will translate into higher graduation rates. Students who began kindergarten in 2010 with equal funding only recently entered high school in Rossburn. It will take even longer to determine the impact on outcomes such as employment, health, and well-being. Still, it is clear that, a decade in, things are headed in the right direction.

Yet Troy finds himself contending with expectations that by now Waywayseecappo's students should already be having the same outcomes as students from Rossburn. When the partnership was first announced, he recalls thinking: *They're finally on a level playing field.* He now recognizes it's not that simple.

Troy plans on sticking around for more of the journey. In 2018, there was a vacancy for the position of principal at Rossburn's elementary school. Once upon a time, it's a job he would have jumped at. But he didn't pursue it. "I didn't want to leave Wayway," Troy explains. "I like the programs we've got going on, and the partnership with the school division is going forward. And I like the kids the most. I didn't want to leave behind the relationships that I've built. I've been here long enough to see how lots of people would leave to go to another school. It wasn't fair to the kids or to the community." In 2019, there was another job opening in Rossburn, this time for principal at the high school. Troy didn't apply to that position, either.

That same year, Troy and Maureen attended an education conference together. One of the speakers talked about the legacy of residential schools, which prompted Troy to share with Maureen the story of how he and his friends had partied at the Brandon residential school on Halloween all those years ago, oblivious to all the suffering that had taken place there. "I didn't have a clue," Troy said. "Nobody told me and I never asked." As

Maureen listened, she found it hard not to get angry. Part of her was thinking, *How the fuck did you not know?* At the same time, she appreciated his honesty. "It takes a lot for someone to say he was wrong," Maureen says.

The two of them agreed that today's students needed to know better. "We need to make sure that the Rossburn kids know," Troy says. "That everybody knows. If we know what happened, maybe we'd understand a bit better what's going on now. Maybe we'd have more empathy. If kids learn about what happened, they won't be as fast or as harsh judging what's happening on the reserve two miles away."

IN JUNE 2019, Rossburn's elementary school invited Maureen to give a presentation about residential schools to a Grade 6 class. She knew this was where her mom had once endured incessant racist put-downs. Maureen hoped she could help improve the behaviour of the next generation.

During her talk, Maureen tried to convey the lasting consequences of residential schools by talking about the effects they'd had on her own family. She described how her parents were taken away from their families at a very young age, then asked the students to imagine what that might feel like. Maureen explained that even things that had happened a long time before she was born could still have a profound impact on her life. "Do your parents say that they love you?" Maureen asked the class. They nodded: *Of course.* "Well, my mom didn't say it to me out loud until I was in my early twenties."

After discussing how residential schools suppressed Native languages and culture, Maureen talked about her own journey as a mother, trying her best to pass along Ojibway traditions. She

278

described the ceremony where her daughter Teagan, then aged one, had received her name in Ojibway. Maureen wrote it out on the chalkboard—Zaagaate Giizis—and invited the students to say it out loud. It was the first time they had heard or spoken words in Ojibway.

Sarah Saley, the class's teacher, recalls that she didn't have to quiet her students once while Maureen was giving her presentation. "Maureen spoke in such a tactful, kid-friendly manner," Saley says. "The kids were attentive, really focused—much more than if I had tried to share the same information with them. There's still so much prejudice, so many stereotypes. There are these things about our neighbours we assume are true, but aren't near true. I'll be honest—I've heard some of my students say these things. Some of my colleagues say things that are just awful. Being able to see Maureen come in and talk about these things so openly, so candidly, it for sure gave the students a lot of information. I don't know if they'll be disagreeing with their parents—I hope so—but at least they'll have a different perspective, a more open-minded perspective."

18

"A GRAND NOTION"

THE TROUBLED RELATIONSHIP BETWEEN INDIGENOUS
Peoples and non-Indigenous Canadians sometimes snaps
into focus: a young Indigenous woman who is supposed
to be in protective care is abandoned in a motel and then found
dead after being raped and thrown from a bridge;[1] a carload of
Indigenous teens seeks help with a flat tire at a farmhouse and one
of them is shot dead by a farmer who assumes they have come
to rob him;[2] hospital workers taunt an Indigenous woman as she
draws her final breath;[3] a patch of overgrown scrub yields up the
bodies of hundreds of Indian children, long buried in unmarked
graves—the horror of which had been whispered for decades.[4]
But it is never long before the news cycle turns and saves us the
trouble of having to look away. Outrage blurs once more into
indifference.

It seems as though nothing has changed, and nothing ever
will. First Nations remain poor, the Indian Act is still valid legislation, and violence stains the Indigenous landscape.

The reserve system has made interactions between Indigenous and non-Indigenous settler people less frequent than they otherwise might be. Poverty goes unseen, violence happens elsewhere, and inequality is a lot easier to stomach when you're not the one losing out. We just don't regard each other as neighbours.

But we *are* neighbours, just as Rossburn and Waywayseecappo have been for more than a century. Yet these two communities show the remarkable extent to which neighbours can remain strangers. Only recently, after all those years sharing the valley of the Birdtail, have they started to see each other differently and cooperate more. The change is limited. But it's a start.

Perhaps the most basic challenge is that Indigenous and non-Indigenous Canadians talk past each other. When we think about our history, Indigenous and settler narratives rarely intersect. The bigger picture, that we are all bound together, entangled in unexpected and uncomfortable ways, is too often obscured.

How many people in Rossburn have heard about the permits that for so long hamstrung Waywayseecappo's farmers? Not many, and perhaps as few as the number of people in Waywayseecappo who are familiar with the bigotry Ukrainians endured for multiple generations. It wasn't until Maureen was attending university that she first heard about the internment of Ukrainian Canadians during the First World War. It reminded her of the pass system that had confined Indians to reserves, and it got her thinking about other parallels she had never really considered. "Rossburn had its own history," Maureen says, "but I had never bothered to look into it."

Clifford Sifton once said that "the history of Canada is one of absorbing and romantic interest." By teaching Canadian history to Canada's students, he hoped the country would develop a sense of "national unity—a Canadian soul and Canadian outlook from coast to coast." He hoped that students would be taught about the contributions immigrants made to the prairies: "The epic story of Canadian pioneering, with the high courage of those whose faith moved mountains, properly told, will thrill our children."[5] And so it did—millions of Canadians such as Nelson Luhowy grew up within the soothing confines of this heroic narrative. But so long as we allow ourselves to be trapped inside narrow stories about the past, reconciliation can never truly begin. Here in the present, the relationship between Indigenous and non-Indigenous Canadians remains broken. The underfunding of reserve schools is merely one symptom of a much deeper sickness: profound inequalities in education, health, and wealth outcomes.

Listening to each other's stories is one way to stitch Canada back together. Reconciliation will require us, at the very least, to acknowledge each other's dignity.

Indigenous Peoples know that there's more to listening than letting a message wash over you. Listening activates our hearts, which allows us not simply to listen to one another but to really hear what is being said. There is a Haudenosaunee ceremony that is a prelude to any meeting between themselves and another Nation: participants begin with an act of compassion—wiping away each other's tears. The ceremony, sometimes called the Three Bare Words, both acknowledges a participant's humanity and underscores a key concept of Haudenosaunee philosophy: we all need help sometimes.

Of course, listening more is one thing, but acting differently— as individuals, as a country—is another. In recent years, Rossburn and Waywayseecappo have provided an example of what meaningful cooperation between Indigenous and non-Indigenous people can look like. Forced to see that each community needs the other, Rossburn and Waywayseecappo were able to imagine a shared future. There are lessons to be learned from their example, or, as might be said in Waywayseecappo, teachings to be heard.

THE INEQUALITY BETWEEN settler and Indigenous communities has been present since Confederation. What is true about on-reserve education is also true of other basic services, like access to health care and child welfare resources: far worse services on reserves are the norm. It is as though Canadians accept this inequality and go to bed each night untroubled by the lack of basic infrastructure in reserve communities. For now, equal outcomes remain beyond reach.

And yet Canadians view themselves as deeply committed to equality. The Constitution and provincial human rights codes enshrine equality rights. But what does it mean for an education system to treat children equally? The answer is more complicated than at first it may seem.

One way to think about the education partnership that began in 2010 is simply as an equalization of resources. With equal funding, the educational outcomes of children living on the reserve quickly improved. And so one might argue that increased spending in other Indigenous communities could work the same magic. To give credit where credit is due, since 2015, the Liberal government of Justin Trudeau has substantially increased spending on Indigenous children. "It is simply not right that young people in Indigenous communities don't have the same dollars spent on education that young people in provincial schools do," Trudeau has said.[6] The year 2021 marked the first time the federal government was providing students on reserves funding roughly comparable to that of students in provincially funded schools.[7]

But although this recent increase in federal investment will surely make a positive difference, there is no talk of making up for all the years of comparative underfunding.

We might use, as a basis for judging equality, the measuring stick of resources. Dollar for dollar, each child should receive the same spending on programs and services. But equal distribution of resources alone cannot address the structural inequalities between First Nations and settler communities. First Nations communities are often small and remote. So a small reserve school could receive, per student, the same funding as a provincial school in a larger school district, but would not have the benefit of increased efficiencies that come with a larger population. That is why, after Waywayseecappo's partnership with the nearby provincial schools, children on the reserve suddenly had access to a speech therapist. For a single school this was an unaffordable luxury, but shared between the fifteen schools in the district, a speech therapist was perfectly affordable.

Another method of measuring equality is to focus our concern not on equality of resources but on equality of outcomes. With respect to school funding, what would matter is not how much money is spent per child but, rather, whether enough money is spent so that children are achieving at roughly the same levels regardless of whether they live on or off reserve. Equality of outcomes allows us to focus on an endpoint of equality, and equality of this sort just costs what it costs.

But this outcomes-focused approach to equality also has shortcomings. We can identify a desired outcome as a marker of equality—for example, scores on standardized tests—but that outcome may not be the priority for First Nations communities.[8] Indigenous Peoples want quality education for their children, just as any parents do. But, also like other parents, Indigenous parents want a say in the contents of that education. They want schools that prepare children for success in the world while also nurturing ties to Indigenous knowledge and ways of being. To give merely the most obvious examples, communities might want to focus more heavily on teaching an Indigenous language or incorporating land-based learning.[9] Equality of outcomes only makes sense if we all value the same outcomes. This simply isn't the case when it comes to bringing standard Canadian education into Indigenous communities.

Back in 1996, the Royal Commission on Aboriginal Peoples described Canada as a "test case for a grand notion—the notion that dissimilar peoples can share lands, resources, power and dreams while respecting and sustaining their differences. The story of Canada is the story of many such peoples, trying and failing and trying again, to live together in peace and harmony."[10]

We are still failing. It is time to try a fundamentally different approach.

THE PRESENT-DAY INEQUALITIES between Indigenous and settler peoples are the inevitable result of governments of all stripes ignoring with impunity the needs of Indigenous Peoples: this is the root of the problem, and this is what must be addressed.

Indigenous Canadians are poorer, get imprisoned more often, attain lower levels of formal education, and have worse health outcomes than their settler neighbours. Hardship and unequal treatment have become endemic and routine. Poking away with new programs here and there and hoping for a brighter future will not meaningfully alter the economic and social outcomes of Indigenous Canadians.

To undertake fundamental change, we need to rethink our approach to two key mechanisms of government. The first is law-making: Who gets to make what kinds of law, and where? The second is financing: Where does the money come from to pay for roads and judges and schools and nurses?

With regard to jurisdiction, our Constitution gives the federal government exclusive authority over issues of national concern (such as banking, national defence, and "Indians, and lands reserved for the Indians"), while the provinces and territories have jurisdiction over issues of more local concern (such as property and civil rights). This is called the division of powers, and it is an arrangement from which First Nations communities are entirely excluded. First Nations governments have only limited decision-making authorities, as set out in the Indian Act, federal legislation that has dictated the nature of Indigenous government, its participants, and capacities for more than 150 years.[11] Band councils such as Waywayseecappo's have authority over such narrow matters as beekeeping and the regulation of trespassers, while other, more meaningful powers (policing, social welfare programs, game and wildlife, mining, forestry, and courts) are held by the provinces. But even if First Nations governments had legal authority to do more, it costs money to pay police, teachers, and nurses, just as it costs money to finance and regulate mining, forestry, and other industries.

Governments tax people and things to raise money, but First Nations have been left as bit players in this regard, with nearly all the powers of taxation taken up by the federal, provincial, and, to a lesser degree, municipal governments. First Nations can charge sales and property tax on their reserves, but reserve economies are so small that there is little revenue to be realized through these avenues.[12]

Because of the widespread myth that Indigenous Peoples in Canada pay no taxes, non-Indians believe that they are the ones holding the bag and subsidizing Indigenous communities. In fact, exactly the opposite is true. To explain how, we need to understand how taxation works, and why taxation has the potential to make Indigenous communities places where hope wins out over despair.

Taxation is the lifeblood of governance. Without tax revenue, there are no schools or any other kind of civic infrastructure. Without the capacity to raise funds, Indigenous communities cannot set and pursue ends of their own. Instead, the money for nearly every expense of an Indian band comes from another government, principally the federal government.[13] To state the obvious, the federal government could underfund on-reserve education only because it controlled the funding.

In an Indigenous community such as Waywayseecappo, there is a rapidly growing population and an extremely limited tax base, where virtually all incoming resources are transferred from the federal government. A community such as this has to make hard choices about what to do with that money: build a community centre or provide home care to elderly residents; fund primary education or repair roads; build additional housing or purchase a fire engine. Of course, all governments have to make similar choices, but non-Indian governments have the ability to raise or introduce taxes, a choice largely denied to First Nations communities. Rather than think about where to increase spending, Indigenous communities are usually only left with choices about what to cut.

★ ★ ★

GIVING FIRST NATION communities the power to tax an adequate land base would be a first step to empowering effective local government. To show what this might look like, we can look at a group of forty-three communities in northern Ontario that are far more remote than Waywayseecappo. Except during the coldest days of winter, when it is possible to construct ice roads, half of these communities are accessible only by air. There are very few signs of federal or provincial Crown presence: no government offices, no hospitals, no high schools, no courthouse. It is hard to understand why federal and provincial lawmakers should govern over places so removed from federal and provincial government services and legislatures.

If we were to take seriously the idea that these forty-three First Nations should be able to govern themselves, what would that mean? What sorts of resources and governmental powers would they need?

To start with, they would have to exercise jurisdiction over a much larger area of the province than the land that makes up reserves—the reserves are tiny compared with the vast expanse of government-owned Crown land in the north.[14] First Nations would need this enlarged territory in order to have sufficient land from which to extract resources for sale or on which to tax the extraction of those resources by others. With jurisdiction over this larger territory, these communities would have the financial resources to do the sorts of things that other local governments are expected to do: operate schools and a justice system, provide clean running water, fix roads, staff a fire department, and provide health services.

The lands of the north are rich. In recent years, the government of Ontario collected about $100 million annually in revenue from Crown timber fees from forestry activities, largely located in the northern parts of the province.[15] Those lands are the Traditional Territories of Cree and Ojibway people and for thousands of years provided Indigenous Peoples the means to live a good life—and they should do so again.

Were we to give Indigenous communities in northern Ontario the ability to govern themselves in this way, we could eliminate dependence on federal money. Some might argue that it is unfair to place Indigenous communities in the position of having to extract natural resources or to tax the extraction of natural resources from their Traditional Territories. But this is just what governments do: tax activities (such as forestry and mining) and people (via sales or income tax), and then spend that money on citizens, community infrastructure (schools, police, hospitals), and connections to other communities (highways, rail corridors). Indigenous governments should be no different, and they should be the ones making the difficult choices about what taxes to collect and which resources to extract.

So now we imagine forty-three First Nations communities in northern Ontario having jurisdiction over their Traditional Territories. It is probably not within the capacity of a small population to govern over such vast territories. Instead, small First Nations communities would need to work together in some form of confederacy to create viable governments capable of making complex land use and spending decisions.[16] The money raised from taxation could then be spent on building adequate schools and housing, paying teachers' salaries, and initiating environmental remediation in lakes and streams. Perhaps most important, Indigenous governments would surely prioritize what the federal government has long neglected: the well-being of Indigenous children.

But solutions to big problems are never cost-free. In the scenario we set out, the Province of Ontario would have a hole in its budget more or less exactly the same size as the revenue generated by Indigenous taxation of northern Ontario. And this provincial revenue loss would not be a minor concern. Across Canada, the vast majority of Crown lands are held provincially, not federally.[17] This means that any effort to redistribute territorial jurisdiction between provinces and First Nations will require not merely provincial cooperation but a willingness to give up territory to Indigenous governments. In other words, to the extent that the territorial jurisdiction of First Nations is enlarged, jurisdiction over provincial land is necessarily diminished.[18] Provincial coffers, likewise, will experience a considerable diminishment of revenues, because a great deal of provincial revenue is raised from taxing resource industries in the north.

We must come to accept that reconciliation between Indigenous and settler peoples will require a redistribution of access to wealth and to the mechanisms of governance. But the provinces will obviously be concerned about a plan requiring them to relinquish their most resource-rich areas. Provincial leadership, and Canadians in general, may be interested in reconciliation, but not at the cost of billions of dollars in annual tax revenue. And yet, to flourish, Indigenous Peoples will need to raise revenues through taxation, and so will require territory of sufficient size and wealth to invest in their communities. And that land will have to come from somewhere. The transfer of jurisdiction from provinces to First Nations may be seen—particularly by Indigenous Peoples themselves—as the righting of a historic wrong. Yet, at the same time, there is likely a large non-Indigenous southern population who would see the present-day transfer of land to First Nations as unfair.[19]

To reconcile these views, we must face a simple truth: the problem is distribution. Readjusting the borders of Indigenous territories means readjusting the borders of what would other-wise be provincial lands. And because the lands of northern Canada are rich in resources, redistribution of those territories is also a massive redistribution of wealth. So it seems that we are at a logjam: First Nations communities need land over which to govern, and the provinces require that same land in order to tax resource extraction.

To find a way through this conundrum, we need to see that the distribution problem we face is not of lands but of resources and wealth. Would residents of Toronto or Vancouver care who governed over their provinces' northern territories if it meant no material change to government services or the rate of taxa-tion?[20] We think not. So, the question isn't who governs, but who benefits.

CANADA'S WEALTH IS not distributed equally among its prov-inces and territories; it varies based on factors such as population density and natural resources, and it fluctuates over time—with the collapse of a fishery, say, or a spike in oil prices.

Nevertheless, a key feature of Canadian federalism is the principle that every citizen, no matter where they live, should receive a similar level of government services. And, except on Indian reserves, Canada largely delivers on this commitment. The guarantee of equal government services at the provincial level is made possible through an economic program called equalization—which, for all its controversies, has enjoyed long-standing and widespread support among Canadians.[21] Through the equalization formula, regional disparities are smoothed out by a federally administered program that allocates federal rev-enue to provincial coffers. Redistribution levels the playing field among provinces. Whether you live in Newfoundland, Manitoba, or Quebec, equalization ensures that you receive comparable quality schooling and medical care. (In 2019–20, for example, Manitoba received an infusion of $2.25 billion.) Without equalization, smaller provinces such as Prince Edward Island simply could not generate enough tax revenue to provide similar services to those living in oil-rich Alberta. Yet no one ever asks whether Prince Edward Island deserves decent schools. It is a given. Prince Edward Island's citizens have decent elementary schools and clean running water, even if this requires redistribution of wealth. Equalization is how Canada balances our provincial and regional inequalities. Yet Indigenous communities neither contribute to nor benefit from equalization. First Nations do not share any part in the redistribution of national wealth. But imagine if this basic principle of equality were extended to Indigenous Peoples and communities.

Under the proposal we offer here, First Nations communities of northern Ontario might collect $1 billion in revenue from taxing resource extraction, the same $1 billion that once financed health care, policing, and education in Toronto, Windsor, and the like. The First Nations in northern Ontario could spend the tax money on community infrastructure to provide decent services for their citizens, and this would very likely cost considerably less than $1 billion annually. And we can then imagine the remaining funds being deposited into the equalization formula for redistribution to Ontario, thus somewhat ameliorating the budget shortfall that would otherwise occur.

In this way, First Nations communities would govern territories and tax resource extraction so as to make finally and abundantly clear that citizens in southern Canada are, and have been, subsidized by the north for at least 150 years. Under our proposal,

First Nations governments would be signing the cheques that underwrite their southern neighbours.

IN MANY REGIONS of the Canadian north, Indigenous Peoples are virtually the only human inhabitants, and always have been. In these areas in particular, it makes sense to think about recognizing a robust third order of government: Indigenous, in addition to federal and provincial. An Indigenous order of government would provide a way for Indigenous Peoples to finally be brought into the Canadian confederation as partners, not subjects. Communities such as these would also be better placed to consider the environmental effects of resource industries. After all, Indigenous Peoples have lived in these territories for thousands of years, and they intend to remain there for thousands more. This means it will be Indigenous Peoples, exercising jurisdiction over their territories, who will keep safe the watersheds and forests that provide southern Canadians with clean water to drink and fresh air to breathe.

Band councils like Waywayseecappo's are ostensibly governments in that they have some governmental powers, but in the absence of a meaningful capacity to tax resources and people, these band councils do not really govern—they merely spend money transferred to them by the federal and provincial governments. Indigenous governance of much larger Traditional Territories is an altogether different proposition, and should become a familiar feature of our political landscape. Crucially, because these communities would be self-governing, and self-financing, they would be immune from the financial vagaries of a federal government that has often not felt the need to treat all its citizens equally.

First Nations communities and Indian reserves are not all located in the north. Many bump right up against cities and towns like Rossburn and Vancouver. In these situations, we would need to consider the manner in which municipalities in the south raise tax revenues. In cities such as Toronto, the primary forms of government revenue are property and land-transfer taxes. To the extent that southern reserve communities were provided expanded territorial jurisdiction under our proposal, these communities would need to draw on the same resources as southern municipalities—namely, property taxes. This in turn means that some residents of southern Ontario might find themselves no longer living within settler-run municipalities but would instead be residents of a First Nations–led municipality. This would not, to be clear, affect who owns what land. Private landowners would simply find themselves paying taxes to a different order of government: an Indigenous municipal government instead of a settler municipal government.

Consider a 2020 U.S. Supreme Court case about an Indian reservation created by a nineteenth-century treaty between the Creek tribe of Indians and the U.S. government. The reservation had been in what was then Indian country, but as soon as oil was discovered, the newly formed state of Oklahoma assumed control of the territory. Oklahomans and the U.S. government acted as though the declaration of statehood was a sufficient legal act to extinguish the Creek Indian reservation. At issue was the question of whether the state diminishment of the Creek Indian reservation was legal. The majority judgment was written by Neil Gorsuch, a conservative judge appointed by Donald Trump:

How much easier it would be, after all, to let the State proceed as it has always assumed it might. But just imagine what it would

mean to indulge that path. A State exercises jurisdiction over
Native Americans with such persistence that the practice seems
normal. Indian landowners lose their titles by fraud or otherwise
in sufficient volume that no one remembers whose land it once
was. All this continues for long enough that a reservation that
was once beyond doubt becomes questionable, and then even far
fetched. Sprinkle in a few predictions here, some contestable com-
mentary there, and the job is done, a reservation is disestablished.
None of these moves would be permitted in any other area of
statutory interpretation, and there is no reason why they should
be permitted here. That would be the rule of the strong, not the
rule of law.[22]

As a result of the McGirt decision, about half of Oklahoma,
including much of the city of Tulsa, is for some purposes once
again recognized as an Indian reservation. Gorsuch noted that
"many of [Oklahoma's] residents will be surprised to find out
they have been living in Indian country this whole time." The
U.S. Supreme Court is untroubled by the result (even if some
Oklahomans are indeed rattled) because the court can clearly
see that no transfer of property is taking place—borders have
changed, but nobody's land was taken.[23]

What happened in Oklahoma could happen in Canada.
Jurisdictions shift, politics adapt, and new relationships become
possible.

FOR MORE THAN 150 years, we have attempted to find a way to live
side by side as Indigenous and settler people, just as the citizens
of Waywayseecappo and Rossburn have lived side by side. What
has made all the difference to Rossburn and Waywayseecappo

has been the realization that they are better off working together rather than against each other. It is important to note that neither the citizens of Rossburn nor the citizens of Waywayseecappo agreed to the partnership out of generosity. Instead, each community understood the arrangement in terms of its own self-interest. And it is in our larger self-interest as Canadians to recognize that the relationship between Waywayseecappo and Rossburn is no different from the broader relationship between Indigenous and settler people. Keeping Indigenous Peoples poor is an expensive proposition for everyone else as well.

Consider the case of education. An estimated 70 percent of new jobs require some amount of post-secondary education, so an Indigenous person without a high school diploma is twice as likely to be unemployed. Lower rates of formal education are also linked to worse health outcomes and higher rates of incarceration. Beyond the direct toll on Indigenous Peoples themselves, the resulting costs to taxpayers are immense, including hundreds of millions in additional dollars spent on income support, health services, and prisons. In Manitoba, for example, 75 percent of persons admitted into custody are Indigenous, even though Indigenous Peoples account for only 15 percent of the province's population.[24] Keeping a single inmate in federal prison costs $125,000 each year. Compared to the alternatives, investing more in education for Indigenous Peoples is a bargain. And yet we haven't, opting instead for an approach that is both cruel and self-defeating.

What's more, because Indians raised on reserves receive cheap, subpar education, they usually don't go on to fill high-paying jobs, and so don't pay as much into the income tax system. Collectively, we also lose out on so much of the talent that they have to offer. It is expensive to keep Indians poor, and we would all benefit from *full access* to the economy, access which comes only with *full access* to education, health care, and clean running water.

Since the release, in 2015, of the Truth and Reconciliation Commission's report on the Indian residential school system, there have been attempts by churches, unions, school boards, and governments to respond meaningfully to calls for reconciliation. Some of the resulting changes, such as the now widespread invocation of the land acknowledgement at public events, will take a generation to bear fruit, as our children grow up in a world where they understand that we all live on Traditional Indigenous Territories and not merely land homesteaded by settlers. In the meantime, while we may acknowledge Traditional Territories, we do nothing to return their governance to Indigenous Nations.

Many Canadians fear or do not believe in the viability of an Indigenous order of government. But the proposals we are making here are based on principles our country knows and has long used: extending policies like the equalization formula to Indigenous communities is just to invite First Nations into Confederation on familiar terms. Reconciliation will require not only a common understanding of the jagged contours of our shared history, but also enacting a fair distribution of resources and the authority to make decisions about land use. To redraw jurisdictional borders and redistribute governmental powers of taxation is to recognize the dignity and equality of Indigenous Peoples.

All across this great land, Indigenous Peoples entered into treaties with the government of Canada. They understood these agreements as sacred: the land was sacred and so were the agreements for its sharing. More and more Canadians are beginning to understand that we are all treaty people. Indigenous Peoples and settlers alike are party to the treaties, and the treaties are not just historical documents—they set out a plan for sharing territory and providing the legal authority to do so. When entering into these agreements, Indigenous Peoples understood the Canadian government's promises to be honourable, good-faith efforts. For nearly three centuries before Confederation, in 1867, Indigenous Peoples worked alongside the British and French as military allies, trading partners, and family members.[25] But, after Confederation, the young Dominion government of Canada turned its back on the very idea that treaties should be honoured and that the land could be shared. First Nations were moved onto tiny reserves and governed as wards of the state. Indeed, settler Canadians have been the only beneficiaries of historic treaties with First Nations.

Pushed aside and given few resources, Indigenous Peoples have suffered an inequality that is more like abject poverty. Without the capacity to raise meaningful resources through taxation, First Nations have been left to eat from the hand of the federal Crown. It is easy to think that we might address these inequalities through increased funding for basic services in Indigenous communities, but that increased funding has rarely arrived, and Canada continues to under-service Indigenous communities.

IN 2000, AN outbreak of *E. coli* bacteria contaminated the water supply of Walkerton, Ontario. Six people died and more than two thousand people were infected. Almost immediately, a boil-water advisory was issued, and the town of Walkerton no longer had access to clean running water. Police began an investigation. Needless to say, once identified, the source of contamination was addressed and the taps were turned back on within days. A public inquiry was called, criminal charges were laid, elected officials were held to account.

In contrast, more than thirty First Nations communities have been living under boil-water advisories for more than a decade.[26] There has been no public inquiry, no one is held accountable, and day after day, year after year, the taps spill out contaminated water, undrinkable and unusable for laundry or bathing yourself or your newborn.

A feature of the pervasive racism toward First Nations people is the ability to so undervalue Indigenous lives that settler citizens sleep comfortably at night, safe in the knowledge that their water is clean and not caring, or even knowing, that First Nations communities have no such luxury. First Nations citizens are too few in number to effectively hold public officials accountable at the ballot box, and so beyond the obvious immorality of the situation, public officials have little incentive to act, and, for the most part, they have not. We are left with an uncomfortable truth: the inequality between settler and Indigenous Canadians results from politics, and, so far, not enough Canadians have been motivated to upend an unfair and unequal system.

In Waywayseecappo, as across Canada, Indians are short-changed, neglected, and impoverished. Even if Canadian citizens and politicians were to muster the political will to fund services in First Nations and settler communities equally, how long would it be before the inequalities began to creep back in, as governments struggled to determine how best to spend limited resources? If 150 years of history is anything to go by, it would be only a matter of time until we reverted to the discriminatory norm.

The Canadian commitment to equality was set out in the 1982 Charter of Rights and Freedoms. Section 15 states, "Every individual is equal before and under the law and has the right to equal protection and equal benefit of the law . . . without discrimination based on race, national or ethnic origin, colour, religion, sex, age or mental or physical disability." And yet, as we have seen, Indigenous Canadians have markedly unequal access to government services of all kinds. We do not think that it is too much to insist on changes that ensure Indigenous Peoples have access to services that are on par with what provinces provide to every other Canadian. The best way to do this is to give Indigenous Peoples the necessary power to ensure a fairer distribution of lands and resources.

The proposals we are making here may seem ambitious, extraordinary even, but Canadians have done this before. Modern-day land claim agreements—treaties—in the Yukon and in the James Bay region of Quebec provide extensive self-government arrangements.[27] There, and in other regions subject to modern-day treaties, First Nations governments exercise jurisdiction over broad territories and many areas of governance. These are no longer experiments: Indigenous-governed territories are now woven into the fabric of Canada. In other words, the future we propose is already a part of our present-day Canadian identity. The only difference is this: modern-day treaties are mostly in British Columbia and Yukon, where no treaties were previously signed. What we are proposing is to implement these same sort of arrangements—modern-day treaties—where it makes sense to do so, including in places like Manitoba where historical treaties negotiated by Alexander Morris have proved inadequate.

And we need look no further than Quebec to see that religious, linguistic, and even legal accommodation is possible. Provincial law in Quebec is governed by a civil code, a set of laws found nowhere else in Canada. Part of what makes Canada great has been our accommodation of difference. To form a country with two official languages, two official sets of laws, and two distinct peoples, was, in 1867, the product of profound imagination.

But just as Canada found a way to accommodate two founding European peoples, now we must find a way to afford Indigenous Peoples in Canada the equality and dignity they deserve.

To see First Nations governance as an integral part of our Canadian culture is not to stretch the imagination—it is to stretch our arms, and embrace each other as equal partners in a vast and complicated land. There is enough to share. Land, resources, wealth: there *is* enough for everyone, and there always has been.

"SHINING SUN"

AUGUST 2019

Traditional songs and dances continue to occupy a special place in the hearts of many Ukrainian Canadians, including Nelson Luhowy's. That is why, during the first weekend of August, Nelson makes the seventy-minute drive from Rossburn to Dauphin for the National Ukrainian Festival. The event is Nelson's best opportunity each year to hear the beats and lyrics of his boyhood. "I like hearing the songs in Ukrainian," he says, "even though I don't really understand them. They just sound good."

The festival draws five thousand attendees and lasts all weekend, featuring buffets of Ukrainian cuisine, booths with traditional arts and crafts, shirtless and sun-burned men dancing while holding overflowing glasses of beer, and—of course—a perogy-eating contest. This year, the champion manages to hoover down a plate of twenty-four perogies within ninety-four seconds.

At night, Nelson stays with his brother Don in a mobile home parked in a sprawling campground infused at dinnertime with the aroma of sausage. During the day, Nelson explores the festival grounds on an electric scooter, his crutches jutting out the rear. At any given moment, there are two or three live performances taking place, some of them given by musicians who flew all the way from the old country. Nelson has plenty of time to watch a whole slew of traditional dances: the *hutzul*, the *poltava*, the *transcarpathian*, the *volyn*. On this weekend at least, the fiddle is king.

This year, Troy, Michelle, and their kids, Reid and Addison, didn't make the drive to the festival. The kids never expended much effort learning Ukrainian folk dances, unlike some of their cousins. "Learning the dances takes a lot of time," Nelson says. "But so does hockey." By August, Reid and Addison have already started their training camps for the upcoming hockey season, and they're just fine with eating perogies at home.

ON THE SAME weekend as the Ukrainian Festival, Waywayseecappo hosts a powwow. More than 350 dancers from across the Canadian prairies and the United States converge for the event. Hundreds more spectators pack the wooden stands. Among them are Linda, Maureen, and Teagan, seated a few rows back from a drum circle.

Teagan does not flinch, even though the drums are so loud her chest vibrates with a second heartbeat. This is her third time at the annual event, and she is not yet three years old. She is mesmerized by the dance circle, a shimmering swirl of movement and colour. The dancers orbit a central wooden pole, moving clockwise on a ring of grass. It is as if buckets of bright paint were being poured into a whirlpool, creating a churn of yellow and green, blue and red, purple and pink. Each dancer wears a distinctive combination of feathers, regalia, and animal skins—the sight would surely make Hayter Reed roll in his grave.

Teagan's own regalia is the work of many hands. Her father's aunt stitched her dress (mostly pink and floral), Maureen sewed beads into the belt (in the shape of yet more flowers), and Maureen's friend Grace made the moccasins (with red and pink beadwork). Like many of the women and girls in attendance, Teagan is wearing a "jingle dress" adorned with dozens of tiny bells that ring out whenever she moves. The dress is associated with a healing dance meant to repair wounds in a community.

Eighteen drumming groups take turns singing and setting the pace for the dancers. In between songs, a loquacious MC keeps up a steady stream of banter and uplift: "Through all the trials and tribulations, ladies and gentlemen, we're still here, we've always been here." More than a century has passed since Waywayseecappo's drums terrified residents in Rossburn. Two-year-old Teagan knows there's nothing to be frightened of, except maybe that man draped in a bear's skin.

The whole spectacle is enough to make Maureen tear up. Someone once told her that when she feels like crying while watching the powwow, that's her ancestors reaching out to her. Maureen likes to think of her ancestors continuing to dance through all those years when the government was trying to stop them.

Over the loudspeaker, the MC announces the Initiation Dance for first-timers: "New dancers, welcome to the dance circle. We're welcoming you to our big family circle. Welcome to the powwow family, for the rest of your lives. Parents, thank you for teaching the young ones." Teagan sits this one out because she was initiated last year, shortly after she started walking. Maureen had held her hand as she completed her first lap around the circle and received blessings from the community.

This year, Teagan's time to shine is the "Tiny Tots" dance. On cue, she joins dozens of toddlers in the dance circle, and the drumming begins anew. Teagan knows what to do: she puts her hands on her hips, grins widely, and starts bouncing. Around her, there is a range of skill. For the smallest dancers, it is an achievement to simply stay on their feet. Teagan clearly feels the music, though her little body can't quite keep up with the rhythm. As she gets older, she will add other elements, like waving a handkerchief or feather fan. For now, she knows the main thing is to keep her hands firmly on her hips while she twirls.

Watching Teagan dance makes Maureen feel like a good mom. "Traditional dancing was something I didn't know much about while I was growing up," she says. "As Teagan learns more, she'll be able to teach me, too."

Teagan will soon start attending kindergarten at Waywayseecappo Community School. Because of all the positive changes in recent years, Maureen is comfortable with this. "I want her school to be up to par, for her not to go through what I went through," she says. "I hope for her not to be behind. I hope that wherever she goes to school, in a city or on a reserve, that she receives a fair education."

The drums are still beating, the chants continue, the song goes on. Maureen leans forward, scanning the circle of diminutive dancers to locate her daughter. There is Teagan, still twirling in her jingle dress. Maureen's face softens, then brightens with a smile.

Zaagaate Giizis, Teagan's name in Ojibway, means "Shining Sun."

AFTERWORD

BY MAUREEN TWOVOICE, BINESI IKWE (THUNDERBIRD WOMAN)

O N July 1, 2021—Canada Day—I woke five minutes before my alarm clock that I set for 5:30 a.m. I
put on my skirt, found my orange T-shirt that reads
"Every Child Matters," and packed my snacks and *nibi*. Before I
left I captured a mental photo of my sleeping husband and our
nidaanisag in our bed, then grabbed my decaf coffee and walked
out the door.

I drove through the valley, heading south along Highway 45.
I enjoy rides through the reserve. Appreciating the landscape,
mishoomis giizis, *mitigoog*, and the silence of *aki*. Imagining what
the community looked like when the gravel roads were dirt
wagon trails, when there was more bush. How beautiful *giizis*
looks when it peeks through *mitigoog*.

I arrived at my friend Marisa's kokom's home, our meeting
place before we started our day further southwest. Marisa has
been my friend since I was eleven years old, when I forged my
mother's signature to attend a week-long cultural camp located in

the valley that divides Wewezhigaabawing and Rossburn. Marisa was there and showed me kindness. We set up camp, working together to create a shelter in case it rained, making our beds, rummaging through our cooler full of food. I was gone for a week, and I felt safe.

Now we continued on the back roads until we reached the Birtle Indian Residential School. Waiting was the pipe carrier, eagle staff, and a gathering of people from First Nations across Manitoba. Ceremony began on the front lawn of the school. As I sat on the ground with my skirt and legs to one side, I looked up at the building: there was the front door, a few shorts steps from the driveway. All I could think was, *My grandparents were dropped off at schools like this, taken from my great-grandparents by law and left alone with hundreds of other children.* My heart started to hurt and my eyes filled with tears. I took a deep breath. This is where intergenerational trauma started for my family. Or maybe it was another generation before my grandparents, but that's a history search for another time.

After the pipe ceremony came the walk from the Birtle Residential School to Wewezhigaabawing. There were at least forty or more Anishinaabeg dedicating their day to walk. Marisa and I followed a group of four ladies as they walked from the school on the left side, through the back, through the tall grass, along the tree line, up to the old train tracks. I looked back and wondered if children running from the school had looked back as they fled into the night. *Giizis* was already getting hot. We walked for about thirty minutes on the gravel road. To the left of us in the pasture were maybe ten black stallions. They came and formed a semicircle facing us, and then they walked with us along the fence. I had a lump in my throat remembering the teaching I received about horses and the healing they bring. It was like they knew we needed healing that day. I am afraid of horses, but that day I embraced what they came to share.

I walked for my maternal mooshum Alvin Jandrew and kokom Thelma Ross, who both attended Birtle Residential School. I walked for my paternal mooshum Michael Twovoice, who attended the Lebret Residential School, and kokom Annie Keewatincappo, who also attended the Birtle school in the early forties. I walked for my mother Linda, who attended the Brandon Residential School, and my father Maurice, who attended Sandy Bay Residential School in the late fifties and early sixties. I also walked for all the other children from our community who attended residential school. I was told once that when you do something as little as walk in honour of someone, their spirit heals.

It was July 1, but I do not celebrate Canada Day. After learning about the atrocities Anishinaabeg across Turtle Island have endured, why would I celebrate a day that praises a country that attempted to assimilate my people? A country that attempted to strip from us Anishinaabemowin, ceremony, teachings, and traditional life skills, a country that set us up for failure through residential school education.

As an Anishinaabeikwe, I am relearning about *mashkiki*, which I was fortunate to identify alongside the road. A sense of pride ran through my body as I was able to identify and share other medicine plants with whoever was walking beside me. I wondered if the cultural disconnect was already present when children were running away from residential schools. One *mashkiki* was the root of bulrushes; one of its purposes is to give you energy if you do not have food. My friend Shirli taught me that while we were looking for *wekay* one summer. These were *mashkiki* my great-grandparents would have known and utilized for minor and major injuries. I was working to reclaim a traditional skill to revitalize my people's ways of knowing and understanding the world around us.

During the walk, I was surrounded by community members, who were exchanging stories. One community member said, "My grandparents went to Sandy Bay School." I shared, "My parents went to Brandon and Sandy Bay." Some wondered about the shoes children were issued—the shoes they wore as they stood in line for meals, the shoes they forgot beside their bed and were struck across the head for, the shoes they wore as they fled into the night. Another said, speaking of our walking today, "This is nothing compared to what our parents went through." And then it hit me again: this is why my family is the way it is. It wasn't just me, or my mom, or even my community. This was a reality for my people for generations.

There was a stretch when I was walking alone and I just cried. I could hear the birds singing in the distance. I could hear the footsteps of the walkers on the gravel road. I could hear laughter, even though we were all carrying a heavy heart that day. I could see all the beauty Mother Earth provides for us, *aki*, *mashkiki*, *noodin*, and *giizis*. I felt alone, walking, thinking of my family who have been deeply affected by residential schools and how directly connected I am to intergenerational trauma, whether I like it or not. I thought about being the first generation not to have attended residential school. I am now thirty years old.

Walking the whole way from the school to Wewezhigaabawing would have taken me eight and a half hours. But after six hours, I could not walk anymore. I developed blisters on the back of my ankles and my toes were throbbing. I imagined young children, alone, running, with whatever shoes that had been given to them. Children like Jim Cote, now one of our most respected Elders. I tried not to complain about my feet until the pain overrode my focus. I imagined how far from the road the children had to hide to continue their journey. How brave they were, how determined to get home. In most cases, they would be brought right back to the doorstep of a residential school when they were discovered by an Indian agent or church official.

I looked up ahead and was surprised to see farmers standing at the end of their driveways handing out freezies and bottles of *nibi*. "I am so glad you're doing this walk," a woman said with her hand placed across her heart. A man had driven from Birtle with his son and was stopping to hand out *nibi* to walkers.

A woman not from the reserve sat in her parked vehicle, holding a tissue as tears fell down her face. I could see she was hurt and showed compassion for the walkers and acknowledged the pain of our people.

Miigwech to those who showed empathy from the surrounding communities. Maybe next time they will walk with us.

I am most grateful for my parents, Linda Jandrew and Maurice Twovoice, for their resiliency during a period of history when the goal was to assimilate every Indigenous child. For all of my grandparents: Michael and Annie Twovoice (née Keewatincappo), and Alvin and Thelma Jandrew (née Ross). Without the generations before me, their strength and their determination, I would not be who I am today. And *gichii miigwech* to leadership from Waywayseecappo First Nation throughout the years who challenged the status quo for a better future.

Lastly, I walked for Zaagaate Giizis and Binesi, my daughters. With their names given through ceremony, they will both know the direction they are going in life. They will know the history of where they come from. They will be familiar with teachings. They will have the tools and knowledge about Anishinaabeg that my husband and I did not receive until later in life. These will help guide them to walk in two worlds, a talent our people require. I will show them how to teach those around them, in a kind way, so that they will be ready to advocate for Anishinaabeg rights for the next generations.

GLOSSARY

aki: earth; land
Anishinaabeg: Ojibway people
Anishinaabeikwe: Ojibway woman
Anishinaabemowin: Ojibway language
binesi: thunderbird
gichii miigwech: big thank you
giizis: sun
kokom: grandmother
mashkiki: medicine
miigwech: thank you
mishoomis giizis: grandfather sun
mitigoog: trees
mooshum: grandfather
nibi: water
nidaanisag: my daughters
noodin: wind
Turtle Island: according to a creation story shared among Anishinaabeg, Canada is part of the turtle's back
wekay: sweetflag/sweet calamus
Wewezhigaabawing: traditional pronunciation for Waywayseecappo
Zaagaate Giizis: shining sun

ACKNOWLEDGEMENTS

WE ARE, FIRST AND FOREMOST, GRATEFUL TO Maureen Twovoice, Linda Jandrew, Jim Cote, and Troy and Nelson Luhowy for their time and generosity of spirit. We have done our best to honour your trust by telling this story accurately and well.

We also wish to thank the many people in Waywayseecappo, Rossburn, and beyond who shared their thoughts and memories, including Norbert Tanner, Hazel Twovoice, Maurice Twovoice, Elizabeth "Tizz" Shingoose, Linda Shingoose, Jackie McKee, Colleen Clearsky, Brad Clearsky, Marellia Cote, Bryan Cloud, Raymond Clearsky, Amanda Cooke, Madaline Whitehawk, Murray Clearsky, Michelle Luhowy, Tammy McCullough, Stephen David, Bob Plachinski, Dennis Kaskiw, Joe Arruda, Brian Brown, Morley Luhowy, John Kostecki, Paulette and Jack Mann, Con Erikson, Larry Huston, Travis Laing, Russ Andrews, Harry Swain, Scott Serson, and Michael Wernick.

A special thanks goes to Lorena Fontaine, for her early support and insights. Esther Sanderson, Louise Garrow, and John Borrows aided us with Cree and Ojibway translations. Paul Williams assisted with the details of the Three Bare Words ceremony. We also appreciate those who provided invaluable feedback and encouragement along the way, including Jody Porter, Justin Ferbey, Sarah Prichard, Allan Sniderman, Anmol Tikoo, Arvind Nair, Raghu Karnad, Bob and Judith Rae, Scott McIntyre, Lea Nicholas-MacKenzie, Sara Robinson, Rosanna Nicol, Jane Gaskell, William Westfall, Julia Sande, Sarah Molinoff, Erin Freeland, Jessica Magonet, Emma Preston-Lanzinger, Sheila Sanderson, Amal Haddad, Elyse Decker, Tiffany Wong-Jones, Hayden Eastwood, Tom Brennan, Arthur Ripstein, Promise Holmes Skinner, John Bonin, Michael Walsh, Jason Baker, Barry Elkind, and Mayo Moran.

This book would not have been possible without the support of a number of institutions, including the University of Ottawa's Human Rights and Education Research Centre (with the unwavering enthusiasm of John Packer), the O'Brien Fellowship program at the McGill University Faculty of Law's Centre for Human Rights and Legal Pluralism (with special thanks to Nandini Ramanujam and Sharon Webb), and the Center for Human Rights and Global Justice at New York University's School of Law (with particular gratitude to Lauren Stackpoole and Philip Alston). Generous financial support from the Wesley M. Nicol Foundation made the initial research for this book possible. And, way back in 2012, Anne Marie Owens and Mark Stevenson at *Maclean's* gave the go-ahead to an intern to write a feature story—everything since flowed from there.

A number of research assistants made important contributions, in part thanks to funding from Swarthmore College and SSHRC. Hope Rumford, Shelisa Klassen, Shay Downey, Henry Lei, CeCe Li, Serene Falzone, and most especially Daniel Diamond: we appreciate your help.

In Winnipeg, Aaron Trachtenberg was always a warm and welcoming host. So too were Heather Dean and Philip Carter on their farm in Sainte-Anne-des-Chênes, where delicious meals and good cheer were in bountiful supply.

In November and December of 2018 and again in December 2019, Andrew had the privilege of being a fellow in the Logan Nonfiction program at the Carey Institute for Global Good in Rensselaerville, New York. Thanks to Carlie Willsie and Josh Friedman for believing in this project, and to Meg Kissinger, Pat Evangelista, and Susan Berfield for their advice and (much-needed) cheerleading.

We were lucky to have the assistance of competent archivists across the country. A most special thank-you goes to David Cuthbert, based at the Winnipeg branch of Library and Archives Canada, who went above and beyond the call of duty. Many thanks, too, to Library and Archives staff in Ottawa, particularly Naïka Monchery. This project also benefited from the assistance of Rob Phillipson at the Provincial Archives of Saskatchewan, Joan Sinclair at the Archives of Manitoba, and Heather McNabb and Jonathan Lainey at the McCord Museum in Montreal. We also wish to acknowledge the work of prior archival researchers, whose footnotes often showed us where to start our own detective work. The research of Sarah Carter, John S. Milloy, J.R. Miller, and Katherine Pettipas proved particularly valuable in this regard.

This book would not have reached its potential without the zealous advocacy of our agent, Michael Levine, at Westwood Creative Artists. We also benefited from early editorial advice from Dan Crissman and Andrea DenHoed. Thankfully, we found a happy home for this book at HarperCollins, and we are grateful to Iris Tupholme, publisher extraordinaire, and to our editor, Jim Gifford, for his wise counsel and deft touch. Copy editor Shaun

Oakey and production editor Canaan Chu also contributed with their considerable talents.

Most of all, we are indebted to our spouses, Mariella and Tanya, who turned pages and calmed nerves and never stopped believing.

ENDNOTES

Authors' Note

1. Natasha Beedie et al., "Towards Justice: Tackling Indigenous Child Poverty in Canada," Upstream and Canadian Centre for Policy Alternatives, 2019; "A Portrait of First Nations and Education," Assembly of First Nations, 2012; Barry Anderson and John Richards, "Students in Jeopardy: An Agenda for Improving Results in Band-Operated Schools," C.D. Howe Institute, Commentary No. 444 (2016), 4.

Prologue: "The Valley of the Birdtail"

1. Marion Abra, *A View of the Birdtail: A History of the Municipality of Birtle 1878–1974* (Altona: The History Committee of the Municipality of Birtle, 1974), 3–4. See also Nathan Hasselstrom, *Pivotal Events: Birtle's Significant Historical Themes and Events* (n.p.: n.p., 2018), 130. Hasselstrom references the alternative theory that "the name was derived from the original Native name which was descriptive of its shape, since branches of the creek at its source resemble a spreading bird's tail."

2. Reita Bambridge Sparling, *Reminiscences of the Rossburn Pioneers* (Rossburn: Rossburn Women's Institute, 1951), 70. For ease of reading, we have changed the original "No where" to "Nowhere" and added a comma after "Birdtail."

3. Statistics Canada, *Rossburn, Municipality, Census Profile*, 2016 Census; Statistics Canada, *Waywayseecappo First Nation, Indian Reserve, Census Profile*, 2016 Census. For the purposes of this paragraph, we use the word "family" to connote what Statistics Canada calls an "economic family." In 2016, the average family income in Rossburn was $58,880; in Waywayseecappo, it was $26,517.

317

2: Linda's Shoes

1. Ian Mosby, "Administering colonial science: Nutrition research and human bio-medical experimentation in Aboriginal communities and residential schools, 1942-1952," *Histoire sociale/Social history* 46, no. 1 (2013): 145-72. Lack of food for Indigenous children in residential schools was not only the result of neglect. Some children were intentionally starved in nutritional "experiments" without their knowledge or consent.

2. There were schools run by various Christian denominations prior to 1880. For example, the Mohawk Institute opened in Ontario in 1831 under the adminis-tration of the Anglican Church. The federal government did not formally assume control of educating Indian children until 1880.

3. House of Commons, Debates, 9 May 1883, 1107-8.

4. Correspondence from A. Sutherland, General Secretary, Mission Board, to Superintendent General of Indian Affairs, 18 January 1890, vol. 6255, file 576-1, part 1, RG10, LAC, Ottawa.

5. John S. Milloy, *A National Crime: The Canadian Government and the Residential School System, 1879 to 1986* (Winnipeg: University of Manitoba Press, 1999), 58-9.

6. Correspondence from Chief Berens to A. Sutherland, 12 August 1891, vol. 6255, file 576-1, part 1, RG10, LAC, Ottawa.

7. Correspondence from A. Sutherland to Chief Berens, 23 September 1891, vol. 6255, file 576-1, part 1, RG10, LAC, Ottawa.

8. Correspondence from Chief Berens to A. Sutherland, 8 January 1891, vol. 6255, file 576-1, part 1, RG10, LAC, Ottawa. Berens adds, "Notwithstanding your oppo-sition to and arguments against local . . . schools, my views on that point are unshaken and as firm as ever."

9. Correspondence from Chief Jacob Berens et al. to E. McColl, Inspector of Indian Agencies, 25 February 1892, vol. 6255, file 576-1, part 1, RG10, LAC, Ottawa.

10. John Semmens, "Notes on Personal History," 1915, Accession 85-28, I.D. 3460, loca-tion PP37, Rev. John Semmens fonds, United Church of Canada Archives, Manitoba Northwestern Ontario Conference and All Native Circle Conference, 94.

11. Correspondence from J. Semmens to McColl, 19 February 1895, vol. 6255, file 576-1, part 1, RG10, LAC, Ottawa.

12. Correspondence from Deputy Superintendent of Indian Affairs to E. McColl, 8 March 1895, vol. 6255, file 576-1, part 1, RG10, LAC, Ottawa.

13. G.H. Wheatley (Indian Agent), "Letter to the Superintendent General of Indian Affairs Re: North-west Superintendency, Birtle Agency," 22 April 1907, in Dominion of Canada, *Annual Report of the Department of Indian Affairs for the Year Ended March 31, 1907* (Ottawa, 1908). Wheatley is speaking generally about the Birtle Agency, which included Waywayseecappo.

14. Dominion of Canada, *Annual Report of the Department of Indian Affairs for the Year Ended June 30, 1903* (Ottawa, 1904); Katherine Lyndsay Nichols, "Investigation of unmarked graves and burial grounds at the Brandon Indian Residential School" (MA thesis, University of Manitoba, 2015), 249–50. The dead in 1903 included Allan Ross on 27 January, Mary Captain on 30 March, Victoria Trout on 11 May, John Hastings on 3 November, David Moar on 26 November, and Annebella Sinclair on 11 December.

15. Semmens, "Notes on Personal History," 97–8.

16. Correspondence from W.W. Shoup (Nelson House) to A. Sutherland, 17 March 1907, box 7, file 127, A. Sutherland Papers, United Church of Canada Archives, as quoted in J.R. Miller, *Shingwauk's Vision: A History of Native Residential Schools* (Toronto: University of Toronto Press, 1996), 349.

17. Kristy Kirkup, "Names of 2,800 children who died in residential schools documented in registry," *Globe and Mail*, 30 September 2019; "Murray Sinclair on the deaths of children in residential schools, and what must be done to help survivors," *The Current*, CBC Radio, 1 June 2021. The National Centre for Truth and Reconciliation has estimated that approximately 1,600 names of deceased students remain unknown. Murray Sinclair estimates that as many as 25,000 Indigenous children died while attending residential schools.

18. Truth and Reconciliation Commission of Canada, *Canada's Residential Schools: Missing Children and Unmarked Burials: The Final Report of the Truth and Reconciliation Commission of Canada*, vol. 4 (Kingston: McGill-Queen's University Press, 2015), 30.

19. "Report of S.J. Jackson, Inspector for Lake Manitoba Inspectorate, Manitoba," in Dominion of Canada, *Annual Report of the Department of Indian Affairs for the Year Ended March 31, 1914* (Ottawa, 1914).

20. Correspondence from J.A. Doyle, "To Indian Agents, Missionaries, Teachers, and Parents or Guardians of Indian Children," 16 March 1931, vol. 6350, file 753-5, part 2, RG10, LAC, Ottawa.

21. Correspondence from J.A. Doyle, "To Indian Agents, Missionaries . . . ," 21 March 1932.

22. To Miss . . . , 16 February 1966, and attached correspondence, file 1/25-20-1, vol. 1, INAC, LAC, as quoted in Milloy, *National Crime*, 284. See also Miller, *Shingwauk's Vision*, 315.

23. Truth and Reconciliation Commission of Canada, "They Came For the Children: Canada, Aboriginal Peoples, and Residential Schools" (Winnipeg, 2012), 51–2; Elizabeth Graham, *The Mush Hole: Life at Two Indian Residential Schools* (Waterloo: Heffle, 1997), 12, as cited in Milloy, *National Crime*, footnote 7 in the Foreword.

24. Agent's Report, J. Waite, Brandon School, 1950, vol. 7194, file 511/25-1-015, MR C 9700, RG10, LAC, Ottawa, as cited in Milloy, *National Crime*, 266.

25. The material relating to Clifford Shepherd, Tommy Douglas, and Oliver Strapp draws on the following sources: T.C. Douglas collection, R-33.1, file 7336, PAS, Regina; correspondence from T.C. Douglas to J.A. Glen, Canadian National Telegram, 28 September 1946, vol. 6259, file 576-10, part 15, RG10, LAC, Ottawa; correspondence from T.C. Douglas to J.A. Glen, 11 December 1946; correspondence from Minister Glen to T.C. Douglas, 2 January 1947, vol. 6259, file 576-10, part 16, RG10, LAC, Ottawa; Truth and Reconciliation Commission of Canada, *Canada's Residential Schools: The History, Part 2: 1939–2000* (Kingston: McGill-Queen's University Press, 2015), 372–3. The Department of Indian Affairs claimed that Clifford should not be staying with his mother on account of her ill health, but Douglas noted that he was informed that "at present" she was "in reasonably good health."

26. Correspondence from G. Dorey to C. Neary, 27 December 1946, vol. 6259, file 576-10, part 16, RG10, LAC, Ottawa. Years later, Rev. George Dorey would publish a book entitled *No Vanishing Race: The Canadian Indian Today* (Toronto: Committee on Missionary Education, United Church of Canada, 1955) in which he wrote: "Scarcely a century has passed since the Christian missionary, with selfless dedication and intrepid courage, first joined battle with the entrenched forces of savagery, paganism and superstition that held a race enthralled."

27. Canada, Royal Commission on Aboriginal Peoples, *Report of the Royal Commission on Aboriginal Peoples, Volume 1: Looking Forward, Looking Back* (Ottawa, 1996), 386. "The diet at Brandon school, which was condemned by nutritionists, was allowed to remain wholly inadequate for more than six years, from 1950 to 1957."

28. Correspondence from Mrs. A. Swaile to R.S. Davis, 6 October 1951, vol. 7194, file 511/25-1-015, MR C 9700, RG10, LAC, Ottawa, as quoted in Milloy, *National Crime*, 266.

29. Correspondence from R.S. Davis to P. Phelan, 1 November 1951, and R.S. Davis to Phelan, 25 October 1951, LAC, Ottawa, as quoted in Milloy, *National Crime*, 266.

30. Indian Act Amendment and Replacement Act S.C. 2014, c. 38. Truancy remained a punishable federal offence for Status Indians until 2014.

31. Milloy, *National Crime*, 268.

32. Correspondence from R.F. Davey to H. Jones, 12 December 1956, vol. 7194, file 511/25-1-015, MR C 9700, IRG10, LAC, Ottawa, quoted in Milloy, *National Crime*, 268.

3: "An Indian Thinks"

1. Michael Twovoice, "An Indian Thinks," *Rossburn Review*, 7 March 1951.

2. Rossburn History Club (hereafter RHC), *On the Sunny Slopes of the Riding Mountains: A History of Rossburn and District*, vol. 1 (Rossburn: RHC, 1984), 294.

3. Peter Lozinski, "Indigenous people of Saskatchewan get full liquor privileges," *Prince Albert Daily Herald*, 27 July 1960. The context that prompted Douglas's comment was the question of whether or not Indians should be admitted into beer parlours.

4. Michael Twovoice, "Farewell Address," *Rossburn Review*, 24 January 1957.

5. Michael Twovoice, "Brief History of Waywayseecappo Band," *Rossburn Review*, 12 November 1959.

6. Waywayseecappo Band, Band Management, Minutes of Council, 1959-01-01–1964-04-30, BAN 2000-01600-6, Box 5, file 57713-6-11, part 1, stack 1, RG10, LAC.

7. Waywayseecappo Band, Band Management, Minutes of Council, 1959-01-01–1964-04-30.

8. Canada, Sessional Papers, 6th Parliament, 1st Session, vol. 16, 3 January 1887. Decades later, Duncan Campbell Scott, who was serving as the government's top Indian education official, described the overarching purpose of the department's policies: "I want to get rid of the Indian problem.... Our objective is to continue until there is not a single Indian in Canada that has not been absorbed into the body politic, and there is no Indian question, and no Indian Department"; correspondence from Hayter Read to the Superintendent General, 15 January 1889, vol. 6255, file 576-1, part 1, RG10, LAC, Ottawa. In 1889, Hayter Reed used the term "assimilate" in his letter about the ideal location for the Brandon Residential School. Reed had hoped that situating Indian students near settlers would "assimilate them with the white population, and save them from relapsing into ignorance and barbarism."

9. Sister G. Marcoux, *History of the Qu'Appelle Indian School* (Lebret, Sask.: n.p., 1955).

10. Michael Twovoice, "Classifieds," *Rossburn Review*, 23 July 1952.

11. Michael Twovoice, "Thanks Extended For Assistance," *Rossburn Review*, 7 March 1968.

12. From 1946 to 1948, a joint committee of the House of Commons and Senate conducted an investigation into Canada's approach to Indians, and at public hearings the committee heard nearly unanimous denunciations of residential schools.

13. R. Davey's remarks, Regional School Inspectors' Conference, 10–11 April 1958, vol. 8576, file 1/1-2-21, MR C 14215, RG10, NAC, as cited in John S. Milloy, *A National Crime: The Canadian Government and the Residential School System, 1879 to 1986* (Winnipeg: University of Manitoba Press, 1999), 195.

14. Correspondence from T.A. Crerar to Rev. G. Dorsey, 20 October 1941, vol. 7185, file 1/25-1-7-3, part 1, RG10, NAC, as quoted in Milloy, *National Crime*, 193. The cost per capita at residential school was $159, while the cost of a day school student was $47.

15. Correspondence from H. McGill to Deputy Minister, 25 November 1942, vol. 6479, file 940-1 (1-2), MR C 8794, RG10, NAC, as quoted in Milloy, *National Crime*, 192.

16. Correspondence from D. Kogawa to R.L. Boulanger, 25 January 1973, file 301/25-13, vol. 4, RG10, NAC, as quoted in Milloy, *National Crime*, 200.

17. Milloy, *National Crime*, 211. Roman Catholics (Oblates) and Anglican bishops were the principal opponents of residential school closures in the 1940s and 50s.

18. R.A. Hoey to the Deputy Minister, 7 June 1944, file 468-1, MR C 7937, vol. 6205, RG10, NAC, as quoted in Milloy, *National Crime*, 194.

19. Canada, Department of Indian and Northern Affairs, *A Survey of the Contemporary Indians of Canada: Economic, Political, Educational Needs and Policies – Part 2 [The Hawthorn Report]* (Ottawa, 1967).

20. Brown v. Board of Education, 347 U.S. 483 (1954). "Does segregation of children in public schools solely on the basis of race, even though the physical facilities and other 'tangible' factors may be equal, deprive the children of the minority group of equal educational opportunities? We believe that it does."

21. Statement Presented by Mr. R.F. Davey on Behalf of Indian Affairs Branch To the Standing Committee of Ministers of Education, 25 September 1963, file 6-2-21, vol. 3, INAC, LAC, as quoted in Milloy, *National Crime*, 196. By 1956, the view of the Department of Indian Affairs was that "the best hope of giving the Indians an equal chance with other Canadian citizens to improve their lot and to become fully self-respecting, is to educate their children in the same schools with other Canadian children."

22. "Memorandum of Agreement between Her Majesty the Queen and the Board of School Trustees of the Consolidated School District of Rossburn," March 1965, file 511/25-11-231, RG10, LAC, Winnipeg.

23. Correspondence from C.M. King to Mr. J. Slobodzian, 7 April 1961, "Rossburn Joint School: Feb 1961 – Dec 1971," file 501/25-11-231-01, vol. 005, RG10, LAC, Winnipeg.

24. Band Council Resolution, 11 April 1961, "Rossburn Joint School: Feb 1961 – Dec 1971," LAC, Winnipeg.

4: "Whitewash"

1. Canada, Department of Indian and Northern Affairs, "Statement of the Government of Canada on Indian Policy (The White Paper)" (Ottawa, 1969). Later published in *Aboriginal Policy Studies* 1, no. 1 (2011), 192–215.

2. W.E. Stefanuk, *One Room and Beyond* (Rossburn: n.p., n.d.) (available in the Rossburn Regional Library). Stefanuk described Minish as an educator with "progressive ideas and methods."

3. Correspondence from A.G. Minish to Jean Chrétien, 22 April 1970, "Rossburn Joint School: Feb 1961 – Dec 1971," file 501/25-11-231-01, BAN no. 2000-01170-5, RG10, LAC, Winnipeg.

4. Correspondence from William Mussell to A.G. Minish, 5 June 1970 "Rossburn Joint School: Feb 1961 – Dec 1971."

5. Memorandum to the Regional Superintendent of Education in Manitoba from J.R. Wright, District Superintendent of Education, Dauphin, 23 June 1970, "Rossburn Joint School: Feb 1961 – Dec 1971." Chief Lynn McKay and Hugh McKay represented the reserve at the meeting.

6. Chief Dan George, "A Talk to Teachers," Ottawa, Department of Indian and Northern Affairs, 1970. George was born with the name Geswanouth Slahoot; like many others, he received his English name at residential school. In a speech George delivered in 1967, entitled "A Lament for Confederation," he said: "But in the long hundred years since the white man came, I have seen my freedom disappear like the salmon going mysteriously out to sea. The white man's strange customs, which I could not understand, pressed down upon me until I could no longer breathe. When I fought to protect my land and my home, I was called a savage. When I neither understood nor welcomed his way of life, I was called lazy. When I tried to rule my people, I was stripped of my authority. My nation was ignored in your history textbooks—they were little more important in the history of Canada than the buffalo that ranged the plains."

7. Correspondence from A.G. Minish to J.R. Wright, 23 October 1970, "Rossburn Joint School: Feb 1961 – Dec 1971."

8. Correspondence from J.R. Wright to A.G. Minish, 28 October 1970, "Rossburn Joint School: Feb 1961 – Dec 1971."

9. Correspondence from A.G. Minish to Jean Chrétien, 21 December 1971, "Education G.S. – Indian Education – Joint Schools – Rossburn," file 501/25-11G/82, vol. 01, 1971-12-01 to 1974-12-31, RG10, LAC, Winnipeg.

10. Correspondence from Jean Chrétien to A.G. Minish, 1 February 1972, "Education G.S.– Indian Education – Joint Schools – Rossburn." Chrétien ultimately declined, but suggested Minish seek more provincial funding.

11. Correspondence from J.R. Wright to A.G. Minish, 10 February 1972, "Education G.S. – Indian Education – Joint Schools – Rossburn."

12. Canada, House of Commons, Report of the Standing Committee on Indian Affairs, 22 June 1971, as cited in Verna J. Kirkness, *Creating Space: My Life and Work in Indigenous Education* (Winnipeg: University of Manitoba Press, 2013), 79.

13. Indigenous Services Canada, "Reducing the Number of Indigenous Children in Care," 2021. Even today, Indigenous children make up more than one half of all children in foster care, even though they are only 8 percent of all children in Canada.

14. Harold Cardinal, *The Unjust Society: The Tragedy of Canada's Indians* (Edmonton: Hurtig, 1969), 90. Cardinal writes, "In spite of all government attempts to convince Indians to accept the white paper, their efforts will fail, because Indians understand that the path outlined by the Department of Indian Affairs through its mouthpiece, the Honourable Mr. Chrétien, leads directly to cultural genocide. We will not walk this path."

15. Indian Tribes of Manitoba, "Wahbung: Our Tomorrow" (Manitoba Indian Brotherhood, 1971), 1, 108, 109, 117.

16. National Indian Brotherhood, "Indian Control of Indian Education" (Ottawa: Assembly of First Nations, 1972), 25.

17. Minister's Address to the Council of Ministers of Education, 23 June 1972, file 501/25-1, vol. 9, RG10, LAC, as quoted in Milloy, *A National Crime: The Canadian Government and the Residential School System, 1879 to 1986* (Winnipeg: University of Manitoba Press, 1999), 199.

18. Bob Rowlands, "MIB presidential election sparks bitterness in ranks," *Winnipeg Tribune*, 24 July 1980.

19. George Stephenson, "Schools issues won't die: Indians," *Winnipeg Sun*, 29 March 1982. Longclaws predicted that many "non-Indian communities will be in trouble because education is a multi-million dollar industry."

20. "Waywayseecappo Education Authority Annual Report," "Education – General – Education Authority – Waywayseecappo First Nation Education Authority, 1983-08-01 to 1985-03-30," 1985, ACC: 2001-00966-6, vol./box 2, file WIN-E-4700-22-285-02, RG10, LAC, Winnipeg. Attendance of students from Waywayseecappo in the Rossburn schools ranged from 40 to 60 percent.

21. Irv Freitag, "Proposal for funding for an analysis and evaluation of educational trends and strategy development at Waywayseecappo," 28 March 1983, "Education – General – Education Authority, Waywayseecappo First Nation Education Authority, 1980-01-01 to 1983-07-30," ACC 2001-00924-0, vol. 13, file WIN-E-4700-22-285-01, RG10, LAC, Winnipeg.

22. "Education – General – Waywayseecappo First Nation, 1981-01-01 to 1982-12-31," ACC 2001-00939-9, vol./box 009, file WIN-E-4700-285-03, RG10, LAC, Winnipeg. On 7 April 1982, a Waywayseecappo band council resolution resolved to create an on-reserve school. The previous year, on 25 May 1981, another resolution had stated "That the Waywayseecappo feel that the children are not getting

the education that they need." The federal government recognized the resolution but said funding for a school on reserve would not be available until "some future year" (15 June 1981).

23. Laura Rance, "Indian Band Seeks Funding for Reserve School," *Brandon Sun*, 22 March 1982.

24. Correspondence from D.G. Biles to John Bagacki, 21 October 1982, "Education – General – Education Authority – Waywayseecappo First Nation Education Authority," ACC 2001-00924-0, vol. 13, file WIN-E-4700-22-285 01, RG10, LAC, Winnipeg; correspondence from Ron Hedley to John Bagacci [*sic*], 16 December 1982, "Education – General – Education Authority, Waywayseecappo First Nation Education Authority," 1980-01-01 to 1983-07-30; Waywayseecappo Band Council Resolution, 13 April 1982.

25. Waywayseecappo Community School, *Yearbook* (Waywayseecappo: 1983).

26. Waywayseecappo Community School, *Yearbook*.

27. Correspondence from Hugh McKay to Ron Penner, 10 November 1982, "Indian Education – Waywayseecappo," file 501/25-1-285-0, RG10, LAC, Winnipeg.

28. Correspondence from Hugh McKay and Robert Shingoose to Gary Maxwell, 5 May 1983, "Education – General – Education Authority, Waywayseecappo First Nation Education Authority, 1980-01-01 to 1983-07-30." Waywayseecappo claimed that it was not receiving sufficient funds to be successful, and that its school was receiving less funding than schools that were federally funded.

29. Correspondence from Jim Manly to John Munro, 23 June 1983, "Education – General – Education Authority, Waywayseecappo First Nation Education Authority, 1980-01-01 to 1983-07-30."

30. Correspondence from John Munro to Jim Manly, 4 November 1983, "Education – General – Education Authority – Waywayseecappo First Nation Education Authority, 1983-08-01 to 1985-03-30." An earlier draft of the letter, dated 2 September, was more frank: "The Department of Indian Affairs and Northern Development is under extreme resource constraints. The budgets passed on the band education authorities and band management units reflects the most equitable allocation of funds that could be devised in view of this restraint. Many of the decisions that had to be taken were as unpalatable to Regional officials as they were to the education authorities who presented them."

31. Correspondence from E. Korchinski to Brian Cloud, 23 April 1986, "Education – General – Waywayseecappo First Nation," WIN-E-4700-22-285 (E 26), Box 24, 1986-01-01 to 1987-12-31, 2001-00939-9, RG10, LAC, Winnipeg.

32. Correspondence from Bryan Cloud to Mr. Korchinski, 14 April 1986, "Education – General – Waywayseecappo First Nation."

33. Correspondence from Robert Shingoose to J. Bagacki, 29 July 1986, "Education – General – Waywayseecappo First Nation."

34. Dan Lett, "Racist slurs drive natives from Rossburn high school," *Winnipeg Free Press*, 16 September 1990.

35. Mr. and Mrs. Norbert Tanner et al., "Parents Comment on Racial Incident," *Rossburn Review*, 18 September 1990.

36. Lyndenn Behm, "Distraught band members disclose 10 years of racism in Rossburn," *Brandon Sun*, 14 September 1990.

37. Dan Lett, "Apology fails to halt switch," *Winnipeg Free Press*, 16 September 1990.

5: "Let Us Live Here Like Brothers"

1. Alexander Morris, *The Treaties of Canada with the Indians of Manitoba and the North-West Territories, including the Negotiations of Which They Were Based, and Other Information Relating Thereto* (Toronto, 1880; Project Gutenberg, 2004).

2. Correspondence from Morris to Alexander Campbell, 11 August 1873, "Correspondence, 1845–1911," Hetchison Collection, as quoted in Robert Talbot, *Negotiating the Numbered Treaties: An Intellectual and Political Biography of Alexander Morris* (Saskatoon: Purich, 2009).

3. David Treuer, *The Heartbeat of Wounded Knee: Native America from 1890 to the Present* (New York: Riverhead Books, 2019), 92. Treuer notes that in the United States, between 1850 and 1975 "it is estimated that at least twenty thousands Indians and eight thousand Anglo settlers and soldiers died in twenty-five years of warfare, although the figure for Indian deaths, based on U.S. Army records, almost certainly should be higher."

4. Correspondence from Alexander Mackenzie to Alexander Morris, 6 December 1873, "Correspondence, 1845–1911," Hetchison Collection, as quoted in Talbot, *Numbered Treaties*, 80–1.

5. Morris, *Treaties*.

6. Morris, *Treaties*; House of Commons, *Debates*, vol. 9, 5 May 1880. Macdonald said: "We must remember that they are the original owners of the soil, of which they have been dispossessed by the covetousness or ambition of our ancestors . . . the Indians have been great sufferers by the discovery of America and the transfer to it of a large white population."

7. Lyle Longclaws and Lawrence J. Barkwell, "The History of Waywayseecappo First Nation," in *History of the Plains-Ojibway and the Waywayseecappo First Nation* (Rossburn: Waywayseecappo First Nation, 1996). The letter was dated 11 October 1873. It is a mystery why the letter was written so formally, or who wrote it in English.

8. Sarah Carter, *Aboriginal People and Colonizers of Western Canada to* 1900 (Toronto: University of Toronto Press, 1999), 38. See also James Daschuk, *Clearing the Plains: Disease, Politics of Starvation, and the Loss of Aboriginal Life* (Regina: University of Regina Press, 2013), 96–8.

9. J.R. Miller, *Skyscrapers Hide the Heavens: A History of Native–Newcomer Relations in Canada*, 4th ed. (Toronto: University of Toronto Press, 2017), 186.

10. Peter Erasmus and Henry Thompson, *Buffalo Days and Nights* (Calgary: Fifth House Books, 1999), as quoted in J.R. Miller, *Compact, Contract, Covenant: Aboriginal Treaty-Making in Canada* (Toronto: University of Toronto Press, 2009), 4. These words were spoken in the context of subsequent 1876 Treaty 6 negotiations.

11. Talbot, *Numbered Treaties*, 79.

12. Philip Goldring, "Cypress Hills Massacre," *The Canadian Encyclopedia*, 4 March 2015.

13. Miller, *Compact, Contract, Covenant*, 159.

14. Morris, *Treaties*. Indigenous treaty discussions frequently employed family and kinship metaphors. By invoking the mother metaphor, Morris was using Indigenous ideas about relationships to propound a lie about what the Indigenous/settler relationships would be.

15. John S. Milloy, "Tipahamatoowin or Treaty 4: Speculations on Alternate Texts?" *Native Studies Review* 18, no. 1 (2009): 110. This story is derived from oral history.

16. Morris, *Treaties*.

17. Bill Waiser, *A World We Have Lost: Saskatchewan Before* 1905 (Markham: Fifth House, 2016), 5–6. These rights had been granted by the Crown to the Hudson's Bay Company in 1670.

18. Morris, *Treaties*.

19. F.L. Hunt, "Notes of the Qu'Appelle Treaty," *The Canadian Monthly and National Review*, March 1876, 180.

20. Danny Musqua, "Treaty Elders Forum," Office of the Treaty Commissioner, Saskatoon, 1997. In 1997, Saulteaux Elder Danny Musqua provided an account that was related to him by his grandfather, who was present at the negotiations as a young boy. An elderly Ojibway asked about a man taking notes for the Treaty Commissioners. On being told that this was a "learned man," the Ojibway man said, "That is what I want my children to have. That kind of education is what my children must have."

21. Morris, *Treaties*.

22. Sheldon Krasowski, "Mediating the numbered treaties: Eyewitness accounts of treaties between the Crown and Indigenous Peoples, 1871–1876" (doctoral thesis, University of Regina, 2011), 189. "The surrender clause was part of the template and was not changed."

23. Hunt, "Notes," 180.

24. Harold Cardinal and Walter Hildebrandt, *Treaty Elders of Saskatchewan: Our Dream Is That Our Peoples Will One Day Be Clearly Recognized as Nations* (Calgary: University of Calgary Press, 2000), 115. Oral histories of Treaty 4 stated that the Cree and Saulteaux did not surrender any of their rights or titles to land. They merely agreed to share the land "to the depth of a plow." As Elder Gordon Oakes states, "There were two nations that negotiated the treaty. You know, this country belongs to the Indian people; the Creator gave us this country. Then the treaties were taking place, that's what they gave up, a tip of the plough, so the people that came from elsewhere, different countries, they can farm, ranch, all that. We never gave up anything more than that."

25. Canada, "Treaty No. 4 between Her Majesty the Queen and the Cree and Saulteaux Tribes of Indians at the Qu'appelle and Fort Ellice." Handwritten copy available at "Correspondence and Report on the Indians in Treaty 4," October 1875, vol. 3625, file 5489, MIKAN 2060606, RG10, LAC, Ottawa.

26. Morris, *Treaties*.

27. Indian Tribes of Manitoba, "Wahbung: Our Tomorrow" (Manitoba Indian Brotherhood, 1971), xii.

28. Sheldon Krasowski, *No Surrender: The Land Remains Indigenous* (Regina: University of Regina Press, 2019), 155. There was a conspicuous absence of a pipe ceremony. By some accounts, the failure to invoke and participate in a pipe ceremony suggests that to the Indigenous signatories the deal was not yet done. A pipe ceremony typically accompanies treaty signings, and indicates a sacred solemnity to the agreement.

29. Longclaws and Barkwell, *History of the Plains-Ojibway and the Waywayseecappo First Nation*. According to Longclaws and Barkwell, Waywayseecappo was born around 1825 and died in 1902 or 1903.

30. Longclaws and Barkwell, *History of the Plains-Ojibway and the Waywayseecappo First Nation*, 18.

31. Heather Devine, "Les Desjarlais: The Development and Dispersion of a Proto-Métis Hunting Band, 1785–1870," in *From Rupert's Land to Canada*, ed. Theodore Binnema, Gerhard J. Ens, and R.C. MacLeod (Edmonton: University of Alberta Press, 2001), 149. It is not entirely clear that this is in reference to the correct person, referring to "Wah-ween-shee-cap-po." This individual was said to be "dreaded" for his knowledge of "Indian medicine and black art."

32. Morris, *Treaties*.

33. "Treaty No. 4," MIKAN 3974413, item 7, vol. 1846, RG10, LAC, Ottawa.

34. Correspondence from and written on behalf of the Earl of Dufferin (author's

name illegible) to the Minister of the Interior, 30 November 1875, vol. 3625, file 5617, RG10, LAC, Ottawa.

35. Dominion of Canada, *Annual Report of the Department of the Interior for the Year Ended 30th June,* 1876 (Ottawa, 1877).

36. Canada, Royal Commission on Aboriginal Peoples, *Report of the Royal Commission on Aboriginal Peoples, Volume 1: Looking Forward, Looking Back* (Ottawa, 1996), 259.

37. Michael Twovoice, "Brief History of Waywayseecappo Band," *Rossburn Review,* 12 November 1959. Michael described the band's Traditional Territory as follows: "a vast tract of land extending from the source of Birdtail, south as far as where Birtle is situated and as far west as to the emptying of the Qu'Appelle River, into the Assiniboine River, north as far as the present townsite of Russell, along the banks of the Assiniboine."

38. Ian Froese, "Waywayseecappo reaches $288M settlement with Ottawa over forced surrender of their lands," *CBC News,* 17 July 2019. Originally, the Waywayseecappo reserve included land to the east of the Birdtail River. Under dubious circumstances, however, this land was "surrendered" by the Waywayseecappo band in 1881, for sale to a group of settlers. In 2012, the Waywayseecappo First Nation brought a legal claim alleging that this sale was improper, and in 2019 the federal government agreed to a $288-million settlement to compensate for the unlawful surrender. For more details about the claim, see documents for claim SCT-4001-12, available on the website of the Specific Claims Tribunal of Canada.

39. J.L. Swanson, *Our Ancestors Arrive in Manitoba* (Winnipeg: de Montfort Press, n.d.). The group waited a week until the ground was dry enough to bear the weight of their carts.

40. Rossburn History Club (hereafter RHC), *On the Sunny Slopes of the Riding Mountains: A History of Rossburn and District,* vol. 1 (Rossburn: RHC, 1984), 369.

41. RHC, *Sunny Slopes,* 2:1. "Samuel Warnock was the first to make a squatters claim."

42. Reita Bambridge Sparling, *Reminiscences of the Rossburn Pioneers* (Rossburn: Rossburn Women's Institute, 1951), 4.

43. Report of J.W. Herchmer (Indian Agent) to the Superintendent-General of Indian Affairs, Manitoba, Fort Ellice, Birtle, 24 October 1882, 42–3. Herchmer was based in Birtle and writing about the whole agency.

44. Sparling, *Reminiscences,* 5.

45. Dominion of Canada, *Annual Report of the Department of Indian Affairs for the Year Ended 31st December,* 1881 (Ottawa, 1882).

46. HTFC Planning and Design, *"See What the Land Gave Us": Waywayseecappo First Nation Traditional Knowledge Study for the Birtle Transmission Line* (2017), 20.

47. RHC, *Sunny Slopes,* 1:24.

48. T.P. Wadsworth's report re: "Way-way-see-cappo's Band," in Dominion of Canada, *Annual Report of the Department of Indian Affairs for the Year Ended 31st December,* 1884 (Ottawa, 1885).

49. L.W. Herchmer, 13 August 1883, in Dominion of Canada, *Annual Report of the Department of Indian Affairs for the Year Ended 31 December,* 1883 (Ottawa, 1884).

50. Aidan McQuillan, "Creation of Canadian Reserves on the Canadian Prairies 1870–1885," *Geographical Review* 7, no. 4 (1980): 392. In 1884, "only 770 of a total of 20,230 Indians in the Territories were not reliant on government relief supplies."

51. Blair Stonechild, "The Indian View of the 1885 Uprising," in *Sweet Promises: A Reader on Indian-White Relations in Canada,* ed. J.R. Miller (Toronto: University of Toronto Press, 1991), 263.

52. Correspondence from J.A. MacRae to Dewdney, 25 August 1884, vol. 3697, file 15,423, RG10, LAC, Ottawa. An account of this meeting is given in Arthur J. Ray, Jim Miller, and Frank Tough, *Bounty and Benevolence: A History of Saskatchewan Treaties* (Montreal: McGill-Queen's University Press, 2002), 197–200. See also Dewdney to Macdonald, 9 February 1885, MG 26A, vol. 117, LAC, as cited in John L. Tobias, "Canada's Subjugation of the Plains Cree, 1879–1885," *Canadian Historical Review* 64, no. 4 (December 1983). The Cree at this meeting were signatories to Treaty 6, which was also negotiated by Alexander Morris. In February 1885, the most senior official in the Department of Indian Affairs, Edgar Dewdney, conceded that the government had violated the treaties.

6: Iron Heart

1. Hayter Reed, "Notes on my early days in the North-West" (1928), P056 (1815–1944), Box 1, Folder 11, Reed Family fonds, McCord Museum, Montreal, 12. The same folder contains two slightly different drafts of this speech.

2. Reed, "Notes on my early days," 31; David Laird, "North-West Indian Treaties," Manitoba Historical Society Transactions, Series 1, no. 67 (1905): "Most of these Indians which met us at Qu'Appelle in 1874 were wild, painted Indians, having buffalo robes or blankets around their shoulders, and a majority of men with only Nature's leggings"; Hayter Reed, "On the Aims of Government in Dealings with our Indians" (undated, but speech delivered in 1899, 1900, or 1901 based on its contents), P056 (1815–1944), Box 1, Folder 12, Reed Family fonds, McCord Museum, Montreal, 12. Hayter went on to observe that the treaties had been more than fair and had "extinguished on liberal terms" Indian land rights.

3. Reed, "Notes on my early days," 20.

4. Hayter Reed, untitled, undated short autobiography (evidently written late in his life), P056 (1815–1944), Box 1, Folder 16, Reed Family fonds, McCord Museum,

Montreal. At the top of the paper is printed: "White Star Line Mediterranean Cruise: On Board S.S. 'Adriatic.'"

5. Reed, "Notes on my early days," 7. A dash has been inserted after "whirlpool" here for clarity.

6. Reed, "Notes on my early days," 4.

7. The threat of violence was not remote or unfounded. A year earlier, in 1868, Thomas D'Arcy McGee, often termed "Canada's first nationalist," was assassinated by the Fenian operative Patrick J. Whelan.

8. "Minutes #1 – 309, September 16, 1870 to December 21, 1878," Executive Council Minutes, A 0070, GR1659, Archives of Manitoba, Winnipeg.

9. Correspondence from Lindsay Russell to Hayter Reed, April 1880, vol. 245, file 23563, D-OO-1, part 1, RG15, LAC, Ottawa.

10. Correspondence from Augusta Draper to John Macdonald, 10 February 1880, microfilm CC-1748, MG 26A, LAC, Ottawa. Hayter got the job with the help of his aunt, who wrote to the prime minister, a family friend, on Hayter's behalf.

11. Aidan McQuillan, "Creation of Canadian Reserves on the Canadian Prairies 1870–1885," *Geographical Review* 7, no. 4. (1980): 391. There were about 1,300 Indians in the district in 1884.

12. Reed, "On the Aims of Government," 24.

13. Hayter Reed, undated memo (circa June 1892), Inspection of Agencies, 1885–1896, vol. 17, Reed Papers, LAC, as quoted in Brian E. Titley, "Hayter Reed and Indian Administration in the West," in *Swords and Ploughshares: War and Agriculture in Western Canada*, ed. R.C. Macleod (Edmonton: University of Alberta Press, 1993), 127.

14. Robert Irwin, "Indian Agents in Canada," *The Canadian Encyclopedia*, 25 October 2018. "The Battleford Indian Agency, situated west of North Battleford, Saskatchewan in the Treaty 6 region, consisted of Cree and Stoney reserves including the Moosomin, Poundmaker, Red Pheasant, Sweet Grass, Thunderchild, Little Pine, Mosquito, Grizzly Bear's Head, Lean Man, and Lucky Man reserves." Hayter wrote that he often travelled fifty or sixty miles a day.

15. Reed, "Notes on my early days," 16, 46, 43.

16. "Valuable Indian relics received," *Montreal Daily Star*, 21 July 1931.

17. Correspondence from E. Dewdney to J.A. Macdonald, 11 April 1884, vol. 212, p. 90065, Macdonald Papers, LAC, Ottawa, as quoted in Titley, "Hayter Reed and Indian Administration in the West," 116.

18. Reed, "Notes on my early days," 40–1. In a speech that Reed delivered some three decades before (see Reed, "On the Aims of Government," 4–5), he attributed this observation to Col. Richard Irving Dodge of the U.S. Army.

19. Reed, "On the Aims of Government," 9, 32–3. Hayter wrote: "True may it be that where the advantages of civilization are viewed in prospect, the Indian may not covet them for himself, or for his children, but suppose his feelings had been consulted in such regard, what would his fate have been today?"

20. Canada, Royal Commission on Aboriginal Peoples, *Report of the Royal Commission on Aboriginal Peoples, Volume 1: Looking Forward, Looking Back* (Ottawa, 1996), 242.

21. Reed, "On the Aims of Government" (bullet point notes attached to the main document). Hayter said that few knew "how often agents, faithful to the interests of the government and to the best interests of the Indians themselves, fairly refused to give supplies to the idle, although their lives were threatened for so doing, while they were being held up to the light of the public in the light of dishonest tyrants." He also handwrote the following bullet points: "No credit ever given to agents" and "Honest though great temptation."

22. Correspondence from Reed to E. Dewdney, 17 March 1883, vol. 3949, file 126886, RG10, LAC, Ottawa.

23. Correspondence from Reed to Indian Commissioner, 18 June 1881, vol. 3755, file 30961, RG10, LAC, Ottawa.

24. Reed to E. Dewdney, 18 June 1881; Headquarters to Assistant Commissioner E.T. Gait, 25 July 1881, vol. 3755, file 30961, RG10, LAC, as quoted in Titley, "Hayter Reed and Indian Administration in the West," 113.

25. Correspondence from, Reed to T.M. Daly, 1893, Hayter Reed fonds, Personnel A-G, vol. 18, LAC, Ottawa.

26. Titley, "Hayter Reed and Indian Administration in the West," 118.

27. Correspondence from E. Dewdney to J.A. Macdonald, 27 September 1883, vol. 211, p. 89923, John A. Macdonald Papers, MG 26A, LAC, as quoted in Macleod, *Swords and Ploughshares*, 113.

28. Harry Loucks, *Voice of the People* (n.p., n.d.), 129, as quoted in Sarah Carter, *Lost Harvests: Prairie Indian Reserve Farmers and Government Policy* (Montreal: McGill-Queen's University Press, 1990), 144.

29. Letter from William Donovan, 30 October 1886, vol. 3772, file 34938, MIKAN 2059746, RG10, LAC, Ottawa.

30. "Education," in Dominion of Canada, *Annual Report of the Department of Indian Affairs for the Year ended 30th June,* 1892 (Ottawa, 1893).

31. Hayter Reed, "Notes on my early days in the North-West—Industrial Schools," P056 (1815–1944), Box 1, Folder 11, Reed Family fonds, McCord Museum, Montreal. In the same document, he refers to the students at the schools as "inmates."

32. "Education - General Remarks," in Dominion of Canada, *Annual Report of the Department of Indian Affairs for the Year Ended 31st December,* 1889 (Ottawa, 1890), 354.

33. Reed, "Notes on my early days in the North-West—Industrial Schools."

34. Father Hugonard to Hayter Reed, 2 December 1887, Hayter Reed fonds, LAC, Ottawa. Hugonard is writing in French. He refers to "nos fugitifs" and their "desertions." A few years later, on Christmas Eve in 1889, a group of students at the school composed an eerie letter directly to Reed: "Considering you as a kind father to us all here, allow the Inmates of our Industrial school to wish you a merry merry Christmas and a thrice happy new year."

35. Reed, "Notes on my early days"; Brian E. Titley, *The Frontier World of Edgar Dewdney* (Vancouver: UBC Press, 1999), 51.

36. Jean Teillet, *The North-West Is Our Mother* (Toronto: HarperCollins, 2019), 386.

37. J.R. Miller, *Skyscrapers Hide the Heavens: A History of Native–Newcomer Relations in Canada*, 4th ed. (Toronto: University of Toronto Press, 2017), 187. In addition to contiguous reserves, they also wanted treaty revisions.

38. Alexander Morris, *The Treaties of Canada with the Indians of Manitoba and the North-West Territories, including the Negotiations of Which They Were Based, and Other Information Relating Thereto* (Toronto, 1880; Project Gutenberg, 2004).

39. Reed, "On the Aims of Government," 24.

40. H. Reed to the Indian commissioner, 28 December 1883, vol. 3668, file 10,644, MIKAN 2057930, 12, RG10, LAC, Ottawa.

41. Reed to T.M. Daly, 1893, Personnel A-G, vol. 18, Hayter Reed fonds, LAC, Ottawa; Titley, *The Frontier World of Edgar Dewdney*, 51. Hayter's tactical achievement thrilled his superior, Edgar Dewdney, who viewed the removal of thousands of Indians "and scattering them through the country as a solution to one of our main difficulties, as it was found impossible at times to have such control as was desirable over such a large number of worthless and lazy Indians, the concourse of malcontents and reckless Indians from all the bands in the Territories."

42. Reed, "Notes on my early days," 31. In handwriting on the typewritten page, Reed wrote: "To make them start pulled tents down."

43. Reed, "Notes on my early days."

44. Correspondence from Reed to the Superintendent General of Indian Affairs, 12 April 1884, vol. 3668, file 10,644, RG10, LAC, Ottawa.

45. Murray Dobbin, *The One-and-a-Half Men* (n.p., n.d.), attributed the quote to James Dreaver, as cited in Teillet, *North-West*, xxi.

46. A.S. Morton, *A History of the Canadian West to 1870–71* (Toronto: University of Toronto Press, 1973), 872, as cited in Teillet, *North-West*, 216.

47. Teillet, *North-West*, 204.

48. Morris, *Treaties*. Otakaonan said, "Now when you have come here, you see sitting out there a mixture of Half-breeds, Crees, Saulteaux and Stonies, all are one, and

you were slow in taking the hand of a Half-breed." Morris replied, "You may rest easy, you may leave the Half-breeds in the hands of the Queen who will deal generously and justly with them."

49. Teillet, *North-West*, 395.

50. Teillet, *North-West*, 400.

51. Teillet, *North-West*, 273.

52. Beverley McLachlin, "Louis Riel: Patriot Rebel," *Manitoba Law Journal* 35, no. 1 (2011): 4. Riel "had won Provincial status for Manitoba against persistent opposition and had secured linguistic and religious recognition for his people."

53. Louis Riel, "Final Statement of Louis Riel at his Trial in Regina," 31 July 1885.

54. Michele Filice, "Mistahimaskwa (Big Bear)," *The Canadian Encyclopedia*, 19 December 2006. Riel met with Big Bear on 17 August 1884.

55. Richard Gwyn, *Nation Maker: Sir John A. Macdonald: His Life, Our Times* (Toronto: Random House Canada, 2011), 433.

56. Bob Beal and Rod Macleod, *Prairie Fire: The 1885 North-West Rebellion* (Toronto: McClelland & Stewart, 1994), 134.

57. Keith D. Smith, ed., *Strange Visitors: Documents in Indigenous–Settler Relations in Canada from 1876* (Toronto: University of Toronto Press, 2014), 56.

58. Correspondence from Crozier to Dewdney, 13 March 1885, 1: 348–51, Dewdney Papers, LAC, Ottawa, as cited in Beal and Macleod, *Prairie Fire*, 137.

59. Patrice Fleury, "Reminiscences," Saskatchewan Archives Board, file A-515, 6.

60. In fact, the government had dispatched none other than Hayter Reed to negotiate with Riel. Hayter set off dutifully toward Duck Lake, but he didn't quite make it before fighting broke out. See "Trouble with Half-Breeds and the Abandoning of Fort Carlton" (undated), P056 (1815–1944), Box 1, Folder 17, Reed Family fonds, McCord Museum, Montreal.

61. Beal and Macleod, *Prairie Fire*, 12–3; Louis Riel, "Final Statement of Louis Riel at his Trial in Regina."

62. George F.G. Stanley, ed., *The Collected Writings of Louis Riel*, vol. 3 (Edmonton: University of Alberta Press, 1985), 60; Item 035, 1885/03/23.

63. Thomas Flanagan, *The Diaries of Louis Riel* (Edmonton: Hurtig Publishers, 1976), 66.

64. George Stanley, *The Birth of Western Canada* (Toronto: University of Toronto Press, 1961), 328. Original quotation in French: "Pour l'amour de Dieu de ne plus en tuer . . . il y a déjà trop de sang répandu."

65. Beal and Macleod, *Prairie Fire*, 156.

66. Charles Pelham Mulvaney, *The History of the North-West Rebellion* (Toronto: A.H. Hovey, 1886), 144. Hayter filed the report on 5 May.

67. Mulvaney, *North-West Rebellion*, 144. His name was Colonel Miller.

68. Desmond Morton, *The Last War Drum: The North West Campaign of* 1885 (Toronto: Hakkert, 1972), 34.

69. Teillet, *North-West*, 413. A hyphen has been added between "sour" and "apple" for clarity.

70. Morton, *Last War Drum*, 41.

71. Reita Bambridge Sparling, *Reminiscences of the Rossburn Pioneers* (Rossburn: Rossburn Women's Institute, 1951), 22–4.

72. Stanley, *The Collected Writings of Louis Riel*, vol. 3, letter 047. The letter is dated 29 March 1885. See also vol. 3, letter 048, and a sequence of letters dated 6–9 April 1885. In early April, Riel wrote his "Dear Relatives": "We have the pleasure to let you know that . . . God has given us a victory over the Mounted Police . . . be courageous. Do what you can. . . . Come and reinforce us."

73. Miller, *Skyscrapers*, 195: "The incident, essentially a bloody act of reprisal against unpopular officials, became unjustifiably known as the Frog Lake Massacre."

74. Blair Stonechild and Bill Waiser, *Loyal Till Death* (Markham: Fifth House, 2010), 117.

75. Sparling, *Reminiscences*, 107, 75, 68–9.

76. Rossburn History Club (hereafter RHC), *On the Sunny Slopes of the Riding Mountains: A History of Rossburn and District*, vol. 1 (Rossburn: RHC, 1984), 24.

77. Sparling, *Reminiscences*, 9.

78. Sparling, *Reminiscences*, 67–8; RHC, *Sunny Slopes*, 1:118.

79. Michael Twovoice, "Brief History of Waywayseecappo Band," *Rossburn Review*, 12 November 1959.

80. L.W. Herchmer to Superintendent-General of Indian Affairs, 4 October 1885, in *Annual Report of the Department of Indian Affairs for the Year Ended 31st December,* 1885 (Ottawa, 1886). Note that "[them]" is substituted for "my Indians."

81. RHC, *Sunny Slopes*, 2:33.

82. Sparling, *Reminiscences*, 39, 107.

83. Correspondence from Hayter Reed to Edgar Dewdney, C-4595, image 305, Northwest Rebellion, MG 27, IC4, vol. 5, Edgar Dewdney fonds, Glenbow Library and Archives.

84. Correspondence from Hayter Reed to Edgar Dewdney, 20 July 1885, vol. 3710, file 19,550-3, RG10, LAC, Ottawa. The assessment of Waywayseecappo occurs at MIKAN 2058918 (item 149).

85. Correspondence from E. Dewdney to J.A. Macdonald, 21 August 1885, vol. 3710, file 19,550-3, RG10, LAC, Ottawa. Macdonald made the additional comment in the margins of Hayter's July memo, which was passed along by Commissioner Dewdney.

86. Gwyn, *Nation Maker*, 458.

87. "Government Report of Riel Transcript 1886," 154, as cited in Martin L. Friedland, "Louis Riel and His Appeal to the Privy Council," *Criminal Law Quarterly* 69, no. 3 (August 2021): 9.

88. Canada, Parliament, Sessional Papers, 1886, Volume 12, No. 43, 143.

89. Gwyn, *Nation Maker*, 461.

90. Gwyn, *Nation Maker*, 474.

91. Correspondence from Reed to Dewdney, 6 September 1885, vol. 5, p. 1240, Dewdney Papers, LAC, Ottawa, as cited in Titley, "Hayter Reed and Indian Administration in the West," 117.

92. Gwyn, *Nation Maker*, 489. Future prime minister Wilfrid Laurier was outraged by the executions: "If I had been on the banks of the Saskatchewan [River], I too would have shouldered my musket to fight against the neglect of government and the greed of speculators."

93. William Cameron, *Blood Red the Sun* (Calgary: Kenway, 1950), 210–1.

94. Alex Williams, *The Pass System*, 2015, documentary film.

95. The letters of recommendations had to come from federal farm instructors.

96. Correspondence from Hayter Reed to Lawrence Herchmer, 16 February 1891, MG 29, E106, vol. 13, Hayter Reed fonds, LAC, Ottawa.

97. Hayter Reed, "Annual report for the fiscal year 1890–91," in Dominion of Canada, *Annual Report of the Department of Indian Affairs for the Year Ended 31st December, 1891* (Ottawa, 1892).

98. David J. Hall, "North-West Territories (1870–1905)," *The Canadian Encyclopedia*, 7 February 2006: "The 1885 census of Assiniboia, Saskatchewan and Alberta reported a total population of 48,362. Of this, 20,170 people (41.7 per cent) were Status Indians."

99. Dominion of Canada, *Annual Report of the Department of Indian Affairs for the Year Ended 31st December, 1889* (Ottawa, 1890).

100. Correspondence from Hayter Reed to Edgar Dewdney, 20 July 1885, vol. 3710, file 19, 550-3, RG10, LAC, Ottawa. "By preserving a knowledge of individual movements," Reed wrote, "any inclination to petty depredations may be checked."

101. Correspondence from Alexander Morris to the Minister of the Interior, 23 October 1875, vol. 3625, file 5489, RG10, LAC. In a conversation with Chief Waywayseecappo a year after he signed the treaty, Morris assured the Chief that "he had the same right of hunting as before."

102. Lawrence Vankoughnet to John A. Macdonald, 14 August 1885, vol. 3710, file 19, 550-3, RG10, LAC, Ottawa, as cited in Laurie F. Barron, "The Indian Pass System in the Canadian West, 1882–1935" in *Immigration and Settlement, 1870–1939*, ed.

Gregory P. Marchildon (Regina: University of Regina Press, 2009), 216. When Prime Minister Macdonald approved the pass system, he acknowledged that "no punishment for breaking bounds can be inflicted & in case of resistance on the grounds of Treaty rights [punishments] should not be insisted on."

103. Correspondence from Hayter Reed to Minister of the Interior, MG 29, EI06, vol. 14, file T.W. Day, RG10, LAC, Hayter Reed Papers, as cited in Barron, "Indian Pass System," 37. Reed, too, acknowledged that "it was especially stipulated ... when [Indians] entered Treaty that they should not be tied down to their Reservations, and although I have often taken the responsibility of employing police to send them home, the greatest caution has to be exercised, for were they to offer resistance and conflict ensue, they have the law on their side."

104. Correspondence from Hayter Reed to Edgar Dewdney, 16 August 1885, MG 27, 2076-87, Dewdney Papers, North-West Rebellion, LAC, Ottawa, as cited in Barron, "Indian Pass System," 37. It is notable that they are implementing the system even before the prime minister approves the memo.

105. Barron, "Indian Pass System," 29.

106. Correspondence from Sergeant R. Burton Deane (Lethbridge, Alberta) to NWMP commissioner, 12 February 1891, MG 29, E106, vol. 12, file R. Burton, 1891, Hayter Reed fonds, LAC, Ottawa.

107. Barron, "Indian Pass System," 36.

108. Correspondence from Hayter Reed to Deputy Superintendent of Indian Affairs, 14 June 1893, vol. 6817, file 487-1-2, part 1, reel C-8539, RG10, LAC, Ottawa: "Unfortunately, however, the Police Department has become alarmed about the risk of assuming its share of responsibility. . . . I cannot refrain from an expression of extreme regret that such order should have been given. . . . Had the order been kept quiet, the Indians might have remained for some time in ignorance, but as I have already seen references to it in the public press, no expectation of withholding it from them need now be entertained."

109. Correspondence from Hayter Reed to Indian Agent in Carlton, Saskatchewan, 15 June 1893, vol. 1597, RG10, LAC, Ottawa. Document courtesy of Sarah Carter.

110. Sarah Carter, "Controlling Indian Movement: The Pass System," NeWest Review (May 1985); Miller, Skyscrapers, 212. Miller has written, "The pass system, however, was never very effective. It was not often enforced in the 1880s, and by 1893 was virtually a dead letter." Carter suggests otherwise, and indeed there is evidence of enforcement as late as in 1941.

111. Correspondence from Harold McGill to Inspectors of Indian Agencies and Indian Agents, 11 July 1941, and correspondence from Alfred G.B. Lewis to I Secretary, Indian Affairs Branch, 24 July 1941, "Correspondence regarding Indian Pass system,"

M3281, Harold and Emma McGill fonds, Glenbow Library and Archives. In 1941, more than half a century after the first passes were issued, McGill, an official in the Department of Indian Affairs, circulated a notice to staff across Canada:"There seems to be a misunderstanding in the minds of some Indian agents and other officials concerning the right of Indians to leave their reserves. Indians are not compelled to remain upon their reserves and are free to come and go in the same manner as other people. No law or regulation exists to the contrary. Please be guided accordingly."To help clear up the "misunderstanding," McGill requested that all remaining passbooks be sent to Ottawa to be destroyed. Two weeks later, an Alberta-based Indian agent named Alfred Lewis mailed a reply. He enclosed one partially used booklet of forms, along with eleven unused booklets. Lewis wrote,"The writer regrets that this action was found necessary as it will be now impossible to control our farming Indians."

112. Kate Armour Reed, *A Woman's Touch: Kate Reed and Canada's Grand Hotels* (Westmount: John Aylen Books, 2017), 87–9.

7: The Young Napoleon of the West

1. Richard Gwyn, *Nation Maker: Sir John A. Macdonald: His Life, Our Times* (Toronto: Random House Canada, 2011), 385.

2. "Sifton: Review of the Young Minister's Career," *Globe and Mail*, 18 November 1896.

3. "Speech Delivered on Receiving Degree of L.L.D. by Queen's University," 1927, vol. 313, Manuscript Group 27, series II D 15, Clifford Sifton fonds, LAC, Ottawa.

4. Clifford Sifton to [illegible], 5 March 1901, C-422, Clifford Sifton fonds, LAC, Ottawa.

5. D.J. Hall, *Clifford Sifton*, vol. 1, *The Young Napoleon, 1861–1900* (Vancouver: UBC Press, 1981), 294; Robert Russell, "The Young Napoleon of the West," *The Busy Man's Magazine*, June 1908; *Winnipeg Free Press*, 10 November 1900.

6. John Wesley Dafoe, *Clifford Sifton in relation to his times* (Toronto: Macmillan of Canada, 1931), 48.

7. D.J. Hall, *Clifford Sifton* (Don Mills, Ont.: Fitzhenry & Whiteside, 1976).

8. Mabel F. Timlin, "Canada's Immigration Policy, 1896–1910," *The Canadian Journal of Economics and Political Science* 26, no. 4 (November 1960), 518.

9. D.J. Hall, "Clifford Sifton and Canadian Indian Administration, 1896–1905," *Prairie Forum* 2, no. 2 (November 1977), 253.

10. Sifton, "The Immigrants Canada Wants," *Maclean's Magazine*, 1 April 1922.

11. Timlin, "Canada's Immigration Policy," 521–2. Sifton wanted to suppress publication of the temperatures but apparently was "dissuaded." Ultimately, he decided a cover-up was worse than the clime.

12. Sifton, "Immigrants Canada Wants"; Dafoe, *Clifford Sifton*. On another occasion, Sifton added: "If you are to settle the rough lands you have to settle them with these people, because the average young Canadians or American farmer will not do it."

13. Sifton, "Immigrants Canada Wants."

14. House of Commons, *Debates*, Fourth Session, 8th Parliament, vol. 1, 7 July 1899, 6859. Sifton added: "Any man . . . willing to till the soil, is a welcome addition to this Western country, and his arrival is a national blessing."

15. Bohdan S. Kordan and Lubomyr Y. Luciuk, *A Delicate and Difficult Question: Documents in the History of Ukrainians in Canada, 1899–1962* (Kingston: Limestone Press, 1986), 17. Sifton insisted that their "strongest desire is to assimilate with Canadians."

16. Paul Yuzyk, *The Ukrainians in Manitoba: A Social History* (Toronto: University of Toronto Press, 1953), 13.

17. Pierre Berton, *The Promised Land: Settling the West, 1896–1914* (Toronto: Anchor Canada, 2011), chap. 2, "The Sheepskin People," Part 1, "The long voyage," Kindle.

18. P.J. Giffen, *Adult Education in Relation to Rural Social Structure: A Comparative Study of Three Manitoba Communities* (Winnipeg, 1947), 110 (viewed at the Manitoba Legislative Library).

19. M.H. Marunchak, *The Ukrainian Canadians: A History* (Yorkton: Redeemer's Voice Press, 1970), 297.

20. Marunchak, *The Ukrainian Canadians*, 71.

21. D.J. Hall, "Clifford Sifton's Vision of the Prairie West," in *The Prairie West as Promised Land*, ed. R. Douglas Francis and Chris Kitzan (Calgary: University of Calgary Press, 2007), 83.

22. Clifford Sifton, *Geography of the Dominion of Canada and Atlas of Western Canada* (Ottawa: Department of the Interior, 1904), 10.

23. Hall, "Vision of the Prairie West," 85, 86; Yuzyk, *Ukrainians in Manitoba*, 30.

24. Michael Ewanchuk, *Pioneer Profiles: Ukrainian Settlers in Manitoba* (self-pub., 1981), 3.

25. William A. Czumer and Vasyl A. Chumer, *Recollections about the Life of the First Ukrainian Settlers in Canada* (Edmonton: Canadian Institution of Ukrainian Studies, 1981), 12–3.

26. Yuzyk, *Ukrainians in Manitoba*, 31.

27. Orest T. Martynowych, *Ukrainians in Canada: The Formative Period, 1891–1924* (Edmonton: University of Alberta Press, 1991), 46.

28. Elsie Lesyk, *Sifton Then and Now: A Reminiscence of the Pioneer Era* (Dauphin: self-pub., 1992), 4–9.

29. Martynowych, *Ukrainians in Canada*, 46; Hall, *Young Napoleon*, 262.

30. Sifton, "Immigrants Canada Wants."

31. D.J. Hall, *Clifford Sifton*, vol. 2, *A Lonely Eminence, 1901–1929* (Vancouver: UBC Press, 1985), 65.

32. Marunchak, *Ukrainian Canadians*, 80.

33. Jaroslav Petryshyn, *Peasants in the Promised Land: Canada and the Ukrainians, 1891–1914* (Toronto: Lorimer, 1985), 60.

34. Dafoe, *Clifford Sifton*, 323; Hall, *A Lonely Eminence*, 957. A total of 115,478 home-steads were issued during Sifton's nine-year tenure.

35. Dafoe, *Clifford Sifton*, 324. Canada went from a million acres producing 14,371,806 bushels of wheat to 3,141,537 acres producing 55,761,416 bushels of wheat.

36. Hall, "Clifford Sifton's Vision of the Prairie West," 77.

37. House of Commons, *Debates*, Fourth Session, 8th Parliament, 27 July 1899, 8655.

38. Dafoe, *Clifford Sifton*, 528.

39. Hall, *A Lonely Eminence*, 158.

40. Dafoe, *Clifford Sifton*, 11.

41. Hall, *The Young Napoleon*, 292.

42. Dafoe, *Clifford Sifton*, 316–7; Hall, *A Lonely Eminence*, 63. During his first full year as minister, in 1897, 16,835 immigrants arrived in Canada. That number rose to 141,465 in 1905, Sifton's last full year as minister.

43. Hall, *A Lonely Eminence*, 42.

44. Lubomyr Luciuk and Stella Hryniuk, eds., *Canada's Ukrainians: Negotiating an Identity* (Toronto: University of Toronto Press, 1991), 289; "scum" comment from the *Winnipeg Free Press*, 17 July 1899.

45. Luciuk and Hryniuk, *Canada's Ukrainians*, 289.

46. Marunchak, *Ukrainian Canadians*, 299, 74; *Winnipeg Daily Nor-Wester*, 23 December 1896.

47. *Winnipeg Telegram*, "Another Siftonian Tragedy," July 1899, as quoted in Berton, *Promised Land*, chap. 2, "The Sheepskin People," Part 2, "Dirty, ignorant Slavs."

48. Winnipeg Free Press, 22 October 1898.

49. O.W. Gerus and J.E. Rea, *The Ukrainians in Canada* (Ottawa: Canadian Historical Association, 2018), 9.

50. "Look out for it," *Winnipeg Tribune*, 22 October 1898.

51. House of Commons, *Debates*, Fourth Session, 8th Parliament, 7 July 1899, 6835.

52. Sifton, "Immigrants Canada Wants."

53. "Mr. Sifton at Winnipeg: Enthusiastic Audience Greets the Minister of the Interior," *Globe and Mail*, 28 October 1899.

54. Hall, *A Lonely Eminence*, 70 (citing a letter from Sifton to Dafoe, 11 November

1901). Sifton refers to "the cry against the Doukhobors and the Galicians." The Doukhobors were another ethnic group from eastern Europe.

55. House of Commons, *Debates*, 9th Parliament, 1st Session, 12 April 1901.

56. "Immigration Discussed," *Globe and Mail*, 13 April 1901.

57. Hall, *The Young Napoleon*, 264.

58. Berton, *The Promised Land*, chap. 1, "The Young Napoleon of the West," Part 4, "The spoils system."

59. Dafoe, *Clifford Sifton*, 547.

60. Dafoe, *Clifford Sifton*, 541.

61. Hall, "Clifford Sifton and Canadian Indian Administration," 192.

62. Hall, "Clifford Sifton and Canadian Indian Administration," 184. The total budget of the federal government doubled in that span.

63. Petryshyn, *Peasants in the Promised Land*, 22; W.T.R. Preston, *My Generation of Politics and Politicians* (Toronto: D.A. Rose, 1927), 215.

64. House of Commons, *Debates*, 1901, col. 2763, 10 April 1901.

65. House of Commons, *Debates*, 18 July 1904, 6946–56; House of Commons, *Debates*, 23 July 1903, cols. 7260–1. Punctuation has been moderately altered for clarity.

66. Hall, "Clifford Sifton and Canadian Indian Administration," 189. The comment was made by Sifton in 1897. Sifton later acknowledged the difficulty of recruiting qualified teachers for these boarding schools, as the department only offered half of the pay available in an urban public school where non-Native Canadians were being educated. House of Commons, *Debates*, 1902, cols. 3043–6, 18 April 1902.

67. Hall, "Clifford Sifton and Canadian Indian Administration," 191. Sifton said, "I have followed the policy of encouraging the establishment of boarding schools"; House of Commons, *Debates*, 1904, cols. 6946–56, 18 July 1904. Indian Affairs finally gave up the distinction between industrial and boarding schools in 1923, when both types of schools were amalgamated into a single category known as residential schools.

68. Hall, "Clifford Sifton and Canadian Indian Administration."

69. Hayter Reed, "Memorandum for the information of the Minister relative to application of the per capita grant system of maintenance to the Brandon Indian Industrial School," 28 January 1897, vol. 6255, file 576-1, part 1, RG10, LAC, Ottawa. Sifton's approval was contingent on "the official consent of the Church."

70. Sister G. Marcoux, *History of the Qu'Appelle Indian School* (n.p., 1955), 14–5. The cost of the rebuild was $125,000. This school was also known as the Lebret Residential School, and was situated close to where Alexander Morris had promised that Indian children would learn the "cunning of the white man" during Treaty 4 negotiations.

71. P.H. Bryce, *Report on the Indian Schools of Manitoba and the North-West Territories* (Ottawa: Government Printing Bureau, 1907).

72. Katherine Lyndsay Nichols, "Investigation of unmarked graves and burial grounds at the Brandon Indian Residential School" (MA thesis, University of Manitoba, 2015), 92.

73. Hall, *The Young Napoleon*, 273, 193. Sifton said "the main reason for making this arrangement is to pacify and keep pacified the North-West Territories" and to avoid "having an Indian trouble on our hands." The superintendent later wrote that he discounted most signed statements by Indians. "It is possible for persons to get the Indians to sign almost any kind of statements, if a little excitement and agitation be got up beforehand, and we are unable therefore to rely to any extent upon written statements that come in signed by Indians."

74. Correspondence from Clifford Sifton to J. Peuder, 13 March 1897, C-403, image 385, Clifford Sifton fonds, LAC, Ottawa.

75. Dafoe, *Clifford Sifton*, 305–6.

76. Sifton, "Immigrants Canada Wants": "While I had many other duties [as minister of the interior], I regarded my most important mission as connected with Immigration."

77. Mrs. J. Skavinski (Annie Danyleyko), "The Early Pioneers" (undated), in Rossburn History Club, *On the Sunny Slopes of the Riding Mountains: A History of Rossburn and District*, vol. 1 (Rossburn: RHC, 1984), 299.

8: "One Load of Barley"

1. Dominion of Canada, *Annual Report of the Department of Indian Affairs for the Year Ended 31st December,* 1889, 7 October 1889 (Ottawa, 1890). A comma between "time" and "this" has been removed for added clarity.

2. Sarah Carter, *Lost Harvests: Prairie Indian Reserve Farmers and Government Policy* (Montreal: McGill-Queen's University Press, 1990), 212.

3. Sarah Carter, "Two Acres and a Cow: 'Peasant' Farming for the Indians of the Northwest, 1889–97," *Canadian Historical Review* 70, no. 1, (March 1989), 44–5. Indians said that lanterns would help them care for cattle after nightfall, but to no avail.

4. Reed to T.M. Daly, (date illegible) 1893, Personnel A-G, vol. 18, Hayter Reed fonds, LAC, Ottawa.

5. RG10, Deputy Superintendent General of Indian Affairs Letterbooks, vol. 1115, p. 220, Reed to Forget, 12 June 1894, as cited in Carter, *Lost Harvests*, 218.

6. Carter, "Two Acres and a Cow," 33.

7. Carter, "Two Acres and a Cow."

8. Hayter Reed, "On the Aims of Government in Dealings with our Indians," P056 (1815–1944), Box 1, Folder 12, Reed Family fonds, McCord Museum, Montreal, 28.

9. McGirr to Reed, MG29, vol. 13, no 960, Hayter Reed Papers, LAC, Ottawa, as cited in Carter, "Two Acres and a Cow," 48.

10. Correspondence from Chas. De Cases to Reed, 19 November 1896, vol. 3964, file 148,285, RG10, LAC, Ottawa. The quotation later continues: "Perhaps in the south where the seasons are longer the system would work successfully, but up here no whiteman attempts to do so."

11. The first threshing machine in Rossburn arrived in 1880.

12. Dominion of Canada, *Annual Report of the Department of Indian Affairs for the Year Ended 31st December,* 1889 (Ottawa, 1890).

13. Sarah Carter, "'We Must Farm to Enable us to Live': The Plains Cree and Agriculture to 1900," in *The Prairie West as Promised Land,* ed. R. Douglas Francis and Chris Kitzan (Calgary: University of Calgary Press, 2007), 122: "by the mid 1890s, per capita acreage under cultivation had fallen to about half of the 1889 level and many had given up farming altogether."

14.

Year	Total acres under crop	Year	Total Acres under crop
1882	76	1891	103 13/32
1883	66	1892	100
1884	70	1893	18 5/16
1885	(data not available)	1894	13 11/24
1886	96	1895	20.61
1887	29 1/4	1896	13
1888	50	1897	16
1889	182	1898	7.88
1890	66 23/48	Sources: Annual reports of the Department of Indian Affairs, 1882-98	

15. The Indian Act, R.S.C. 1886, c. 43, s. 30. The prohibition on selling livestock appears in 1930 revisions to the act, and the permit system was limited to Alberta, Manitoba, Saskatchewan, and the Territories.

16. Reed to T. Mayne Daly, 13 March 1893, Hayter Reed Archives, LAC, Ottawa.

17. House of Commons, *Debates,* 24 March 1884, at 1063, as cited in Carter, "Two Acres and a Cow," 37.

18. McGirr to Reed, 8 March 1893, Hayter Reed Papers, LAC, vol. 13, no 960, as cited in Carter, "Two Acres and a Cow," 48.

19. *Virden Chronicle,* 11 January 1894 (viewed at the Manitoba Legislative Library).

20. Correspondence from J.A. Markle to the Secretary, Department of Indian Affairs, "Timber: Waywayseecappo Reserve No. 62, Brandon District," 11 June 1900, file 577/20-7-11-62, vol. 7057, MIKAN 2047064, RG10, LAC, Ottawa; correspondence from J.D. Maclean to J.A. Markle, 18 June 1900. The restrictions even extended to trees cut for firewood. On 11 June 1900, Markle, Waywayseecappo's Indian agent, wrote his superior to ask "whether it is necessary for [an] Indian to procure a permit to cut and remove a single load of wood to procure food for himself and family." Maclean, a senior official, replied from Ottawa one week later. He told Markle that "no deviation can be made from previous instructions," which specified that "Indians have not the right to cut timber on their Reserves for sale ... without the sanction of the Department." He added, by way of explanation: "If an Indian can, without permission, cut and sell one load of wood, he might urge this plea of necessity for continuous cutting and selling and there would be no control over his operations." A version of this restriction remains in Article 93 of the Indian Act as of January 2021.

21. Carter, *Lost Harvests*, ix.

22. Carter, *Lost Harvests*, 193.

23. House of Commons, *Debates*, 19 May 1880, 1610; Walter Hildebrandt, "From Dominion to Hegemony: A Cultural History of Fort Battleford" (unpublished manuscript, 1988), Department of Environment, Parks, Prairie Region, as cited in Carter, "Two Acres and a Cow," 36.

24. Annual report of G.H. Wheatley (Indian Agent) to the Superintendent General of Indian Affairs Re: North-west Superintendency, Birtle Agency, 10 July 1906, Dominion of Canada, *Annual Report of the Department of Indian Affairs for the Year Ended June 30, 1906* (Ottawa, 1907).

25. Inspector of Indian Agencies, Birtle Agency, Dominion of Canada, *Annual Report for the Department of Indian Affairs for the Year Ended March 31, 1908* (Ottawa, 1908).

26. RCMP Report re: "Joe MENTUCK et al. (Treaty Indians) Selling timber on reserve without permit," Timber–Waywaysucappo Reserve No. 62 from 1893 to 1989, C-12967, 4 March 1942, file 577/20-7-11-62, vol. 7057, RG10, LAC, Ottawa.

27. Correspondence from A.G. Smith to the Secretary, "Timber: Waywayseecappo Reserve No. 62, Brandon District," 13 March 1942, "Portage La Prairie Agency – Correspondence and reports concerning licence to cut timber; trespass, removal and illegal sale of timber on the Waywayseecappo (fishing station) and Lizard Point reserves," file 577/20-7-11-62, vol. 7057, RG 10, LAC, Ottawa.

28. Correspondence from T.R.L. MacInnes to A.G. Smith, "Timber: Waywayseecappo Reserve No. 62, Brandon District," 4 April 1942, "Portage La Prairie Agency."

Smith's superior (MacInnes) replied, "It is impossible to give any general directions on a subject of this kind," but each case should be decided based on "its merits and in accordance with your best discretion and judgment."

29. Alex Williams, *The Pass System*, 2015 (documentary film).

30. By the year of its repeal, the prohibition applied only to Indians in Alberta, Saskatchewan, and Manitoba.

31. "Waywayseecappo Reserve," *Rossburn Review*, 21 October 1943.

32. James H. Gray, *Bacchanalia Revisited: Western Canada's Boozy Skid to Social Disaster* (Saskatoon: Western Producer Prairie Books, 1982), 117.

9: Reasonable Amusement

1. Cynthia Cooper, *Magnificent Entertainments: Fancy Dress Balls of Canada's Governors General, 1876–1898* (Fredericton: Goose Lane Editions, 1997), 70.

2. Cooper, *Magnificent Entertainments*, 75.

3. *The Lounger*, July 1896.

4. Marcel Trudel, *The Beginnings of New France: 1524–1663*, Canadian Centenary Series (Toronto: McClelland and Stewart, 1973), 44.

5. That Cree was the language he spoke at the event is an educated guess. We know that he spoke what sounded like an Indigenous language to onlookers, and that he had picked up some language skills on the plains. The likely bet for the language is Cree, given that this was the predominant language in the Battleford region where he had first served as an Indian agent.

6. Cooper, *Magnificent Entertainments*, 89.

7. J.G. Bourinot, *Illustrations of the Historical Ball Given by Their Excellencies the Earl and Countess of Aberdeen in the Senate Chamber, Ottawa, 17th February, 1896* (Ottawa: John Durie, 1896).

8. *The Lounger*, July 1896.

9. Cooper, *Magnificent Entertainments*, 96.

10. Bourinot, *Illustrations of the Historical Ball*.

11. Cooper, *Magnificent Entertainments*, 88. "Even Lady Aberdeen repeatedly lamented not having thought of organizing a war dance."

12. Giveaways are a common feature of many Indigenous ceremonies. For example, witnesses to a naming ceremony receive small and useful items like tea towels or more personal items for close relations and friends. On the West Coast, the potlatch ceremony involves the distribution of vast numbers of goods, the purpose of which is both distributive and demonstrative of a Chief's ability to manage property in a productive manner. See also Katherine Pettipas, *Severing the Ties that Bind* (Winnipeg: University of Manitoba Press, 1994), 252–3. In 1903, a judge in

Saskatchewan ruled that the provision of tea and bannock at a dance was sufficient to make the ceremony illegal.

13. Hayter Reed, memo re: "suggested Amendments to the Indian Act," 20 December 1889, vol. 3832, file 64,009, MIKAN 2060836, RG10, LAC, Ottawa.

14. Hayter Reed, "Notes on my early days in the North-West," 1928, P056 (1815–1944), Box 1, Folder 11, Reed Family fonds, McCord Museum, Montreal, 29.

15. Hayter Reed, "On the Aims of Government in Dealings with our Indians," P056 (1815–1944), Box 1, Folder 12, Reed Family fonds, McCord Museum, Montreal, 25: "the inculcation of this spirit of individualism is one of the most strenuously marked features of the Department's Indian policy."

16. *An Act providing for the organisation of the Department of the Secretary of State of Canada and for the management of Indian and Ordnance Lands*, S.C. 1868, c. 42, s. 149.

17. HTFC Planning and Design, *"See What the Land Gave Us": Waywayseecappo First Nation Traditional Knowledge Study for the Birtle Transmission Line* (2017), 44.

18. Harold Cardinal and Walter Hildebrandt, *Treaty Elders of Saskatchewan: Our Dream Is That Our Peoples Will One Day Be Clearly Recognized as Nations* (Calgary: University of Calgary Press, 2000), 14.

19. Reita Bambridge Sparling, *Reminiscences of the Rossburn Pioneers* (Rossburn: Rossburn Women's Institute, 1951), 47.

20. Correspondence from Clifford Sifton to Bishop of Calgary and Saskatchewan, 28 January 1901, C-440, image 1276, Clifford Sifton fonds, LAC, Ottawa.

21. Names of Chiefs and Minor Chiefs in Canada, 1894, Box B-8-ak, vol. 12010, no. 5103711, RG10, LAC. Ottawa.

22. J.A. Markle to the Indian Commissioner, 13 June 1896 and 16 June 1896, vol. 3825, file 60,511-1, RG10. LAC, Ottawa.

23. Correspondence from Forget to Office of the Indian Agent, Blood Agency, 11 July 1898, vol. 3825, file 60,511-1, RG10, LAC, Ottawa. Forget invokes "material withdrawal of assistance." Regarding trespass, see letter of 9 June 1896 in the same file.

24. W.P. Stewart, *My Name is Piapot* (Maple Creek: Butterfly Books Limited, 1981), 103–4. The conversation took place in 1899.

25. Correspondence from Sifton to Governor General in Council, 18 January 1898, vol. 1121, C-9002, RG10, 399–400.

26. John L Tobias, "Payipwat (Piapot, Hole in the Sioux, Kisikawasan, Flash in the Sky)," *Dictionary of Canadian Biography*, vol. 13. "I have no doubt he has been too harshly dealt with," Lord Minto said of Piapot; D.J. Hall, *Clifford Sifton*, vol. 2, *A Lonely Eminence, 1901–1929* (Vancouver: UBC Press, 1985), 48. In 1902, Lord Minto said this of Clifford Sifton: "Speaking generally, while fully recognizing the great success of Canadian administration of Indian affairs, it has seemed to

me that there is a want in many cases of human sympathy between the white administrator and the Indian, and that possibly . . . somewhat narrow religious sentiments have not conduced to a sympathetic understanding of the Indian races."

27. Correspondence from Scott to Graham, 4 October 1921, vol. 3826, file 60, 511-4A, RG 10, LAC, Ottawa. See also Brian Titley, *A Narrow Vision: Duncan Campbell Scott and the Administration of Indian Affairs in Canada* (Vancouver: University of British Press, 1986), 177.

28. Stan Cuthand, "The Native Peoples of the Prairie Provinces in the 1920's and 1930's," in *Sweet Promises: A Reader on Indian-White Relations in Canada*, ed. J.R. Miller (Toronto: University of Toronto Press, 1991), 389–90.

29. Correspondence from Lazenby to Assistant Deputy and Secretary, July 1923, vol. 6609, file 4106-6P, 28, P.G., RG10, LAC, Ottawa: "If the Missionary would devote his entire time to his Missionary work, as he should do, there might be a better chance of improving the moral status of this band, which is, to say the least, at present deplorable."

30. Correspondence from C.L. St John to Department of Indian Affairs, 18 June 1925, vol. 3827, file 60,511-4B, RG10, LAC, Ottawa.

31. Correspondence from A.M. Messner to Minister of Interior, 20 June 1925.

32. Correspondence from P.G. Lazenby to Assistant Deputy and Secretary, Department of Indian Affairs, 29 June 1925.

33. In the same letter, Lazenby says he gets a call from Inspector Christianson: "instructions had been received from the Commissioner's office."

34. Correspondence from P.G. Lazenby to the Assistant Deputy and Secretary, Department of Indian Affairs, 29 June 1925.

35. Correspondence from Sergeant Mann to the Officer Commanding, "Re: Lizard Point I.R. – Rossburn, Man – Assistance to Indian Dept," 11 July 1925. Mann acted per instructions from Commissioner Graham.

36. Correspondence from Sergeant Mann to the Commissioner, RCMP, 11 July 1925, vol. 3827, file 60,511-4B, RG10, LAC, Ottawa. Mann added: "I stayed round the camp for some time that evening. . . . With regard to those Indians, they have . . . been very orderly and well behaved, this much credit is due to them."

37. Mann further added: "Now the main point I have in mind is that there is a possibility in the future of like circumstances reaching an impasse as many of the Indians know as far as the Act is concerned they are doing nothing unlawful, which is liable to bring about a delicate state of affairs as far as the police are concerned when called upon by the dept to stop these dances," Correspondence from Sergeant Mann to the Commissioner, RCMP.

38. Correspondence from Duncan Campbell Scott to A.M. Messner, 30 June 1925, vol. 3827, file 60,511-4B, RG10, LAC, Ottawa. This letter is directed at one of the lawyers. There was indeed an exchange of letters between Scott and Graham, but in this particular government file only Graham's side of the conversation was preserved.

39. Correspondence from W.M. Graham to D.C. Scott, 4 July 1925.

40. Indian Act, 1927, R.S. 1927, c. 98, s. 141: "Every person who, without the consent of the Superintendent General expressed in writing, receives, obtains, solicits or requests from any Indian any payment or contribution . . . for the prosecution of any claim . . . for the benefit of the said tribe or band, shall be guilty of an offence and liable upon summary conviction for each such offence to a penalty not exceeding two hundred dollars and not less than fifty dollars or to imprisonment for any term not exceeding two months."

41. "Lord Tweedsmuir Wins His Way Into Hearts of Interlake Folk," *Winnipeg Evening Tribune*, 22 September 1936.

42. Oleh W. Gerus and Denis Hlynka, eds., *The Honourable Member for Vegreville: The Memoirs and Diary of Anthony Hlynka, MP* (Calgary: University of Calgary Press, 2005), 160.

43. "Lord Tweedsmuir Wins His Way." Tweedsmuir wished the audience "health and prosperity" in Ukrainian.

44. Clifford Sifton, "The Immigrants Canada Wants," *Maclean's Magazine*, 1 April 1922. Sifton also said: "I am just as much opposed to interference with the rights of property as anybody alive."

45. Sarah Carter, *Lost Harvests: Prairie Indian Reserve Farmers and Government Policy* (Montreal: McGill-Queen's University Press, 1990), 162. Under clause 70 of the 1876 Indian Act, an Indian could not take up a homestead unless he was willing to give up Indian status.

46. "Speech Delivered on Receiving Degree of L.L.D. by Queen's University," vol. 313, Manuscript Group 27, series II D 15, Clifford Sifton fonds, LAC, Ottawa.

10: "Never Forget"

1. Rossburn History Club (hereafter RHC), *On the Sunny Slopes of the Riding Mountains: A History of Rossburn and District*, vol. 1 (Rossburn: RHC, 1984), 344.

2. Lubomyr Luciuk and Stella Hryniuk, eds., *Canada's Ukrainians: Negotiating an Identity* (Toronto: University of Toronto Press, 1991), 302.

3. Luciuk and Hryniuk, *Canada's Ukrainians*, 294.

4. Oleh W. Gerus and J.E. Rea, *The Ukrainians in Canada* (Ottawa: Canadian Historical Association, 1985), 11; Orest T. Martynowych, *Ukrainians in Canada: The Formative Period, 1891–1924* (Edmonton: University of Alberta Press, 1991), 323.

5. Bohdan S. Kordan, *Enemy Aliens, Prisoners of War: Internment in Canada During the Great War* (Montreal: McGill-Queens University Press, 2002), 70. Kodro was in the Castle Internship camp.

6. Bohdan S. Kordan and Peter Melnycky, eds., *In the Shadow of the Rockies: Diary of the Castle Mountain Internment Camp, 1915–1917* (Edmonton: Canadian Institute of Ukrainian Studies Press, 1991), 6; Bohdan S. Kordan, *No Free Man: Canada, the Great War, and the Enemy Alien Experience* (Montreal: McGill-Queens University Press, 2016), 130 As his father continued to work for his release, John managed to escape by making a mad dash into the bush during a day of forced labour on a bridge.

7. House of Commons, *Debates*, 1917, 5889: "among [eastern Europeans]" substituted for "among the Galicians, Kukovians, and Rumanians."

8. Frances Swyripa and John Herd Thompson, eds., *Loyalties in Conflict: Ukrainians in Canada During the Great War* (Edmonton: Canadian Institute of Ukrainian Studies Press, 1983), 75.

9. Linda and Darcy Yaskiw, *Our Heritage: Vladimir (Dick) Yaskiw, Lucia Drewniak: A Collection of Data, Photographs and Stories Contributed by Their Descendants* (Canada, 2012).

10. Marge and Mike Sotas, "The Early Birdtail Valley Settlers (1879–1914)," in RHC, *Sunny Slopes*, vol. 2, 25.

11. P.J. Giffen, *Rural Life: Portraits of the Prairie Town, 1946* (Winnipeg: University of Manitoba Press, 2004), 71.

12. Giffen, *Rural Life*, 79, 119, 86.

13. Giffen, *Rural Life*, 86.

14. Giffen, *Rural Life*, 86, 87.

15. P.J. Giffen, "Adult Education in Relation to Rural Social Structure: A Comparative Study of Three Manitoba Rural Communities" (master's thesis, University of Toronto, 1947), 150 (viewed at the Manitoba Legislative Library).

16. Giffen, *Rural Life*, 84.

17. Giffen, *Rural Life*, 88, 83.

18. Giffen, *Rural Life*, 117.

19. Giffen, "Adult Education," 208.

20. Giffen, "Adult Education," 139.

21. Ibram X. Kendi, *How to Be an Antiracist* (New York: One World, 2019), 218.

12: Bloodvein

1. An all-weather road connecting the provincial highway to the reserve wouldn't come for another eighteen years.

13: "The Way It Works"

1. Canada, Office of the Parliamentary Budget Officer, "Federal spending on Primary and Secondary Education on First Nations Reserves" (Ottawa, 2016), 2. The 1 percent figure is after inflation.

2. Nick Martin, "Higher education: Funding puts reserve school on par with public system," *Winnipeg Free Press*, 19 May 2012.

14: "Stark and Obvious"

1. Canada, *House of Commons Debates*, vol. 142, no. 110, 2nd Session, 39th Parliament, 11 June 2008.

2. Canada, Office of the Auditor General of Canada, *Report 5—Socio-economic Gaps on First Nations Reserves*, Indigenous Services Canada, 2018. "Our calculations showed that, on average, only about one in four (24%) students actually completed high school within 4 years." The overall graduation rate, allowing for more years to complete high school, is about 40 percent. See also Matthew Calver, *Closing the Aboriginal Education Gap in Canada: Assessing Progress and Estimating the Economic Benefits*, CSLS Research Reports March 2015, Centre for the Study of Living Standards, 18, 19, 36.

3. "How Stanley Redcrow and First Nations activists reclaimed the Blue Quills Residential School," *CBC News*, 10 May 2017.

4. Correspondence, 5 November 1984, 2001-00966-6, 002, WIN-E-4700-22-285 0c, RG10, LAC, Winnipeg.

5. Correspondence from David Crombie to Charles Mayer, 14 February 1986, E-4700-22-285, RG10, LAC, Winnipeg. Crombie also noted that funding was "equitable in the sense" that all bands received comparable funding, which is to say that when it came to education funding, all Indian bands were shortchanged by the same amount when compared with provincial schools.

6. Michael Mendelson, "Improving Education on Reserves: A First Nations Education Authority Act" (Ottawa: Caledon Institute of Social Policy, 2008), 6–7. Federal policy was to deliver provincial-level education on reserves, though without guaranteeing comparable funding. Mendelson writes, "The harsh reality is that the Department's confidence in the parity of its funding is misplaced, since it simply does not know. There are no regular data collected to compare provincial and federal education funding levels, nor is there any mechanism in the budget-setting process for First Nations education to ensure that funding levels are indeed comparable to those in provinces."

7. Harry Swain's prediction eventually came true. In 2006, the First Nations Children and Family Caring Society and the Assembly of First Nations brought a complaint

alleging that the federal government "discriminates in providing child and family services to First Nations on reserve and in the Yukon, on the basis of race and/or national or ethnic origin, by providing inequitable and insufficient funding for those services." After a ten-year legal battle, the Canadian Human Rights Tribunal found a *prima facie* case of discrimination against First Nations children and families. See First Nations Child and Family Caring Society of Canada et al. v. Attorney General of Canada (Representing the Minister of Indian Affairs and Northern Development Canada) 2016 CHRT 2, 6, 456.

8. "School Buildings – Waywayseecappo First Nation," 1986-02-01 to 1981-06-30, ACC: 2001 - 01057-5, vol./Box 4, file number WIN-E-4965-285 02, RG10, LAC, Winnipeg.

9. Scott Serson, "The Canadian Government Knowingly and Deliberately Maintains First Nations in a State of Poverty," Submission to the Special Rapporteur on the rights of Indigenous Peoples, 14 October 2013.

10. Andrew Stobo Sniderman, unpublished interview with Paul Martin, August 2012. Martin continued: "Let's say the cap was reasonably fair for four or five years because it was an increase at a time when other departments were getting cut. But then it stayed on for a number of years too long. The first thing that I did when I became [prime minister] was to move to eliminate the gap. That's what the [2005] Kelowna [Accord] money was all about. Did the cap last longer than it should have, and was a Liberal government in office when it did? Yes, the answer is yes."

11. Truth and Reconciliation Commission of Canada, *Executive Summary* (Kingston: McGill-Queen's University Press, 2015), 148. See also Canada, Office of the Parliamentary Budget Officer, "Federal Spending on Primary and Secondary Education on First Nations Reserves" (Ottawa, 2016), 1–2. Between 1996 and 2006, provincial funding to provincial schools increased annually by an average of 3.8 percent, while Ottawa maintained its 2 percent limit. These figures actually understate the extent of the problem, because the number of students in provincial schools was stagnating or dropping overall, but the number of Indigenous students was skyrocketing. This aggravated the disparity in per student funding between public schools and reserve schools. One factor that somewhat alleviated the gap was that Indigenous and Northern Affairs Canada was reallocating some infrastructure funding to invest more in services. This was likened to "robbing Peter to pay Paul." Steve Rennie, "Aboriginal Affairs short of cash for education, social programs: document," *CBC News*, 10 November 2014. This diversion of funding from infrastructure is one of the reasons why so many reserves are suffering from an infrastructure crisis.

12. Andrew Stobo Sniderman, "Aboriginal students: An education underclass," *Maclean's*, 8 August 2012.

13. Canada, Office of the Auditor General, *Report of the Auditor General on Indian and Northern Affairs Canada's Elementary and Secondary Education Programs* (Ottawa, 2004), 5.2, 5.27; Canada, Office of the Auditor General of Canada, June 2011 Status Report, "Chapter 4—Programs for First Nations on Reserves," 4.17.

14. For the full text of the motion, which was passed on 27 February, see Canada, House of Commons, *Debates*, 16 February 2012, 5359. The motion declares "that all First Nation children have an equal right to high-quality, culturally-relevant education."

15. Kate Hammer, "B.C. First Nations students to get equal funding," *The Globe and Mail*, 27 January 2012; Canada, "Agreement with Respect to Mi'kmaq Education in Nova Scotia," 1997; Bill Graveland, "Harper unveils retooled First Nations education plan," *Global News*, 7 February 2014. The major exception was in British Columbia, where the federal government committed over $15 million a year in funding for on-reserve education, in order to equalize funding with respect to provincial schools. In 2014, Stephen Harper also introduced legislation that would have committed the federal government to annual budget increases of 5 percent for the education of students on reserve, but the bill never became law.

16. Jody Porter, "First Nations students get 30 per cent less funding than other children, economist says," *CBC News*, 14 March 2016; Office of the Parliamentary Budget Officer, "Federal spending on Primary and Secondary Education on First Nations Reserves," 29. See also John Paul Tasker, "First Nations education a cash-strapped 'non-system,' bureaucrats tell Minister," *CBC News*, 5 October 2016.

15: "People Say We're Racists"

1. John S. Milloy, *A National Crime: The Canadian Government and the Residential School System, 1879 to 1986* (Winnipeg: University of Manitoba Press, 1999), xxxix; Sheila Carr Stewart, "First Nations Education: Financial Accountability and Educational Attainment," *Canadian Journal of Education* 29, no. 4 (2006): 998–1018. In residential schools, "chronic underfunding" was a "persistent flaw." As for the federal "day schools" on reserves—which many Indigenous students attended before the shift to integrated education—these schools were "notoriously under funded, poorly equipped and constructed, [and teachers were] paid less than their colleagues in neighboring public schools," according to evidence submitted to Parliament.

2. Canada, Department of Indian and Northern Affairs, *A Survey of the Contemporary Indians of Canada: Economic, Political, Educational Needs and Policies – Part 1 [The Hawthorn Report]* (Ottawa, 1967), 344.

3. See First Nations Child and Family Caring Society of Canada et al. v. Attorney General of Canada (Representing the Minister of Indigenous Affairs and

Northern Development Canada) 2016 CHRT 2, Canada (Canadian Human Rights Commission) v. Canada (Attorney General), 2012 FC 445, and other associated litigation.

4. Ipsos, "On Immigrants and Aboriginals: Majority (72%) of Canadians Disagree That Canada Should Admit More Immigrants than Current Levels, Split on Whether Immigration has Been Positive (40%) or Negative (34%)," 30 June 2012. "Nearly two in three (64%) 'agree' (27% strongly/36% somewhat) that 'Canada's Aboriginal peoples receive too much support from Canadian taxpayers.'"

5. Indigenous Peoples are the descendants of Canada's first inhabitants. "Status Indians," or "treaty Indians," are Indigenous Peoples deemed to be official "Indians" by the government. "Non-Status Indians" are Indigenous Peoples who lack the status designations, and are, therefore, not legally Indians.

6. Charlie Angus, *Children of the Broken Treaty: Canada's Promise and One Girl's Dream* (Regina: University of Regina Press, 2015), 56.

7. Angus Reid Institute, "Truths of reconciliation: Canadians are deeply divided on how best to address Indigenous issues," 7 June 2018.

8. Arlie Russell Hochschild, *Strangers in Their Own Land* (New York: The New Press, 2016), 52.

9. Chelsea Vowel, "The Myth of Taxation," in *Indigenous Writes: A Guide to First Nations, Métis and Inuit Issues in Canada* (Winnipeg: Portage and Main Press, 2016), 135–42; Aleksandra Sagan, "First Nations pay more tax than you think," *CBC News*, 24 April 2015.

10. Canada, Royal Commission on Aboriginal Peoples, *Report of the Royal Commission on Aboriginal Peoples, Volume 1: Looking Forward, Looking Back* (Ottawa, 1996), 248; John F. Leslie, "The Indian Act: An Historical Perspective," *Canadian Parliamentary Review* 25, no. 2 (2002), 23–7; John S. Milloy, "The Early Indian Acts: Developmental Strategy and Constitutional Change," in *As Long as the Sun Shines and Water Flows: A Reader in Canadian Native Studies*, ed. Ian A.L. Getty and Antoine S. Lussier (Vancouver: UBC Press, 1983), 56–64; John L. Tobias, "Protection, Civilization, Assimilation: An Outline History of Canada's Indian Policy," in Getty and Lussier, *As Long as the Sun Shines and Water Flows*, 39–55.

11. Dominion of Canada, *Annual Report of the Department of Indian Affairs for the Year Ended December 31st, 1899*. In 1899, David Laird, chief negotiator of Treaty 8, promised Indians the treaty would not lead to the imposition of taxes. He said: "We assured them that the treaty would not lead to any forced interference with their mode of life, that it did not open the way to the imposition of any tax."

12. Mitchell v. Peguis Indian Band, [1990] 2 S.C.R. 85.

16: "Kids Are Kids"

1. "Waywayseecappo First Nation LOU and Pilot Project with Park West School Division," Information for Deputy Minister, Originator: Derek Bradley, 22 November 2010, Unclassified – MB 13735. Accessed through Access to Information request.

2. Nick Martin, "Higher education: Funding puts reserve school on par with public system," *Winnipeg Free Press*, 19 May 2012.

3. "Waywayseecappo First Nation LOU."

4. Bruce Carson, 14 *Days: Making the Conservative Movement in Canada* (Montreal: McGill-Queen's University Press, 2014), 170.

5. In 2016, the Paul Martin Initiative began to operate in the Waywayseecappo Community School, investing notably in literacy programs. Because of this additional intervention, we do not cite further data from the school after this date, because improvements in student outcomes could not be attributed as directly to the partnership with the Park West School Division that began in 2010.

6. Andrew Stobo Sniderman, "Aboriginal Students, an education underclass," *Maclean's*, 8 August 2012.

7. Andrew Stobo Sniderman, "Equal education funding gets big results on Manitoba reserve," *Maclean's*, 26 April 2016.

17: "Bury the Hatchet"

1. J.R. Miller, *Residential Schools and Reconciliation: Canada Confronts Its History* (Toronto: University of Toronto Press, 2017), 173, 172, 180–1.

2. This metaphor comes from the Iroquois Confederacy. At the founding of the Confederacy, once-hostile warriors were said to have buried their hatchets alongside the roots of the great Tree of Peace.

3. Statistics Canada, *Rossburn, Town, Census Profile*, 2016 Census; Statistics Canada, *Waywayseecappo First Nation, Indian Reserve, Census Profile*, 2016 Census.

4. Brian Brown, "Hockey players not the only people mistreated," *Crossroads This Week*, 13 December 2019.

5. Murray Clearsky, "Ignorance and misinformation," *Crossroads This Week*, 20 December 2019.

6. Kerry Lawless et al., "Rossburn council comments on letter," *Crossroads This Week*, 20 December 2019.

18: "A Grand Notion"

1. "Missing and Murdered: The Unsolved Cases of Indigenous Women and Girls," *CBC News*, n.d.

2.   Guy Quenneville, "What happened on Gerald Stanley's farm the day Colten Boushie was shot, as told by witnesses," *CBC News*, 9 August 2016.

3.   Benjamin Shingler, "Investigations launched after Atikamekw woman records Quebec hospital staff uttering slurs before her death," *CBC News*, 29 September 2020.

4.   "More unmarked graves found near another school that housed Indigenous children in Canada," *CBC News*, 30 June 2021.

5.   Clifford Sifton, "Natural Resources of Canada," Speech delivered to the Women's Art Association, Clifford Sifton fonds, vol. 313, Manuscript Group 27, series II D 15, LAC, Ottawa.

6.   Jason Warick, "Trudeau not honouring $2.6B education promise, First Nations leaders say," *CBC News*, 13 September 2018.

7.   Canada, Office of the Parliamentary Budget Officer, "Federal spending on Primary and Secondary Education on First Nations Reserves" (Ottawa, 2016), 29.

8.   John Rawls, "Justice as Fairness," *The Philosophical Review* 67, no. 2 (April 1958). The philosopher John Rawls, in thinking about the idea of equality, once set out a list of basic items needed for citizens to flourish in a system of background equality. He termed these "the primary goods," and they include enough resources to adequately feed and house ourselves, and civil and political liberties, but Rawls called the most important of these goods "the social basis of self respect." Rawls understood that to flourish, each citizen must see their values reflected in social institutions lest we be forced to pursue a conception of the good different from our own. This is the reason that Indigenous schooling will look different from off-reserve schools: the reserve school curriculum is designed to affirm the dignity of Indigenous values and cultures.

9.   Nunavut, Department of Education, "Educator Toolkit for Nunavut Schools" 2020–2021. In 2020, Nunavut issued an educator toolkit that focuses on core curriculum like reading and writing, but does so in the context of land-based learning. Curricular activities include berry picking, drying/smoking fish, hunting, carving, and skinning/cleaning caribou, to name just a few activities.

10. Canada, Royal Commission on Aboriginal Peoples, *Highlights from the Report of the Royal Commission on Aboriginal Peoples* (Ottawa, 1996).

11. Modern-day treaties like the Nisga'a or James Bay treaties remove those populations from the Indian Act and provide those treaty nations with a set of jurisdictional powers that is negotiated between the federal, provincial, and Indigenous governments.

12. The Indian Act and the First Nations Fiscal Management Act provide for property taxation, and this has been a boon for Indian reserves located in areas where

the real estate market is booming, such as near North Vancouver and Kelowna. The First Nations Sales Tax Act authorizes the taxing of alcohol, tobacco, and automobile purchases, while the First Nations Goods and Services Act authorizes a tax on retail transactions. Modern-day treaties can provide for the collection of personal income tax, and the First Nations Fiscal Management Act combined with the Indian Act authorize the collection of property taxes. For the most part, these various acts require reserve governments to enter into agreement with the federal government for the collection of these taxes.

13. First Nations reserves are almost wholly funded by transfers from the federal Crown, with the provinces doing all that they can to avoid spending on reserve communities. Nevertheless, most provinces do have some form of financial transfers ("Resource Revenue Sharing") paid to First Nations communities or provincially paid services that provide access for Indian people to provincial services (e.g., Native Child and Family Services, whose funders include several provincial ministries and the City of Toronto).

14. Indian reserves comprise just 11,000 square kilometres. Combined, the more than six hundred reserve communities equal about 0.2 percent of Canada's total land mass, or the size of two Prince Edward Islands.

15. In 2015, Ontario also brought in a further billion dollars in revenue from goods manufactured in the forestry and logging industry in Ontario. Statistics Canada, *CANSIM Table 301-0009: Logging Industries, Principal Statistics by North American Industry Classification System* (Ottawa, 2015).

16. Indeed, many of the forty-three northern communities are already bound together in a political territorial organization known as the Nishnawbe Aski Nation (NAN), and, at a still more local level, communities are also bound together in collectives known as tribal councils.

17. David Treuer, "Return the National Parks to the Tribes: The jewels of America's landscape should belong to America's original peoples," *The Atlantic*, May 2021. The main categories of federally held lands are national parks, military bases, airports, and Indian reserves. In the U.S., there has been recent discussion about the social, political, juridical, and economic benefits of handing back U.S. National Park lands to Indigenous Peoples. Given that the land mass of Canada's National Parks system is fifteen times the total area covered by Indian reserves (3.3 percent vs 0.6 percent), Treuer's suggestion might have relevance here in Canada as well.

18. Sidney B. Linden, *Report of the Ipperwash Inquiry* (Toronto: Ministry of the Attorney General, 2007). In addition to national parks, military bases may have a role to play as well.

19. Douglas Sanderson, "Against Supersession," *Canadian Journal of Law and Jurisprudence*, 24, no. 1 (January 2011), 155–82. In British Columbia, where no treaties were ever signed, Indigenous Peoples find it difficult to understand what is unjust about control over lands being returned to Indigenous Peoples, when those lands were never sold or ceded by the land's rightful owners. Returning the land is, on this view, simply righting a past wrong. Historic injustices do not simply go away.

20. There are, of course, more than public interests at stake. Even if urban citizens experienced no increase in taxes and received the same level of service, private investment in resource extraction may not be able to deliver the same level of returns when First Nations are the ones issuing permits. These losses could be felt not just by the resource companies but by the pension funds and other sources of private capital.

21. Confederation of Tomorrow, 2020 *Survey of Canadians, Report 2: The Division of Powers and Resources* (Toronto, 2020). Prince Edward Island and Quebec are perennial beneficiaries of the equalization formula, while Ontario, Alberta, and British Columbia are the funds' primary depositors. In October 2021, a referendum in Alberta suggested that most voters were dissatisfied with the existing practice of equalization.

22. McGirt v. Oklahoma, No. 18-9526, 591 U.S. __ (2020), 28.

23. *McGirt* does not transfer the property of Oklahomans to Creek Indians. Nevertheless, considerable confusion has arisen with respect to criminal prosecutions resulting from *McGirt*. By arguing that the original reservation boundaries remained intact, McGirt called into question the validity of his trial because it was conducted in state, not federal court. Federal criminal law, not state law, applies on an Indian reserve. McGirt was then tried in federal court and sentenced to three life counts.

24. Jamil Malakieh, Canadian Centre for Justice and Community Safety Statistics, *Adult and youth correctional statistics in Canada, 2017/2018* (Ottawa: Statistics Canada, 2019). Among the provinces in 2017/2018, Aboriginal adults represented three-quarters of admissions to custody in Manitoba (75 percent) and Saskatchewan (74 percent).

25. Robert A. Williams, *Linking Arms Together: American Indian Treaty Visions of Law and Peace*, 1600–1800 (New York, Routledge, 2000); Bruce Morito, *An Ethic of Mutual Respect* (Vancouver: UBC Press, 2012); William Fenton, *The Great Law and the Longhouse: A Political History of the Iroquois Confederacy* (Norman: University of Oklahoma Press, 2010).

26. "Ending long-term drinking water advisories," Indigenous Services Canada, accessed 16 June 2021. The number of communities under boil-water advisories

has diminished in recent years, following significant investments by successive governments.

27. Canada, Yukon Land Claims and Self-Government Agreements, 1994; Canada, The James Bay and Northern Quebec Agreement (JBNQA), 1975; Canada, The Northeastern Quebec Agreement, 1978. In addition to these agreements, there is the Nisga'a Final Agreement, as well as seven other comprehensive treaties finalized in British Columbia in the past twenty years.

INDEX

Aberdeen, Lady, Ishbel Hamilton-Gordon, 164–6, 168–9, 345n11

alcohol: alcoholism, 46, 264–5; fetal alcohol syndrome, 11; prohibited on reserves, 128, 205; Rossburn Hotel bar, 8–9, 44, 161–2, 197, 205, 247; for teenagers, 23–4

Allen, Duncan, 239

Anglican Church, 318n2

Angus, Charlie, 248

Anishinaabemowin. *See* Ojibway Peoples (Anishinaabe) and language (Anishinaabemowin)

Assembly of First Nations, 241, 350–1n7

assimilation: aim of Indian Act, 96–7; in integrated public schools, 62; J.A. Macdonald on, 56; Hugh McKay on, 79; vs partnership, 263; Reed on, 321n8; in residential schools, 32, 62, 136, 148, 309, 311, 321n8; Michael Twovoice on, 56–7, 79; for Ukrainian immigrants, 136, 192, 339n15; White Paper, 73

Assiniboine, 108, 110–12, 336n98

Astakeesic, George, 158

Astakeesic, Prince, Chief, 51, 158, 171–2

Austria-Hungary, 136, 138, 185

Banff National Park (Alberta), 187

Barkwell, Lawrence J., 328n29

Barron, F. Laurie, 128, 337n103

baseball, 195, 251

Batoche (Saskatchewan), 116, 121

Battleford region (Saskatchewan), 106, 109, 331n14, 345n5

Berens (Nauwigizigweas), Jacob, Chief, 33–4, 318n8

Big Bear (Mistahimaskwa), Chief, 110–12, 115, 120, 173

Birdtail River and valley: descent into, 5, 11; name, 1, 317n1; settlers, 98, 100, 106; and Waywayseecappo border, 7, 11, 28, 97, 177, 233, 329n38

Birtle (Manitoba), 30, 171, 201, 318n13, 329n43

Birtle Residential School, 38, 43, 63, 195, 308–12

Blackfoot Peoples, 108, 166

Blake, Hilda, 144

Bloodvein First Nation Reserve (Manitoba), 211–14, 217–19, 222, 349n1

Bond, Ford, 45

Borden, Robert, 146

Brandon (Manitoba), 134, 187, 216